976.4284 From the ashes.
F

$54.00

From the Ashes

Making Sense of Waco

From the Ashes

Making Sense of Waco

James R. Lewis, Editor

Rowman & Littlefield Publishers, Inc.

ROWMAN & LITTLEFIELD PUBLISHERS, INC.

Published in the United States of America
by Rowman & Littlefield Publishers, Inc.
4720 Boston Way, Lanham, Maryland 20706

3 Henrietta Street, London WC2E 8LU, England

Copyright © 1994 by Rowman & Littlefield Publishers, Inc.

British Cataloging in Publication Information Available

Library of Congress Cataloging-in-Publication Data

From the ashes : making sense of Waco / James R. Lewis,
editor.
p.   cm.
Includes bibliographical references and index.
1. Waco Branch Davidian Disaster, Tex., 1993.   2. Branch
Davidians.   3. Koresh, David, 1959–1993.
BP605.B72F76   1994   976.4'284063—dc20   93–48400 CIP

ISBN 0–8476–7914–4 (cloth : alk. paper)
ISBN 0–8476–7915–2 (pbk. : alk. paper)

Printed in the United States of America

 The paper used in this publication meets the minimum requirements of
American National Standard for Information Sciences—Permanence of
Paper for Printed Library Materials, ANSI Z39.48–1984.

Contents

Selected Responses

Selected Letters to Public Officials

Acknowledgments

Many thanks to my wife and partner, Eve, without whose support this project might never have been completed, to Cosby Steuart, who typed most of the final manuscript, and, of course, to the contributors, who trusted me with the fruit of their labors. I am also grateful to Maureen Muncaster and Jonathan Sisk at Rowman & Littlefield Publishers who went out of their way to accommodate this project.

My understanding of the Davidians has been shaped by conversations with several people. I would particularly like to express gratitude to Stan Silva, who gave me many invaluable insights into his community and who supplied the "Christian Holocaust" piece included in the present volume. I am indebted to Jesse Amen—one of the outsiders to cross FBI lines and enter Mt. Carmel during the siege—for the information with which he provided me. Also, a special word of thanks to Jim Tabor and Phil Arnold (contributors to this anthology), with whom I have had lengthy telephone conversations regarding their personal involvement in the Davidian drama.

My understanding of the assault and siege has been shaped by information from sources not normally consulted by academics. Chief among these was an informative series of articles by James L. Pate published in *Soldier of Fortune* magazine (June—November 1993), and I would like to thank Lynne Robertson of *SOF* for her assistance. Information on the Bureau of Alcohol, Tobacco, and Firearms was obtained from the information and research library of the National Rifle Association, and I would like to thank Robert Nagle for his assistance. Finally, I would like to thank Linda Thompson for a copy of her revealing videotape, *Waco—The Big Lie,* which, though I disagreed with certain of her interpretations, provided vivid images for some of our worst suspicions.

Introduction

Responses to the Branch Davidian Tragedy

In its May 24, 1993 issue, *Time* magazine printed a selection of responses to the Waco holocaust in its letters section. While some readers expressed outrage at the FBI attack, others supported the agency's efforts to blame the Branch Davidians:

> The standoff may have come to a devastating end, but the responsibility for the slaughter of innocent children remains with the deluded megalomaniac who wanted to retain the upper hand at any cost, not with the FBI agents, whose main goal was to give the Davidians safe passage.

Other readers expressed support for the assault, at the same time expressing dissatisfaction that it had not been staged *sooner:*

> Not only do I support Attorney General Janet Reno's decision to use teargas and attack Koresh's Waco complex, but I feel the action was long overdue.

Finally, *Time* reprinted a statement from one reader who was not just angry that the FBI had wasted so much time negotiating with Koresh, but was also angry about the further "waste" that was to be incurred by the government's investigation of the fiasco.

> Koresh and his followers are responsible for their own untimely death. I fault the FBI for not concluding the ridiculous situation in seven days rather

than seven weeks, for they have only encouraged other two-bit lunatics who may believe they can use women and children as hostages. Now I fear more taxpayers' money will be spent investigating what should be a closed book.

This strange and frighteningly brutal statement apparently represents the opinion of many otherwise well-meaning Americans.

In America, conflicts and tragedies quickly find expression as slogans in bumper stickers and on T-shirts. The Branch Davidian fiasco was no exception. In Waco, and especially in the general vicinity of Mt. Carmel, one could find vendors hawking T-shirts boasting such mindless slogans as:

I SUPPORT THE ATF.

(As if supporting the ATF was comparable to supporting Desert Storm.) Another, with words drawn across an image of the burning community, said:

HI VERN, WEIRD ASSHOLE, COME OUT.

Yet another one, that pictured Koresh's face in the cross-hairs of a gun sight, sported the chilling assertion:

A SIGHT WE'VE BEEN WAITING TO SEE.

Scholars who have studied new religious movements (NRMs) found the public response to the immolation of the Branch Davidians (over 80% approved of the ill-conceived assault in which ninety men, women, and children were burnt alive) more disturbing than usual. Since at least the mid-1970s, part of the stereotype of alternative religions has been that members are brainwashed—a portrayal which clearly implies that they should be regarded as innocent, duped victims of the leader rather than as conscious co-conspirators. This was the case with the public's response to the Jonestown murder/suicides, in which only Jim Jones was blamed for the killing of his followers and Congressman Leo Ryan.

The response to the Davidian tragedy, however, has been markedly different. While most Americans would still be willing to agree with the assertion that Koresh's followers were "brainwashed," many would also be willing to ascribe to the opposite, contradictory assertion that the Davidians have only themselves to blame for becoming involved with David Koresh. This is clear from the above statement about Koresh and his followers being "responsible for their own untimely death."

To understand our society's increasing hostility to non-traditional religions, we might refer to the classic sociological dictum which asserts that societies need enemies. External threats provide motivation for people to overcome internal divisiveness in order to work together as a unit. Having an enemy one can portray as evil and perverse also provides support for the normative values and institutions of one's society: "They" are communists; "we" are capitalists. "They" are totalitarian; "we" are democratic. And so forth.

One of the more interesting corollaries of this general line of thinking is that in situations where external enemies no longer threaten, a society will find groups or individuals within itself that it can construe as threatening and evil. Such enemies become particularly important to communities passing through a crisis in which fundamental values are being called into question; in the words of Albert Bergessen, from his important study, *The Sacred and the Subversive* (1984), "a community will commence to ritually persecute imaginary enemies—conduct a witchhunt—to manufacture moral deviants as a means of ritually reaffirming the group's problematical values and collective purposes." This general theoretical perspective sheds light on our current social situation.

As a potent international threat, communism has largely disappeared. The only significant remaining communist power is Red China, and the Red Chinese are more interested in cooperating with the West than in challenging it. Other threats, such as Iraq, flare up and pass rather quickly. The lack of pressing external enemies in combination with our current, ongoing social crisis would lead the sociologically informed observer to anticipate that our culture will seek out groups within society to take the place of the communists.

Unless there are groups that are consciously anti-social or criminal like the Mafia, the deviations from the norm that a community chooses to perceive as threatening are somewhat arbitrary. The people our culture have traditionally construed as "deviants" have been racial (e.g., blacks), ethnic (e.g., Jews), and sexual (e.g., homosexuals) minorities. In recent years, however, it has become less socially acceptable to persecute these traditional groups, at least in the overt manner in which they have been attacked in the past. This leaves few groups of any significant size to persecute.

Among the few minorities that liberals have been slow to defend are non-traditional religions. This is due to a number of different factors, including the resistance of traditionally conservative religions to liberal change. The failure of normally open-minded people to protect religious pluralism has allowed contemporary witchhunters to declare open season on "cults." The media response to Waco has also served to make non-traditional religions the preferred object of attack.

Another disturbing aspect of this whole affair was that scholars of alternative religions—many of whom have devoted their careers to the study of such religions—were not consulted, either prior to the initial raid of the Davidian community or during the siege. Law enforcement officials insisted on regarding the Branch Davidians as a criminal organization parading under the guise of religion. Thus no specialized knowledge of the dynamics of a *religious* group was required. Had the ATF or FBI consulted and followed the advice of mainstream academic experts, the Waco tragedy might well have been avoided. Federal law enforcement officials were acting partially on the basis of the widely prevalent stereotype of "cults" as criminal organizations ready to commit the worst atrocities at the drop of a hat. Based on many years of research and analysis, mainstream scholars have thoroughly debunked this stereotype as inaccurate. But the ATF and FBI failed to consult these voices of reason.

Finally, academic specialists were disturbed by the role played by the anti-cult movement in the Waco killing fields. With few exceptions, law enforcement officials and reporters were more receptive to self-appointed "cult experts" associated with this movement than to legitimate scholars. Anti-cult groups have a vested interest in promoting the worst possible stereotypes of non-traditional religions. Instead of balanced information, such groups tend to paint alternative religions in the exaggerated colors of fear and fanaticism. It is the two-decade-long interaction between the anti-cult movement and the media that has been responsible for the widespread view that all "cults" are dangerous organizations, this despite the fact that comparatively few such groups constitute a genuine threat, either to themselves or to society. The general atmosphere of distrust toward minority religions contributed significantly to public support for the ATF assault on Mt. Carmel, and probably even explains why the ATF picked a group like the Davidians for their dramatic, public raid.

While there were comparatively few *direct* connections between the ATF and the anti-cult movement, they were significant. In particular, the testimony of deprogrammed former Davidians was used to support the contention that Koresh had to be served a search warrant (reports of deprogrammees about their former religious group are notoriously suspect). Also important was the advisory role that Rick Ross played with the ATF prior to the attack.

Before the blood had even dried in the fields surrounding Mt. Carmel, Ross was busy promoting himself to the media on the basis of his role as advisor to the ATF. What were the qualifications that allowed this person to have the ear of the ATF? Ross's only credentials were that he was a deprogrammer who had "deprogrammed" several Branch Davidians. In common with almost all deprogrammers, he had no professional training in counseling. Rather, Ross's background was that he was an ex-con with an extensive psychiatric record. After completing an apprenticeship in petty crime, he graduated to the more lucrative career of deprogrammer. And as someone who makes his living kidnapping "cult" members for money—at $35,000 to $50,000 a hit—Ross clearly has a vested interest in portraying non-traditional religions in the worst possible light. It is easy to see how ATF's distorted impressions of the Branch Davidians could have been created by misinformation received from Ross and others of his ilk.

Now that the Branch Davidians have been incinerated—and there is no business to be made deprogramming members of that religious group—the anti-cult movement has shifted public attention to other small religions, marketing the fear that non-traditional religions are pseudo-religious "cults," all more or less guilty of abusing their members. The facts are that mainstream scholars have found such stereotypes to be almost completely unfounded. While a few destructive groups exist, the majority of alternative religions are psychologically healthy organizations whose chief "crime" is that their beliefs and practices diverge significantly from our society's presently accepted religious and cultural traditions. To collapse distinctions within this complex spectrum and imply that *all* such religions are potential Jonestowns/Branch Davidians is inaccurate, misleading, and dangerous.

Despite the attorney general's promise to investigate the Waco incident thoroughly, no legitimate scholar with a specialization in the study of new religious movements has yet (at the time of this writing) been consulted by the federal government. The general feeling among knowledgeable academics and others who have been following the Branch Davidian drama is that the Clinton administration is holding its breath, hoping the incident will be forgotten by the American public so that the many questions that have been raised about the conduct of the ATF, the FBI, the attorney general, and the president will never require an answer.

The holocaust of the Branch Davidian community is a threshold event in U.S. history that will be the subject of analysis for many years to come. The present volume represents a preliminary attempt to begin sorting through some of the issues that such an event raises. While most of the following essays were written by academics, an effort has been made to include non-academic contributors whose expertise and experience offered other kinds of insights. Press releases and letters to public officials that provide different perspectives on the incident have also been incorporated.

Authors were encouraged to write shorter, less purely academic essays than they might compose for a scholarly journal. Beyond this guideline, contributors were not restricted in any way, and the reader will find a variety of opinions expressed in the following pages. In selecting pieces from non-academics, an effort was made to sample the political spectrum from right to left. While politically diverse, the striking aspect of this collection of authors is that they are all highly critical of ATF/FBI actions with respect to the Branch Davidians.

The *Introductory Essays* section, as the name indicates, is intended to set the stage for the volume with essays that lay out a few analytic and comparative considerations. The second section, *Understanding the Branch Davidians,* will be the most interesting for the religious studies scholar wishing to understand the "world" in which Koresh and his followers operated. James Tabor and Phillip Arnold are two biblical scholars who communicated with the Davidian leader, and who had successfully convinced Koresh to surrender a few days before the FBI's ill-conceived assault. Bill Pitts' essay traces the history of the Davidians from the work of Victor Houteff to David Koresh. The papers in *Millennialism and the Waco Confrontation* examine the role and impact of millennialism/apocalypticism in the Waco drama.

Law Enforcement and Tactical Assessments contains a series of essays that critically discuss ATF and FBI involvement. Of particular importance are the detailed assessments by Col. Charlie Beckwith, retired founder of the U.S. Army's elite Delta Force, and Moorman Oliver, a retired criminal investigator with the Santa Barbara County Sheriff's Department. *Mass Suicide?* asks the question expressed in the title of one essay, "Who Started the Fires?" While the anti-cult movement was not directly responsible for initiating the Waco tragedy, it contributed in several important ways that are examined in *The Role of the Anti-cult Movement. Dynamics and Impact of the Media* assesses the contribution of the mass media to public perceptions of alternative religions and of the Branch Davidians.

Polygamy and Accusations of Child Abuse examines the most sensationalistic accusations made against David Koresh. Martha Bradley's essay examines Davidian polygamy and compares it with Mormon polygamy. Larry Lilliston's and George Robertson's pieces dwell on child abuse accusations. *Academic Reflections* contains a series of essays, the themes of which did not fit comfortably into the other sections of the present anthology, but which raise important issues, such as establishing a formal mechanism through which law enforcement officials might consult appropriate scholars in the future.

Selected Responses samples a broad variety of responses to Waco, from the measured responses of mainstream religious bodies to the incisive observations of social critic Eldridge Cleaver. Also included is a Branch Davidian response, authored by the children of one of the individuals to die in the final inferno. This poem was passed on to me by long-time member Stan Silva, who himself lost a wife and several children in the Mt. Carmel fire. The short section *Selected Letters to Public Officials* represents a small sampling of the many letters from academics, religious leaders, and others— letters that Washington has thus far ignored. The concluding *Epilogue* is authored by J. Gordon Melton, widely recognized as a leading scholar of non-traditional religions in North America.

Chapter 1

The Crime of Piety:
Wounded Knee to Waco

Chas S. Clifton

On December 15, 1890, a few days before the Wounded Knee Massacre, Sitting Bull, the mystic leader of the Unkpapa band of the Sioux Indians, died in a shabby scuffle at his cabin door near Fort Yates, North Dakota. A detachment of forty-three Indian police backed by an Army cavalry unit had come to arrest him, based on the following scintillating bureaucratic logic.

The "Ghost Dance" cult, a highly Christianized millennial movement, was led by a charismatic Paiute from Nevada named Wovoka. Wovoka identified himself with Christ, returned this time as an Indian to renew the world. His followers, the Ghost Dancers, would be the only people spared as a cataclysm rolled over the land: they would inherit a country filled with wild game and cleansed of greedy settlers, missionaries, soldiers, and gold miners.

Earlier that year eleven Sioux men had left their reservations in the Dakotas, taken the train to Nevada, heard Wovoka's message, and learned the "Ghost Dance," so called because Wovoka's followers believed that their relatives killed in battle with the soldiers would be reborn after the great cleansing that was about to happen.

The new movement spread rapidly in the Dakotas and elsewhere in the West. Sitting Bull, whose prestige remained high no matter how much the federal government tried to ignore or belittle him, asked one of the eleven, Kicking Bull, to tell him about it. While not joining the movement himself, Sitting Bull gave it his tacit approval. Perhaps he could not realistically have done otherwise. He rightly feared that the Indian Bureau and the Army would not like the Ghost Dance, but Kicking Bull told him that when Wovoka's followers wore their "ghost shirts," long muslin shirts painted with mystic symbols, soldiers' bullets could not harm them.[1]

The Ghost Dance was entirely nonviolent and pacifist, but its sudden spread in the latter months of 1890 baffled Indian agents and military commanders. On the Sioux reservations up and down the Missouri River in the Dakotas, the Indians clearly were up to no good. "No pupils appeared at the schoolhouses, the trading stores were empty, no work was done on the little farms."[2] And since Sitting Bull retained his spiritual leadership, clearly he was in back of it. Sitting Bull therefore had to be arrested. Ignorance produced fear; fear produced a violent reprisal.

A few days before Sitting Bull's murder and the subsequent Christmas-time massacre of about three hundred Sioux by the Seventh Cavalry at Wounded Knee, one former Indian agent, Dr. Valentine McGillycuddy, trying to negotiate a peaceful outcome to this manufactured crisis, took a comparative approach to the Ghost Dance, recognizing its similarity to the millennial movements of his own people.

"I should let the dance continue," he said. "The coming of the troops has frightened the Indians. If the Seventh-Day Adventists prepare their ascension robes for the second coming of the Savior, the United States Army is not put in motion to stop them. Why should not the Indians have the same privilege?"[3]

Dr. McGillycuddy referred to the adventist movement of the early 1840s, whose own charismatic figure, William Miller, a Baptist farmer from Low Hampton, New York, gained a huge following when he began preaching the literal return of Jesus Christ, set to occur in 1843 or 1844. From these "adventists" grew the Seventh-Day Adventist denomination, and, of course, from it sprang David Koresh's Branch Davidians. (One more irony: McGillycuddy was probably wrong in thinking that "Millerites"waited for the Second Coming dressed in long, white robes. As David Rowe wrote in *Thunder and Trumpets*, "the public came to identify ascension robes so closely with the Millerites that the story persists to the present."[4])

A century passed between Sitting Bull's death and the federal assault on the Branch Davidians, but the pattern remains. "Cults," and I use the term broadly to accommodate any group that would separate itself from larger society, are the "wild Indians" of our time. And they are still treated like Sitting Bull.

Likewise, the sight of the Federal Bureau of Investigation leading the second assault on the Branch Davidians' home and then ordering the ruins bulldozed "for safety" should not surprise the historian of America's new religions and marginal political movements. Throughout its history, the FBI has been as active in enforcing America's socio-religious orthodoxy as it has been in pursuing actual dangerous criminals. For example, Master Fard Muhammad, a founder of the Nation of Islam (i.e., the "Black Muslims"), was the subject of lengthy FBI investigation, and some continue to lay his mysterious disappearance circa 1934 at that agency's door. In 1942 the FBI arrested his successor, Elijah Muhammad, on charges of "sedition" and also scooped up eighty followers, one of whom said that federal agents and Chicago police "tore the place apart trying to find hidden weapons, since they believed we were connected with the Japanese."[5]

In its own way, the FBI is the successor to the Seventh Cavalry at Wounded Knee. Attorney General Janet Reno's acceptance of responsibility for the Waco massacre, while perhaps comforting to Americans used to bureaucratic dissimulation, does not change the facts.

Consequently, the agency has long involved itself in harassing "dissidents," including civil rights activists, the American Indian Movement, and "underground" newspapers and anti-war groups of the Vietnam War era. During the Eisenhower administration, in the early 1950s, the FBI, "charged with investigating the loyalty of all current and perspective government employees, initiated a widespread system of surveillance to keep homosexuals off the federal payroll."[6]

Agencies like the FBI function like herbicide in chemical agriculture. Nothing must interrupt the smooth, monocultural perfection of straight rows of corn, not the biggest, prickliest thistle nor the smallest blade of grass. Insects of all sorts die, bird populations dwindle, even the farmer himself—cavalierly ignoring the warnings on the herbicide label—slowly absorbs the poisons. But the field looks the way it should.

Thus, an important American story is preserved—that our differences are only skin deep. By "making nice" and profoundly exchanging platitudes like "all religions have the same goal," we bury our conflicts and true differences. Only when someone like the Branch Davidians comes along, drawing and enforcing a boundary between themselves and the larger society, does the mask come off. Such action threatens the myth of monotheistic oneness that holds the United States together, "one nation, indivisible, under God."

We fought our own war over the issue of oneness in the 1960s, and today we are obsessed by whether or how to respond as Yugoslavia, for example, disintegrates into warring nations. When the mask does come off, we are ready to believe any slander about people who threaten our myth: that they were caching illegal weapons, that they were brainwashed killer zombies, that they were abusing children, et cetera. My wife and I, both college teachers, were stunned after the Waco incident by the vehemence with which most of our students believed that the Branch Davidians "deserved to die." At my school, the University of Southern Colorado, the student newspaper editorialized to the effect that "they brought it upon themselves," while in one of my writing classes, one of the older (late twenties) students insisted that he knew that the Branch Davidians had cases of hand grenades. (Perhaps he had heard the allegation that empty grenade shells had been sent to the compound.)

The national media, meanwhile, treated the entire Waco incident as a football game, content to eat the free hot dogs in the press box and to report the story solely in terms of the body-count: Feds 14, Davidians 4.

Our myth of oneness is indeed important to national survival. Who wants to end up like Yugoslavia? Its death throes fascinate us because they present the worst-case scenario of our own concerns about an America divided according to lines of ethnicity, sexual preference, or race. (Nothing new: consider Josiah Strong, a Congregational minister and author of *Our Country: Its Possible Future and Its Present Crisis*, writing in 1885 about [particularly non-Protestant] immigration and the creation of "little Germanies here, little Scandinavias there, and little Irelands yonder."[7])

But here the greatest danger arises. Our desire for superficial unity dovetails with an undying political principle: the State distrusts all loyalties other than to itself. Let a religion generally accede to the State's goals and it will flourish; let it run crossways to them, however innocently, and its adherents, like Antigone, will find that they have committed "the crime of piety." So the nonviolent, essentially Christian Sioux Ghost Dancers died at Wounded Knee for the crime of believing the messiah had come and changing their lives (in defiance of government policy) as a result. Sitting Bull died because his name was on a list of "fomenters of disturbances" compiled by the Indian Bureau.

Likewise, consider the long and tortuous history of conscientious objection, of the repeated trials over whether or not Jehovah's Witnesses could be forced in public schools to salute the American flag or say the Pledge of Allegiance, an action which the Witnesses equate with idolatry. These examples could be multiplied many times, and for every Justice Jackson affirming that "no official, high or petty, can prescribe what should be orthodox in politics, nationalism, religion, or other matters of opinion,"[8] there is another zoning board, school principal, or senator all too willing to determine those very things.

I have no personal connection with the Branch Davidians nor great sympathy for David Koresh's apocalyptic doctrine, which his followers evidently died to defend. What we must all do, however, is regard the dead Davidians as martyrs in the long struggle against State-sponsored religious conformity. Even in the United States, which claims and which, happily, sometimes even defends religious freedom, the potent combination of our belief in uniformity and innate governmental arrogance can still produce a smoking ruin filled with the corpses of dead dissenters.

Notes:

[1]Dee Brown, *Bury My Heart at Wounded Knee* (New York: Holt, Rinehart & Winston, 1970), 433-34.

[2]Brown, 435.

[3]Brown, 437.

[4]David L. Rowe, *Thunder and Trumpets: Millerites and Dissenting Religion in Upstate New York, 1800-1850* (Chico, California: Scholars Press, 1985), 102.

[5]Prince-A-Cuba (W. Don Fajardo), "Black Gods of the Inner City," *Gnosis* 25 (Fall 1992) 56-63.

[6]John D'Emilio and Estelle B. Freeman, *Intimate Matters: A History of Sexuality in America* (San Francisco: Harper & Row, 1988), 293.

[7]Quoted in Edwin Scott Gaustad, *A Religious History of America* (San Francisco: Harper & Row, 1990), 193.

[8]Quoted in Gaustad, 315. The reference is to a 1943 case arising from West Virginia Jehovah's Witness children being forced to salute the flag.

Chas S. Clifton is the author of *The Encyclopedia of Heresies & Heretics* (1992), a contributing editor of *Gnosis: A Journal of the Western Inner Traditions*, and editor of Llewellyn Publications' series on modern Wicca, including *The Modern Craft Movement* (1992) and *Modern Rites of Passage* (1993).

Chapter 2

Misinterpreting Religious Commitment

Timothy Miller

The anti-cult forces are having a field day in the wake of the Waco debacle, trying, with fair success, to convince the country and the world that destruction of lives is the inevitable end toward which every "cult," whatever that might mean, is hurtling. Cults, we are told daily, are led by power-mad dictators who turn their compliant followers into robots that in their brainwashed stupor do whatever the leader says, even unto death. David Koresh may have been reduced to ashes, but where one cult leader falls a dozen more rise up, Hydra-like, to lure still more lambs to the slaughter.

That explanation is as attractive as it is simplistic. Unfortunately, it dismisses as fraudulent, or at least obsolete, the erstwhile virtues of religious commitment and moral dedication. Carried to its logical conclusion, the brainwashing/mind-control thesis of leaders and followers means that there is no such thing as valid religious conversion.

As long as we dismiss religious conversion and commitment as properties of the lunatic fringe we will see Waco repeat itself, and we will fail to comprehend a driving force in the human psyche. Our secularized society tends to regard commitment as fanaticism and to dismiss it as a manifestation of ignorance, of primitive superstition. Even followers of mainstream religions often see serious commitment as pathological. So what

7

appears as commitment must have some sinister origin. A mad cult leader fills that hole nicely.

Ironically, we adore commitment as long as it's safely in the past. Thousands of early Christians died for their faith, refusing to recant their beliefs even as hungry lions advanced on them. Anabaptist martyrs of the sixteenth century were burned at the stake singing hymns of praise. The Jews of Masada who chose death over surrender were models of religious devotion. This very Sunday thousands of sermons will exhort believers to lead committed lives, and in response those in the pews will vigorously sing, "To the death I'll follow thee." But woe to the person who takes that exhortation seriously.

A further irony lies in the fact that some of those who denounce certain venues of commitment are, or have been, themselves deeply committed to their own moral causes and principles. The anti-war movement of the late 1960s and early 1970s resounded with high moral dedication; those who endured the billyclubs and tear gas of Mayor Daley's finest at the 1968 Democratic National Convention in Chicago were not there because someone had manipulated them into attending, but because their consciences demanded their presence.

A decade earlier the freedom riders and other civil rights activists who endured physical brutality and, in several cases, death were not zombies who unquestioningly followed sinister leaders; they were passionate seekers of justice, persons just naive enough, it would now seem, to believe the American promise of human equality and justice for all.

Similar dedication to a cause energizes today's anti-abortion activists, who in many cases have abandoned comfortable lives in favor of picket lines and civil disobedience and have often ended up in jail and sometimes penniless in the process. Whatever one may think of Randall Terry and his cause, one can hardly argue that he is a ruthless commandant whose followers do what they do because he has manipulated them into doing it.

Perhaps the saddest fallout of Waco is that thousands of committed souls will suffer unjustly for the sins of others, just as they did when an anti-cult rage swept the country in the wake of Jonestown. Anti-cult activists have already identified a wide range of groups of highly committed individuals as dangerous, and have taken justice into their own hands by engaging in what they call "deprogramming," which consisting of kidnapping followed by the application of psychological pressure designed to wrench the target individual from the group with which she or he has chosen to affiliate.

The "cult" participation of some who have been abducted by these zealots, whose commitment bears a remarkable resemblance to that of the persons they work over, has consisted of joining a Catholic religious community, membership in which requires the taking of a vow of total obedience. Another target of many anticultists, despite its obvious benignity, is Mormonism—after all, its leader claims to be able to receive messages directly from God, it had a period of over half a century in which many of its top male leaders practiced polygamy, it has secret rituals from which non-members are barred, and it exercises very considerable psychological control over the lives of its members.

The Mormons' vast numbers and financial clout discourage deprogrammers. Individuals committed to causes with large and influential followings probably have little to fear. But legions of Americans committed to perfectly harmless but small and socially marginal groups are almost certainly in for some very hard times.

Reproduced, with permission, from Pacific News Service, April 20, 1993.

Timothy Miller is a member of the faculty of the Department of Religious Studies at the University of Kansas and a past chair of the New Religious Movements Group of the American Academy of Religion. Among his books is the edited volume *When Prophets Die: The Postcharismatic Fate of New Religious Movements* (1991).

Chapter 3

Tailhook and Waco:
A Commentary

Franklin H. Littell

Now that the Pentagon's inspector general has completed his work, as many as 175 Navy officers face discipline. The 1991 "Tailhook" convention, held at the Las Vegas Hilton, was attended by about four thousand, and some twenty-nine hundred interviews were used in documenting the thick report. Among those implicated are thirty flag officers, two Marine Corps general officers and three Navy Reserve general officers. When the process of trial and punishment sets in, those convicted face the possibility of reduction in rank and dismissal.

The report charges that a growing pattern of misconduct had developed over years, with each annual meet trying to outdo the previous year, and that this revealed a pattern of irresponsibility at the highest level. The "sport" indulged in included not only general rowdiness and drunkenness, but "streaking," "mooning," "ballwalking" and other forms of indecent exposure. Varieties of sexual abuse of women were admitted, frequently consensual. Apparently the latter misbehavior, which slid over into pinching, biting and mauling of some females who were not consenting, brought about the first semi-public rumblings that did not die down as usual. Harassment of women can no longer pass the test of political correctness.

Shift scenes, and go back three months in 1993. As the end of February approached and pieces of the new administration's budget were falling into place, the Bureau of Alcohol, Tobacco, and Firearms faced severe cuts and even the whispered possibility of termination. Governmental relationship with the alcohol industry was stabilized. The tobacco industry was on the defensive in the United States. Although some states were attempting to carve out small patches of order in the prevailing jungle wilderness of weapons, the prospect of federal firearms control was nil.

Faced with this anguishing prospect of the loss of public support and privilege, the chief bureaucrats of the BATF looked desperately around and found a heavenly gift—if not from the gods, at least from a self-styled messiah. On the plains west of Waco, Texas, there was a self-contained community of "cultists." They were said to be expecting Armageddon, a consummate military conflict.

The charismatic leader of the "cult" was said to call himself a "messiah." If that were properly publicized, Christians and Jews would be offended. If that were insufficient, the charge that he called himself "Jesus Christ" should do the trick with the majority of the religious. There was the rumor that the community practiced polygamy. Much more serious offenses to the moral code were promoted in the movie and TV industry, but "Mt. Carmel" was a far less dangerous target to attack than Hollywood.

For harassing women, a number of "Tailhook" officers will be punished. As to "Waco" (the communications center nearest to "Mt. Carmel"), through press conferences that lasted for seven weeks the public has been subjected to a constant flow of official propaganda. The official PR—much of it consisting of conflicting reports and stories—was intended to erase any possible sympathy or even compassion for the targeted "Branch Davidians." When the time of lies, half-truths, self-serving "cult" bashing and cover-up has passed, what will be done with those officials who on the flatland west of Waco, Texas, have disgraced America on the world's TV screens far more grievously than the rowdies of "Tailhook"?

Some tears have been shed publicly for the "little children." Who will shed tears for adult Americans who were victims of an abuse of police power worthy of Hitler, Stalin—or the *milicia* of a banana republic?

"Is it nothing to you, all ye that pass by?" (Lam. 1:12)

April 25, 1993, Philadelphia Center on the Holocaust, Genocide, and Human Rights.

Franklin H. Littell is President of the Philadelphia Center on the Holocaust, Genocide, and Human Rights; Emeritus Professor of Religion, Temple University; and a member of the U.S. Holocaust Memorial Council, 1979-1993.

Chapter 4

The Waco Tragedy:
An Autobiographical Account of One Attempt to Avert Disaster

James D. Tabor

It was 7:25 p.m. on Sunday, February 28, 1993. My attention was suddenly riveted to an unfamiliar voice, edged with an appealing intensity, coming over CNN on the television in the next room. Anchorman David French had someone on a phone hookup who was quoting biblical passages in a steady stream. A photo of a young man with glasses and long wavy hair, which was later to become familiar around the world, was on the TV screen against a backdrop of a map of Texas with a place marked as "Mt. Carmel," near Waco. Regular CNN programming had been interrupted. It was obvious that some emergency situation was unfolding. I had not yet heard of the Alcohol, Tobacco, and Firearms Bureau raid on Mt. Carmel that very morning at 9:55 a.m. which resulted in a two-hour gun battle with the Branch Davidians, the religious group which lived there, leaving four AFT agents dead and fifteen wounded. For the moment my attention was drawn to two things which fascinated me. The young man from Texas called himself David Koresh, and he was talking about the "seven seals" of the Book of Revelation. As a biblical scholar I knew that Koresh was the Hebrew word for Cyrus, the ancient Persian king who destroyed the

Babylonian empire in 539 B.C.E. I was intrigued that anyone would have such a last name. Also, I was quite familiar with the mysterious seven seals in the last book of the Bible, and how they unfolded in an apocalyptic sequence leading to the Judgment Day and the "end of the world." Like any good newsperson, CNN anchorman French kept trying to get David Koresh to talk about the morning raid, how many had been killed or wounded from his group, and whether he planned to surrender. Koresh admitted he was wounded badly, that his two-year-old daughter had been killed, and some others were killed and wounded from his group. But it was clear that he mainly wanted to quote scriptures, mostly from the Book of Revelation. He said he was the Lamb, chosen to open the Seven Seals. He challenged religious leaders and Biblical scholars from around the world to come to Texas and engage in debate with him on the Bible, and particularly to try and match his understanding in unlocking the mystery of the Seven Seals.

The phone conversation over CNN went on for about forty-five minutes. I was utterly taken with this whole scene. Here we were in the year 1993 and this young Cyrus, would-be challenger of modern Babylon, was actually delving into the details of the Book of Revelation at prime time, over a worldwide television network. I pulled out a Bible and turned to Isaiah 45, where I recalled the ancient Persian king Cyrus was addressed by God Himself:

> Thus says the LORD to his *anointed,* to Cyrus [Koresh],
> whose right hand I have grasped to subdue nations before him
> and strip kings of their robes, to open doors before him.

Here Cyrus is actually called "messiah," that is, one who is anointed. The Greek translation of this Hebrew word, *mashiach,* is "Christos," from which we get our term "Christ." So, one could accurately say that this ancient Persian king was called Christ. David Koresh also claimed to be such a "Christ." This biblical terminology led to endless confusion and miscommunication between the secular media and the FBI on the one hand, and the followers of Koresh who lived and breathed these ancient texts. It was widely but incorrectly reported, even by the most responsible media, that David Koresh claimed to be Jesus Christ, or even God Himself. This confusion resulted from a lack of understanding of the biblical use of the term "anointed." In biblical times both the high priests and the kings of Israel were anointed in a ceremony in which oil was poured over the head and beard (see Ps. 133). In other words, in this general sense of the term the Bible speaks of many "christs" or messiahs, not one. The word comes to refer to one who is especially selected by God for a mission, as was the Persian king Cyrus.

It was in this sense that David Koresh took the label "Christ" or messiah. He believed he was the chosen one who was to open the seven seals of the Book of Revelation and bring on the downfall of "Babylon." The early Christians were quite fond of the same kind of coded language. They routinely referred to the Roman empire as "Babylon." The letter of 1 Peter closes with such a reference: "She who is at Babylon [i.e., Rome], who is likewise chosen, sends you greetings" (1 Pet. 5:13). The Book of Revelation is essentially a cryptic account of the destruction of "Babylon," which was understood to be Rome (Rev. 19). I was later to learn that the children of the Branch Davidians routinely referred to the FBI and any other "outsiders," as Babylonians.

Over the next few days, as the FBI took over control of the siege of the Mt. Carmel complex, it became clear to me that neither the officials in charge, nor the media who were sensationally reporting the sexual escapades of David Koresh, had a clue about the *biblical* world which this group inhabited. Their entire frame of reference came from the Bible, especially from the Book of Revelation and the ancient Hebrew prophets. I realized that in order to deal with David Koresh, and to have any chance for a peaceful resolution of the Waco situation, one would have to understand and make use of these biblical texts. In other words, one would need to enter into the apocalyptic world of David Koresh and his dedicated followers. It was obvious that they were willing to die for what they believed, and they would not surrender under threat of force. I decided to contact the FBI and offer my services.

I called my friend Phillip Arnold, director of Reunion Institute in Houston, Texas. Dr. Arnold, like me, is a specialist in biblical studies and we share a special interest in both ancient and modern forms of *apocalypticism.* The term comes from the Greek word *apocalypsis,* which means "to uncover, to reveal." The Book of Revelation is often called the Apocalypse. An apocalyptic group is one which believes that the end of history is near and that the signs and secrets of the final scenario have been revealed to them. The followers of Jesus are properly understood as an apocalyptic movement within ancient Judaism, as was the group which produced the Dead Sea Scrolls. Since the third century B.C.E. many such groups, first Jewish and later Christian, have proclaimed the imminent end of the world on the basis of their understanding of biblical prophetic texts. Dr. Arnold agreed with me that it was urgent and vital that someone who understood the biblical texts become involved in the situation.

The first FBI agent Dr. Arnold contacted in Waco admitted that they were hopelessly confused when David Koresh went into one of his lengthy expositions of scripture, which occurred regularly in their daily telephone negotiations. In later interviews with survivors of the Waco tragedy the one point that they made repeatedly and consistently was that the source of their attraction to David Koresh was his knowledge of the scriptures, particularly the Book of Revelation. The FBI does not routinely pack Bibles when facing what they had categorized as a hostage situation. This FBI agent told us how they had been frantically reading through the Book of Revelation in the Gideon Bibles in their hotel rooms. This image struck me as almost comical, but at the same time frightening. The agent also told us they found the Book of Revelation, and David Koresh's extended biblical monologues, wholly incomprehensible. He asked, "What is this about the seven seals?" We began to explain to him this reference to a mysterious scroll mentioned in the Book of Revelation, which was sealed with wax stamps, and could only be opened by a figure variously referred to as the Lamb, the anointed one (i.e., Christ), or the "Branch of David." David Koresh claimed to be this person, sent to the world before the end of the age and empowered to finally open this scroll. He interpreted the seven seals of the Book of Revelation by the use of certain key chapters from the Psalms, which he took to be the enigmatic "key of David" mentioned in Revelation 3:7. Psalms 40 and 45 were especially important to his self-understanding and Koresh connected these to the meaning of the first seal—the rider on the white horse who goes forth with a bow to conquer. He understood himself to be that rider, a so-called "sinful messiah" who was written of in a scroll:

> Then I said, "Here I am; *in the scroll of the book it is written of me.* I delight to do your will, O my God; your law is within my heart. . . . For evils have encompassed me without number; *my iniquities have overtaken me, until I cannot see; they are more than the hairs of my head,* and my heart fails me. (Ps. 40:7-8, 12)

Psalms forty five, which he understood to refer to the same figure, namely himself, speaks of a mighty king, anointed by Yahweh, who rides victoriously, marrying princesses and bearing many sons who will rule the earth (v. 4-7, 10-16). This psalm explains why Koresh felt he was supposed to father children with the former wives of his male followers. He was the Branch of David who was to build up a dynasty which would someday rule the world from Jerusalem (Jer. 23:3-5). Koresh argued that these and many other passages, which were applied to Jesus Christ by mainstream Christianity, simply could not refer to him. Jesus was said to be without sin, he never married and bore children, and the Branch of David is to be raised up only at the end time, when the Jewish people return to the Land. Koresh insisted that if the scriptures be true, a latter-day messiah must appear, fulfilling the details of these prophecies.

Over the next few weeks Dr. Arnold and I spent many hours in technical and lengthy discussions with Livingston Fagan, an articulate member of the Branch Davidians who had been sent out of the compound by David Koresh as a spokesperson and was being held in jail. With our knowledge of the prophetic texts of the Bible, and especially the Book of Revelation, we slowly began to attain some understanding of David Koresh's interpretation.

It became obvious to us that the Branch Davidian group understood itself to be actually living through the events of the seven seals, found primarily in chapter six of the Book of Revelation. We became persuaded that they understood themselves to be "in the fifth seal." The text reads:

> When he opened the fifth seal, I saw under the altar the souls of those who had been slaughtered for the word of God and for the testimony they had given; they cried out with a loud voice, "Sovereign Lord, holy and true, *how long will it be* before you judge and avenge our blood on the inhabitants of the earth?" They were each given a white robe and told to wait *a little season*, until the number would be complete both of their fellow servants and of their brothers who were *soon to be killed* as they themselves had been killed. (Rev. 6:9-11)

We discussed the chilling implications of these verses with the FBI. For the Koresh group the Book of Revelation was like a script, setting forth in vivid detail what would transpire, and instructing them as to what they should do. The reason they refused to come out of their compound was that they felt God was telling them in these verses to wait "a little season." But the verse goes on to predict that they, like the others in the February 28 ATF raid, would then be killed. David Koresh once told the federal agents, "I knew you were coming before you knew you were coming." On the morning of that initial raid David had said to ATF undercover agent Robert Rodriguez, who was spying on the group, "What thou doest, do quickly" (John 13:27). David had been studying the Bible with agent Rodriguez for weeks, even though he had figured out he was working for the ATF, and now considered him a Judas figure, who had been given an opportunity to know the truth but rejected it. It was as if the entire situation in Waco was locked into a predetermined pattern, set forth in a book written around 96 C.E., during the reign of the Roman emperor Domitian. What worried us all was the very real possibility of a self-fulfilling prophecy. If the Koresh group found itself living "in the fifth seal," did that mean it was inevitable that the remaining eighty-seven men, women, and children in the Mt. Carmel compound must also die? Might they not provoke a violent end to things simply because they felt it was the predetermined will of God, moving things along to the sixth seal, which was the great Judgment Day of God? We were fascinated by the way in which the literal words of this text dominated the entire situation. David Koresh insisted to the FBI that God had told him to "wait" an unspecified time, and the FBI constantly pushed him, asking, "How long?" The entire drama was being played out according to a biblical script.

Through hours of conversations with one another, and consultation with Livingston Fagan, we slowly began to map out the apocalyptic scenario or "script" that David Koresh and his followers were expecting. We were absolutely convinced that David would never surrender from pressure or harassment. Given his understanding of himself as the messenger, or "anointed one," who had been given the secret of the seven seals, he would only act as he felt God was leading him. And the text of the Book of Revelation was his primary guide. According to his reading of the seven seals, five had now been fulfilled and God was telling him to wait. Given such a view, he simply would not come out and surrender as the FBI demanded. To Koresh and his followers such a move, before the proper time, would have been inconceivable. They would have seen it as disobedience to God. Slowly we formulated a plan to approach David Koresh with an alternative scenario, seeking to meet him within his own interpretive world.

Our first step was a radio broadcast over KGBS, the Dallas radio station which Koresh and his followers tuned to each morning on their battery operated transistor radios. It was April 1, thirty three days since the siege had begun. The talk show host, Ron Engelman, who had been critical of the federal authorities since the February 28 ATF raid, allowed us full use of air time to begin a dialogue with Koresh. Dick DeGuerin, Koresh's attorney who had been meeting with him for the past four days, was clued into our plan. He assured us that Koresh and his followers would be listening to our discussion. What we presented, in give-and-take dialogue form, was a rather technical discussion of an alternative interpretation of the Book of Revelation, which we thought David Koresh might accept. As academics, we were not presenting this interpretation as our own personal view. Rather, our approach was hypothetical—given Koresh's general world view, and the interpretation he was following of the seven seals, what about an alternative understanding? Three days later, on Sunday, April 4th, Dick DeGuerin also took a cassette tape we had made of our discussion of the Book of Revelation into the Mt. Carmel compound so that David Koresh and his followers would have it to listen to and study. Passover was approaching, an eight-day holiday which the Branch Davidians observed. Koresh had announced that following the Passover festival he would announce his plan for surrender.

On Wednesday, April 14th, just five days before the fire that consumed the compound, David Koresh released a letter through his lawyer. It was to be his last. He said that at long last his wait was over; that he had been instructed by God to write an exposition expounding the secrets of the seven seals of Revelation. He wrote:

I am presently being permitted to document in structured form the decoded messages of the seven seals. Upon the completion of this task, I will be freed of my waiting period. I hope to finish this as soon as possible and stand before man and answer any and all questions regarding my activities.... I have been praying for so long for this opportunity to put the Seals in written form. Speaking the truth seems to have very little effect on man. I have been shown that as soon as I am given over to the hands of man, I will be made a spectacle of and people will not be concerned about the truth of God, but just the bizarrity of me in the flesh. I want the people of this generation to be saved. I am working night and day to complete my final work of writing out these seals. I thank my Father, He has finally granted me this chance to do this. It will bring new light and hope for many and they won't have to deal with me the person. As soon as I can see that people like Jim Tabor and Phil Arnold have a copy, I will come out and then you can do your thing with this beast.

Dr. Arnold and I were elated. We felt we had been successful at last. In our tapes to David Koresh we had argued this very point. We had tried to convince him that he was not necessarily "in the fifth seal" of Revelation chapter six, which would mandate the death of the group. We also argued that the "little season" mentioned in Revelation 6:11 could be an extended period. It was logically correlated with the "delay" of Revelation 7:1-3, which we maintained, given such a literal interpretation, could last several years. Further, on the basis of chapter ten we had stressed the idea of a message written in a "little book" which would be given to the world (Rev. 10:11). We had pointed out to David Koresh that although he had appeared on the covers of *Time, Newsweek,* and *People* magazines all in the same week, and was being mentioned hourly on CNN and daily on the network news reports, no one remotely had a clue as to his message. We told him that most people had the idea that he was an insane sex pervert who molested children and claimed to be Jesus Christ, or even God. He had apparently accepted our arguments. We, along with the attorneys, were absolutely convinced he would come out and that this writing of the seven seals, in his mind, was the answer from God he had been talking about for the past six weeks. This has to do with the dynamics of apocalypticism. It always operates through a complex play between the fixed text or "script," the shifting circumstances of outside events, and the imaginative casting of the interpreter. We had not been trying to manipulate David, but we did honestly feel that given his literalist view of the text, there were other viable alternatives.

The FBI had a different reaction. Following Passover week they stepped up their pressure tactics, demanding once and for all that Koresh and his people surrender. They took this latest move on David's part as one more in a long series of delay tactics. In their daily press briefings over the next few days they belittled Koresh as a grade school drop-out who would hardly be capable of writing a book. They said he was a manipulating madman who thought he was God, who interpreted the Bible through the barrel of a gun. He was mockingly pictured as the cartoon character Lucy, who always "moves the football" at the last moment. Nonetheless they did allow writing supplies to be delivered to the Mt. Carmel compound on Sunday evening, April 18, the very evening before the tear gas assault. The authorities had clearly lost all patience. At 5:50 a.m., Monday morning they called the compound and informed the group that if they did not surrender the place would be gassed. What took place in the Mt. Carmel compound from that point on is uncertain. One survivor of the fire with whom I talked told me that the last time he saw David Koresh was about five a.m. that morning. David had come down from his room and looked very tired. He said he had been working most of the night on his manuscript on the seven seals.

When the FBI began their tear gas assault that Monday morning David must have been profoundly disappointed and confused. He had become convinced that God not only was going to graciously allow him to write this most important explanation of the seven seals for the world, but that this was part of the apocalyptic script. In a split second, as the buildings shook, the walls were punched with holes, and the tear gas was injected, he must have thought to himself, "Well, I guess I was right all along. We are in the fifth seal after all, and we must die like the others." It is obvious that one does not write a manuscript if the walls of one's home are being broken down. The actions of the FBI forced David to revise his apocalyptic understanding. Any fulfillment of Revelation 10:11, which he had become convinced would now take place, became impossible. There was not a chance in the world that he or his followers would "come out and surrender to proper authority" as the FBI loudspeakers urged them that morning. To them the only proper authority was God, not the forces of the wicked Babylonians. In their minds, based on Revelation 6:11, they saw their deaths as a necessary martyrdom, a self-sacrifice which would lead to the final collapse of the enemy and the coming of Jesus Christ. Like the famous biblical scene at ancient Mt. Carmel, the contest between the forces of good and evil is decided by a burnt offering (1 Kings 18). For Koresh's followers, the fifth seal has been fulfilled and all that remains is the sudden revelation of the "Great Day of God's Wrath," associated with the sixth seal (Rev. 6:12-17). Modern Babylon has been weighed in the balance and found wanting; her final collapse is imminent.

There is a final bit of historical irony in the Waco tragedy. The defenders of Masada had also died at precisely the same time of year, a few days after Passover in the year 73 C.E. after a lengthy siege by the Roman military forces. Like David Koresh they were serious students of the prophecies of Daniel, the text upon which the Book of Revelation is mainly based. Daniel 11:33 says that in the final battle the remnant of God's true people would die "by sword and by flame." David knew about Masada. He also said he was familiar with the newly released Dead Sea scrolls and had been following the debates surrounding them. It is worth noting that one of the most disputed texts, by one possible translation, speaks of a "Branch of David" being wounded and killed by the authorities. David Koresh, born Vernon Howell, like the Jesus he claimed to emulate, died at age thirty-three, around the time of Passover.

There is not the slightest doubt in my mind that David Koresh would have surrendered peacefully when he finished his manuscript. After the fire some federal agents said they doubted that he was even working on such a project. They took David's talk about being allowed by God to finally write the interpretation of the seven seals as a ploy to further delay things. We now know this was not the case. Ruth Riddle, one of the survivors of the fire, had a computer disk in the right pocket of her jacket. She had been typing David's hand-written manuscript the day before the fire. On that disk was his exposition of the first seal. The disk is in the possession of the federal authorities.

James D. Tabor is Associate Professor in the Department of Religious Studies, University of North Carolina at Charlotte.

Chapter 5

The Davidian Dilemma—To Obey God or Man?

J. Phillip Arnold

For fifty-one days the Branch Davidians waited inside their religious center at Mt. Carmel, refusing to obey federal authorities who demanded their immediate surrender. Why did nearly one hundred members of this Judeo-Christian religious community volunteer to remain inside Mt. Carmel despite the fact that massive firepower was arrayed against them and their messiah David Koresh?[1]

Americans apparently have no problem understanding why a few hundred men went to their deaths in 1836 in a standoff with government authorities at another Texas religious center south of Mt. Carmel at the Alamo mission in San Antonio. In fact, the Alamo defenders are remembered as American martyrs who sacrificed their lives for freedom from a foreign foe. But moderns do not understand or admire the Davidians for refusing to surrender to authorities. After all, the Davidians certainly made no claims to represent the nation-state, and the authorities surrounding Mt. Carmel were not stereotypical "evil foreigners."

Although the Davidians thought that they were defending individual liberty and freedom of religion, this was not the major reason *why* they refused to come out, go to trial, and continue their religious mission from prison if convicted. The question remains why nearly one hundred people adamantly refused to exit their religious center at Mt. Carmel and acquiesce to the demands of the American government.

The Branch Davidians knew full well why it was impossible for them to comply with the authorities' demand to exit Mt. Carmel. Their resistance had nothing to do with their guilt or innocence. It had everything to do with their belief in God. The Davidians believed that *God* had commanded them to remain inside the center until God permitted them to leave the building. Obedience to God was more important to them than submission to human authority—when the two were in conflict, God was to be obeyed.

Federal authorities and the media failed to take seriously the crucial importance of Davidian religious faith. By not factoring in the determinative role that religious faith played for the Davidians, federal negotiations with the group were doomed from the start. Instead of expressing profound insight into the importance of Davidian faith, the authorities and the media constantly demeaned the Davidians by reducing them to "cultists," "con men," "zombies," and victims of "brain-washing." These pejorative and value-laden concepts prevented any crisis-resolving communication to develop between the negotiators and the Davidians.

The inability to understand and relate to the religious beliefs of the Davidians illustrates an abysmal lack of understanding of the phenomenon of religious faith. The absence of empathetic knowledge about this dimension of human experience severely crippled any chance for a peaceful resolution of this crisis and will continue to frustrate the efforts of authorities in future crises as we near the year 2000.

But it is not enough to grant the fact that the Davidians possessed deeply held religious beliefs which determined their decision-making. We also must enquire as to what was the specific *content* of their religion which necessitated—in their minds—their refusal to exit Mt. Carmel. What caused them to conclude that God wanted them inside and *not* outside Mt. Carmel?

The Davidian belief that it was against God's will for them to exit Mt. Carmel was based on prophetic scripture, especially the fifth seal of the Book of Revelation. It is crucial to grasp the fact that the Branch Davidians are a people of the text. For them the words of the Bible are the authoritative revelation of God directed primarily to God's remnant people living at the "end time." Although Koresh was believed to be an inspired prophet figure, even his revelations had to have a basis in the text of scripture. Using the ancient Jewish *pesher* method of interpretation, the Davidians saw the fulfillment of specific biblical prophecies in their particular group at Mt. Carmel—much like the Essenes found scriptural prophecies fulfilled in their community at Qumran.[2]

It is important to realize that for several years Koresh had preached that the "seven seals" of the Book of Revelation were in the process of being fulfilled. That is why the Davidians expectantly awaited the unveiling and fulfillment of each seal in order. They came to believe that the first seal was fulfilled in 1985 when their prophet David Koresh became the white-horse rider of Revelation 6:2. About this time Koresh began to expound the seals, using the prophetic writings of the Bible and the Psalms of David as the primary hermeneutical key.[3] After the fulfillment of the first seal the Davidian community awaited the opening of the second seal. Specific events in the life of the community soon convinced them that the second seal was coming to pass. Confirmed in their faith and inspired by these wondrous fulfillments, the Davidians eagerly awaited in faith the opening and closing of the remaining seals. Within a few years it seemed to them that seals three and four had been fulfilled by important events which took place between 1985 and 1992.[4] The entire church now confidently awaited the catastrophic fifth seal which would precede the direct intervention of God in seals six and seven.

The fifth seal is catastrophic because it clearly predicts the violent deaths of the faithful people of God in the end time. The text in Revelation 6:9-11 states:

> And when he had opened the fifth seal, I saw under the altar the souls of *them that were slain* for the word of God, and for the testimony which they held: And they cried with a loud voice, saying, *How long,* O Lord, holy and true, dost thou not judge and avenge our blood on them that dwell on the earth? And white robes were given unto every one of them; and it was said unto them, that they should *rest* yet for a little season, until their fellow-servants also and their brethren, that should be *killed* as they were, should be fulfilled.

It is crucial to note that the slaying of God's people predicted in the fifth seal occurs in *two phases.* In the first phase only some of the people are to be slain by their enemies. The remainder of God's people are to be slain after a special *waiting* period which lasts for a "little season." Only after these two killing sprees will God directly aid the people by divine intervention as described in seals six and seven. The Davidians believed that this passage commanded the survivors of the first killing episode to patiently await God's supernatural intervention which would occur after a "little season" of waiting. This means that after the fulfillment of the first four seals the Davidians were expecting the opening of the fifth seal which, in their view, predicted that they would be slain by enemies in *two* separate attacks. But they did not know exactly when these tragic events would transpire. Soon, but how soon?

Time was shorter than they thought. When the Davidian community saw the ATF approach them in force on February 28, 1993, the Davidians believed that the moment had come for the dreaded fifth seal to open. That is why Koresh could say that he had known that the government was coming long before the ATF had known. From the Davidian viewpoint, the ATF began shooting at the people of God—killing a number of them. The actual killing of a number of their members confirmed for the Davidians that Revelation 6:9 was fulfilled on Sunday morning February 28. They concluded that phase one of the fifth seal, which predicted the first killing spree, had been fulfilled.

What were they to do? They were driven to the text for direction. Revelation 6:11 informed them that God would intervene in apocalyptic fury to avenge the slaying of the remnant people very soon. God's instructions urged patience and spoke of a short waiting period—a "little season." After this brief period the remainder of the people of God would be killed.[5] The Davidians believed that this interpretation was confirmed by Isaiah 26:20 which commanded the people of God to "enter thou into thy chambers, and shut thy doors about thee: hide thyself as it were for a little moment [a "little season"], until the indignation be overpast." In obedience to their understanding of the text the Davidians did exactly that—for fifty-one days they waited because God told them to in Revelation 6:11! For them it was a matter of conscience—of faithful obedience to God's word. From the Davidian point of view the truth of God was non-negotiable.

Confronted by such religious faith, the authorities found it difficult to negotiate with the Davidians. But had negotiators fully understood the importance of the biblical text to the Davidians, they may have convinced them to leave Mt. Carmel. The Davidians would have exited the center had they been convinced from scripture that God wanted them to leave. In April, the authorities came close to doing just that.

On Sunday, April 4th, they permitted the Davidians to have an audio tape made by Dr. James Tabor and me which spoke to Koresh in biblical language he could understand. We argued from scripture that the "waiting period" was much longer than the "little season" of less than three months which he had expected. The second phase of the fifth seal could be years away. We offered biblical reasons for the possibility that the "waiting period" included time for him to have a trial and to continue his ministry worldwide. Granting his presuppositions for the moment, we pointed him to Revelation 10:11, which "predicted" that "he" had *another* prophetic mission *yet* to be fulfilled. He must "prophesy *again*" to many nations. After hearing our suggestions during Passover week, Koresh decided to lead his people out from Mt. Carmel and let the system do what it would to him. For the first time he confirmed in writing that he had finally received the long-awaited authorization from God to leave the center.[6] But first he must write his interpretation of the seven seals for the world to read—perhaps the "little book" of Revelation 10:8-10. If the world would wait for this written revelation, it would prove itself worthy and could be spared the catastrophes prophesied in the seals.

But on the morning of April 19, with the tanks knocking on his door and dangerous CS gas spreading throughout Mt. Carmel, Koresh became convinced that his original time-table for the fifth seal was correct and that Tabor and Arnold were wrong. It was evident to him that the world was rejecting the seals and that phase two of the fifth seal was now crashing down. Unable to disobey God and "submit" to mere human authority, Koresh and his fellow-believers read scripture, prayed, and accepted their "prophesied" fate. The "little season" was past—the waiting period was over.

Government authorities mistakenly believed that the Davidians would come out of the center once it was infiltrated with painful CS gas. If the children were traumatized, it was hoped that parents would usher them outside to safety. Again, the authorities failed to reckon with the nature of religious faith. They failed to perceive the qualitative difference between a group of religious zealots and a group of bandits or counterfeiters. The Davidians really believed that God's authoritative command in Revelation 6:11 and Isaiah 26:20 took precedence over the sufferings of their loved ones.

Had the government authorities seriously researched Davidian faith and practice they would have realized that successful negotiations with them would have never forced them to choose between obedience to divine authority and human authority. By demanding that the members disobey their understanding of God's commands and "submit to lawful authority," the negotiators created a no-win situation for the Davidians. Once they were confronted with such an alternative, it was a foregone conclusion to those with an awareness of the power of religious faith that the Davidians would remain obedient to their understanding of God's command. In effect, the church members were told to choose between obedience to finite human authority and what they perceived to be infinite divine authority. They believed they should place their lives and their children's safety in the hands of the living God rather than in the hands of government forces. Their decision to remain within the center despite the infusion of CS gas set the stage for the final conflagration where the remainder of the people were slain in what the Davidians would call the final phase of the fifth seal.

The origins of the fire which followed upon the infusion of CS gas remains a mystery. It may have started accidently due to tanks knocking over kerosene lanterns—as reported by survivors. Or, it may have been deliberately set by certain leaders inside the center. Either way, most church members went to their deaths believing that their enemies were destroying them on schedule as prophesied in Revelation 6:11. From the Davidian viewpoint, what role did the fire on April 19 play in their understanding of scripture and prophecy?

It is certain that the Davidians were familiar with the numerous biblical references to the role that fire would play in God's final judgment—"fervent heat," "flaming fire," "ashes" are well-known images in apocalyptic passages. Many of these passages confirm that fire would be the means by which God would melt away the old world order and usher in the new. In Malachi 4:1-3 we read that "the day cometh, that shall burn as an oven; and all the proud, yea, and all that do wickedly, shall be stubble: and the day that cometh shall burn them up. . . . for they shall be ashes under the soles of your feet." In verse 5 this "great and dreadful day" of the Lord's fiery wrath is associated with the coming of an "Elijah" who arrives shortly prior to the last day. The Davidians believed that their church was a typological fulfillment of this Elijah prophecy. As the end-time work of Elijah they would fulfill the role of Elijah immediately prior to the coming of the Lord in "flaming fire taking vengeance" (2 Thess. 1:8).

A further association of the work of Elijah with "fire from heaven" is evinced in 1 Kings 18 where Elijah calls down fire which in verse 38 "consumed the burnt sacrifice, and the wood, and the stones, and the dust, and licked up the water." Verse 19 locates this remarkable event as taking place at Mt. Carmel! It may be that the fire of April 19 was called down from heaven as a typological fulfillment of Elijah's conflagration at the earlier Mt. Carmel.

Given the important role that eschatological fire plays in scripture and in Davidian exegesis, it is likely that David Koresh and the church members considered the burning of their sacred center as the prophesied fire which would immediately precede the opening of the sixth seal. For them, the burning of Mt. Carmel could be the spark which would ignite the worldwide conflagration ushering in the "day of the Lord" when the earth "shall be burned up" (2 Pet. 3:10). The Davidians also were familiar with Daniel 11:33 which predicts that the people of God in the last days would be consumed by fire. The passage states: "and those among the people who are wise [the Davidians] shall make many understand, though they shall fall by sword and *flame*." The Davidians also knew the Second Apocalypse of Baruch which states in 10:19:

> make haste and take all things, and cast them into the fire. . . and the flame sends them to him who created them, so that the enemies do not take possession of them.

Some find it difficult to believe that David Koresh could have planned the fire since scripture indicates that the end-time holocaust is to be started by heavenly beings, not humans. But we know that Koresh saw himself in more than human terms. He portrayed himself as the Persian King Cyrus and as King David.[7] He regarded himself as the Lamb of the Book of

Revelation who must be slain (Rev. 5:6,9) before assuming his avenging role as a conquering king. And remarkably he signed two of his last letters as "Yahweh Koresh." Also on a radio interview after the original ATF raid Koresh identified himself as the one who spoke to the woman at the well two thousand years ago in John 4. He also seems to have identified himself with the angel in the Book of Revelation who had in his hand the book with seven seals. Apparently, this same angel fills a vessel with fire and throws it on the earth in Revelation 8:3-5. The text states:

> And *the angel* took the censer, and *filled it with fire* of the altar, and cast it into the earth: and there were voices, and thunderings, and lightnings, and an earthquake.

We do not know whether David Koresh considered this passage to be a prophecy that his last act on earth would be to start the eschatological fire beginning with Mt. Carmel. But his last words may have resonated those of an earlier David three thousand years ago, recorded in 2 Samuel 23:1-7. And these words conclude with a reference to "fire":

> Now these be the *last words of David*. . . . The Spirit of the Lord spake by me, and his word was in my tongue. . . . and they shall be utterly *burned with fire* in the same place.[8]

Perhaps, in those final moments as the fifth seal drew to a close, Koresh saw himself as a Davidic messiah who brings in the final conflagration. Unable to surrender to the enemies of God's people, did Koresh repeat King David's last words and proceed "in flaming fire" to take "vengeance on them that know not God" (2 Thess. 1:7,8)?

It is impossible to know with certainty how the blaze started. But, whoever started the fire, Koresh and his followers considered their own deaths to be a type of martyrdom. The Davidians were familiar with the tradition of self-inflicted martyrdom in Jewish history. The biblical account of the deaths of Saul and his sons would have been known to them as well as the Masada story.[9] At Masada in 72 C.E. Jewish resistance fighters committed mass martyrdom rather than surrender to Roman authorities. After setting fire to their compound, the Masada defenders drew lots and took one another's lives rather than submit to pagan captivity and death. In the last moments their leader, Eleazar, said:

> It is very plain that we shall be taken within a day's time; but it is still an eligible thing to die after a glorious manner, together with our dearest friends. . . . But first let us destroy. . . the fortress *by fire*.[10]

Josephus writes that the fortress wall "was chiefly made of wood, it soon took fire; and when it was once set on fire, its hollowness made that fire spread to a mighty flame!"[11]

Like the Masada defenders the Davidians believed that God did not want them to surrender to their enemies. For this reason David Koresh and his followers refused for fifty-one days to leave their religious center at Mt. Carmel until they had fulfilled God's plan. They perished in a fiery furnace rather than disobey what they believed was God's command to first explain the seven seals in writing before surrendering to the authorities.

Notes

[1]Branch Davidian theology is characterized by
- A. an apocalyptic-prophetic tradition
- B. a Torah-observant practice, including the Sabbath and festivals of Leviticus 23
- C. a mystical orientation, perhaps related to Luriac Kabbalah

[2]*Jesus and the Dead Sea Scrolls,* ed. James H. Charlesworth (New York, 1993).

[3]Koresh concluded that the "key of David" in Revelation 3:7 was a reference to the Psalms written by David. Ingeniously, Psalms 45 was used by Koresh to interpret Rev. 6:1. He argued that since the author of Revelation used symbols drawn from the Hebrew prophets, a correct interpretation of the book must integrate the prophetic writings—especially in view of Revelation 10:7. Since the Davidians preferred the KJV all citations herein are from it.

[4]These prophetic fulfillments included the conceiving of a number of children who were believed to be divinely ordained to rule over the messianic kingdom as the "House of David" in Israel (Ps. 45:16;8:2). Although Koresh intended to explain these fulfillments to the public in writing prior to surrendering to authorities, no detailed account has been given by surviving members.

[5]They understood a "little season" to be less than three months. Since Passover was less than a "season" from February 28, the Davidians believed that their redemption might draw nigh during that holy season. They also relied on the Second Apocalypse of Baruch 28:2 which predicted that physical calamity would fall upon the people of God (read Davidians) after seven weeks or forty-nine days. Thus, it is probable that the Davidians expected trouble from the federals about day fifty-one.

[6]This was the long-awaited "word" from God which the authorities and media continually said they were waiting for him to receive. There is evidence that Koresh may have wanted to observe another Passover one month after the first one in obedience to Numbers 9:10,11 and 2 Chronicles 30. Not understanding the antiquity of this Jewish tradition, the authorities would have seen in this second observance only stalling tactics by a "con man." But the practice is well known and respected in Torah-observant faiths. Read 2 Chronicles 31:1: where

the enemies of God are defeated only *after* a faithful observance of a *second* Passover by a purified people of God.

[7]Surprisingly, there was another Koresh. Cyrus R. Teed changed his name to Koresh after a divine vision in 1869. He, too, founded a community—the "Koreshans" in Chicago and Florida. This first Koresh also proclaimed himself messiah and wrote on the seven seals of Revelation. He died in 1906 after a violent altercation with a marshal in Ft. Myers, Florida. *The Encyclopedia of American Religions,* ed. J. Gordon Melton (Wilmington, NC, 1987), II, 37.

[8]Do not underestimate Koresh's photographic recall of scripture. He informed the ATF that he knew the Psalms backward and forward because *he* wrote them! Israelis said he knew the "*Tanach* cold." Immediately after the ATF raid, Koresh said on Dallas KRLD radio that Psalms 89 would now begin its tragic fulfillment: verses 38ff predict the rejection and death of a David. And in verse 46 *fire* plays a role in the resolution of the crisis.

[9]1 Samuel 31:3-6: "And the battle went sore against Saul, and the archers hit him; and he was sore wounded of the archers. Then said Saul unto his armourbearer, Draw thy sword, and thrust me through therewith; lest these uncircumcised come and thrust me through, and abuse me. But his armourbearer would not; for he was sore afraid. Therefore Saul took a sword, and fell upon it. And when his armourbearer saw that Saul was dead, he fell likewise upon his sword, and died with him. So Saul died, and his three sons, and his armourbearer, and all his men, that same day together." Arthur Droge and James Tabor, *A Noble Death: Suicide and Martyrdom Among Christians and Jews in Antiquity* (San Francisco, 1992).

[10]See Josephus, *Wars of the Jews,* Bk. VII, Chapt. 8, 5-7.

[11]Ibid.

J. Phillip Arnold received his Ph.D. in Religious Studies from Rice University. He has been a Professor of Religion and History at Houston Graduate School of Theology (1983-1986), and is currently Executive Director of Reunion Institute.

Chapter 6

The Davidian Tradition

Bill Pitts

The Davidians are a small religious group whose message is firmly anchored in millennialist thought. For decades hardly anyone paid this movement any attention. The ATF siege in February 1993, and the Branch Davidian response produced deaths on both sides and began an exhausting standoff which received extended media coverage in the United States and around the world. David Koresh's success in defying the government for weeks, compounded with the tragic holocaust at Mt. Carmel, made the Branch Davidians and David Koresh household names. It would not be surprising to find reference to this episode in history texts generations from now. The event has far-reaching implications for American religion and society and provides occasion for reflection on several significant issues. What, for example, should the church and its biblical interpreters do with apocalyptic materials? How does a religious leader acquire power over others and why do they concede the direction of their lives to someone else? How much power should the state exercise over religious groups and how free are Americans? How has the event affected people's views of religion? Will the Davidian movement survive?

Davidians: Adventist Reformers

The Davidians, like most new groups in church history, set out to reform the church, but ended by creating yet another denomination.

Victor Houteff's Millennial Message

Victor Houteff, founder of the Davidians, immigrated from Bulgaria to America and converted from his national Orthodox church to Seventh-Day Adventist teachings. He believed that the Adventists understood the message of Christianity correctly: (1) Sabbath day worship was a commandment which had not been abrogated anywhere in scripture; (2) Christ would return soon; (3) Old Testament dietary regulations pointed toward a vegetarian diet; and (4) no Christian should kill another, even under conditions of war. He believed, however, that the Seventh-Day Adventist Church had compromised too much with the world. He denounced motion pictures and ball games as a frivolous waste of time, and he refused to allow women to wear make-up. He especially blamed Adventist ministers for failing to produce a disciplined church. He used much biblical imagery in support of his views: the lukewarm Laodicean church, the infidelity of Gomer, and the tares which grew with the wheat. His mission was to convince 144,000 fellow Adventists to reform themselves. Only when this pure church was created would it be possible for the second Advent to occur.

Houteff began his teaching in Los Angeles in 1929. He believed that scripture was correctly interpreted by stages. Luther, Wesley and Ellen White had each offered significant new insights. Houteff believed that he had a message never before revealed to the church. He spoke of his teachings as "Present Truth," that is, new insights into scripture. He called his teaching "Shepherd's Rod," explaining that the rod was the correct interpretation of scripture.

Houteff did not address his message to the general public nor even to the churches at large. Instead, his message was designed for the Seventh-Day Adventists. The Seventh-Day Adventist Church was aware of Houteff's teaching from the start. They interviewed him in 1935 and discussed his teaching when the movement grew very aggressive in its proselytizing efforts. The Seventh-Day Adventists wanted to prevent schism and loss of membership. Houteff wanted the full church to accept his teaching. Both had an interest in keeping lines of communication open, but in the end they separated. Since the larger Seventh-Day Adventist Church in California was not receptive to his teaching, Houteff and his followers therefore scouted the mid-section of the country for a new home. They selected land near Waco, Texas, moved there in 1935, and named their new home Mt. Carmel. Houteff believed that the end of the age was imminent, that the Davidians would be at their new residence less than a year, and that God's Kingdom of 144,000 faithful would presently be established in Palestine.

Life at Mt. Carmel

In order to accomplish their purpose the Davidians separated themselves physically from Waco and psychologically from the mainstream of American life. Two miles away from town they began to build facilities for worship, eating, housing, storage and water supply at Mt. Carmel center. All of this effort was simply the means to a larger end. They had gathered to set up a printing press in order to publish and disseminate Houteff's teachings. His *Shepherd's Rod* was a series of 80-100 page tracts, setting forth his biblical interpretations. *The Symbolic Code* was the Davidian news publication. The title indicates that scripture contains a secret code. Houteff's task was to break the code. Despite hardships of the Depression era, the community succeeded. All of the sixty or so residents worked at the community or took jobs in nearby towns. They contributed two tithes and an offering for their religious endeavors. The children were taught the Bible, academic subjects and a trade at the Mt. Carmel school. Houteff led the group in Bible study each evening and provided authoritarian leadership within the community. The Davidians placed a clock in the floor of their main building with the time set near 11:00. The symbol was a clear reminder to all that the present age is nearing its end and that the Davidians were to be instrumental in inaugurating the last stages of history. The series of tunnels connecting the buildings suggests a sense of impending crisis. Millennialism shaped the life and thought of these people. Their active proselytizing won followers from the Seventh-Day Adventist churches from as far away as Washington, South Carolina, California and Canada.

World War II presented a particular problem for Houteff's followers. He wanted his young men to enjoy conscientious objector status historically associated with Seventh-Day Adventists. Since his group was not recognized by the SDA Conference, he was forced to incorporate, and in 1942 he changed the name of the group from Shepherd's Rod to Davidian Seventh-Day Adventists.

The Great Disappointment

Houteff's death in 1955 shocked his followers. He was supposed to be a new Elijah who should announce the coming of the messiah. Greater shock soon followed. His wife, Florence, assumed leadership of the group and took a step that Houteff had deferred for twenty-five years. She announced in *The Symbolic Code* the beginning of the new era for April 22, 1959: the true church of 144,000 would gather, or war would break out in the Middle East, or the Kingdom of God would be reestablished in Israel. About nine hundred people sold homes and businesses and gathered at Mt.

Carmel. They were deeply disappointed when the date came and passed and nothing dramatic occurred; most soon left the area. But some remained faithful to Davidian teaching, regretting the fact that Florence had set a date and thereby embarrassed the movement. In the interim, in 1957, the Davidians had sold their original site and moved ten miles east of Waco to New Mt. Carmel. About fifty followers remained at the new site. The classic era of the Davidians was finished, but the work of Houteff would continue to shape the essential lines of the movement. It would remain millenarian, sabbatarian, authoritarian, and communal.

Branch Davidian Beginnings

Former members contested for land and money accumulated by the group, and court cases went on for years. Differences among them also led to the establishment of splinter groups. Ben Roden led the most notable of the new groups and called his following the Branch Davidians. The Roden family led the Davidians for the next generation, 1960-1987. Ben Roden was intensely anti-Catholic. Davidian tradition blamed the papacy for shifting worship from the biblical Sabbath to Sunday; this change had no biblical justification in their view. Roden was also particularly committed to taking the Davidians to the promised land. He visited Israel, planned for followers to live there, and noted that five Seventh-Day Adventist families had settled in Israel in 1966. This development was, in his view, an important sign of the beginning of the new age. Following the death of her husband, Lois Roden led the small group until her death, at which time the son, George Roden, assumed leadership.

From Millennialism to Apocalypticism

In its most recent stages the Branch Davidian movement has grown more radical in every key element of its life and practice.

Radical Apocalyptic Thought

The most recent stage of development has been led by Vernon Howell. By virtue of his ability to quote scripture and persuade his hearers, Howell was accepted as their prophet by several of the Davidians. He took them to Palestine, Texas, to organize for the future. In 1987 he and seven of his followers attacked George Roden, and the two sides exchanged gunfire. In the court proceedings which followed, George was declared mentally incompetent, and the Mt. Carmel property was awarded to Howell's group. As with every other stage of this movement, millennialism was the central idea around which the thought and life of the community was organized. However, Howell radicalized the movement's millennial teaching. His apocalyptic imagery focused on his teaching regarding the seven seals of Revelation. His vision of Christian teaching was not based on familiar gospel teachings of love for neighbor and even love for one's enemy, but rather on a titanic apocalyptic struggle between the forces of good and evil. He took the name "David," suggesting renewal of the Israelite Kingdom, and "Koresh," suggesting that his role would be like that of Cyrus, who defeated the Babylonians and allowed the Jews to return to their homeland. Koresh's emphasis fell on Cyrus not simply as deliverer but also as avenger. In a letter he issued during the siege he quoted the prophets, Psalms and Revelation. Taken together, the verses cited set forth a scenario of battle in which Yahweh would fight for Israel and conquer her foes.

The Elect and the Enemy

Koresh envisioned the federal government as the enemy of the Davidians. He must therefore build and fortify a compound and amass weapons to prepare for the inevitable war with its agents. For him this fight was to be fulfillment of his teaching. Whereas Houteff addressed himself to the larger Seventh-Day Adventist Church, Koresh shifted the message to violent conflict with the U.S. government. While Houteff followed traditional Seventh-Day Adventist conscientious objector teaching, Koresh created an armed camp. Both his survivalist mentality and his teaching anticipated potential armed conflict. It was his amassing of arms which prompted government investigation, followed by the attempt to issue the warrant and then the exchange of gunfire. The outside world is no longer interpreted as merely a hindrance to the church's fulfillment of its intended potential. Under Koresh, the government is evil personified and battle with the government was necessary to bring in God's Kingdom.

Community and Control

Koresh, like his predecessors, presided over his community in an authoritarian fashion. Followers have always conceded authority to Davidian leaders because they believe them to have special insight into biblical interpretation which could be found in no other place. They believed that their leaders were inspired with present truth or special insight into the meaning of scripture and the end of history. Again Koresh radicalized this aspect of the community. Whereas Houteff accepted the hardships of communal life, Koresh apparently indulged in amenities—better food, air conditioning, and a good car. Moreover, one of his more controversial revelations suggested that all of the men were to refrain from sex, and that Koresh was to mate with their wives so that the seed of the New Kingdom would all be his offspring. Whereas the Houteffs and the Rodens claimed and were accorded prophet status, Koresh claimed messianic status.

Koresh was a reasonably successful recruiter. He visited Seventh-Day Adventist centers in many parts of the world. Hence he won followers from around the world, and at the time of the siege there were at the compound people from Australia, the United Kingdom and Israel as well as from the United States.

Implications and Reflections

Advocates of the Davidians were quick to point out that they should have had freedom of religion, freedom of speech, and the right to bear arms as long as they harmed no one. Moreover, their defenders pointed out, the Davidians did not begin the siege at Mt. Carmel. Defenders of the government action argued that the amassing of arms included illegal weapons that were potentially dangerous to the lives of others; therefore serving a warrant was justified. Observers divided on this church-state legal issue from the first day; it will continue to be debated. The violence will perhaps be the best remembered aspect of the episode. It will, in turn, provide a discussion point for the never-ending and essential debate over human rights versus state authority. In this case the results for both religion and government were disastrous. There was no winner. It was a lose-lose situation. A great worry is the possible recurrence of religiously motivated violence. How does the state go about encouraging the respect of all its citizens?

A second important issue raised by this episode is the way the church and its biblical scholars interpret millennial and apocalyptic passages. Conversations with Roman Catholic priests and Protestant ministers during the crisis indicated that their parishoners wanted to know about the seals, but that seminary training did not prepare the clergy to handle these texts. The canon within the canon has effectively neutralized these texts for many traditions. If the millennial hermeneutic is suspect (certain events fulfill this prophecy; therefore, the end is near), it is also widely adopted in evangelical circles as an argument to persuade people to be converted. It would seem that there is need to work on approaches other than (1) ignoring the apocalyptic texts, (2) interpreting these texts as ancient prophecy for fulfillment in the twentieth century, or (3) scaring people into religious commitment.

A third key issue is the reaction to the Mt. Carmel episode from institutional churches and the press. Both older Davidians and Seventh-Day Adventists were deeply embarrassed by the Mt. Carmel violence and sought to distance themselves from Koresh following the ATF raid. Other religious leaders were quick to denounce Koresh, chiefly for his messianic claims. Much of the secular press capitalized on sensationalist journalism and reinforced stereotypes with pejorative language (cult, fanatic, etc.). The usually respected *London Times* fell into the trap of reporting astonishingly distorted accounts of Texas, guns and religion. In Europe the picture of the United States as a violent society was strongly reinforced by the episode.

A fourth key issue evolves around the authority of the religious leader. With Koresh it was formidable. The key factor was his ability to persuade his followers that he had the ultimate truth. The fact that the compound was removed from society contributed to his success. Koresh may have elevated the level of authority he was able to exercise, but he did not invent it. Houteff's idea of separating from society, his long hours of indoctrination, along with his domineering personality and organizational structure assured that his will was always carried out. Virtually all religious teachings concede some level of authority to their ministers. The ministers want loyalty, attendance, money, and respect from members. In American society this is usually granted voluntarily. It is worthwhile to examine the basis for the exercise of religious authority. Is the authority exercised in alternative religions different in kind or only in degree? Already books are appearing assessing Koresh as alternatively (1) a con artist, (2) crazy or (3) committed to his belief. Each thesis tries to explain his behavior and his authority. If the third suggestion is correct, what does this say about the larger issue of religious commitment and leadership?

A related issue concerns the people drawn to Koresh. Students of alternative religions have developed many theories regarding reasons for joining alternative religions. Some interpreters stress the significance of the marginalized or disinherited person who finds acceptance; other scholars find the clue in hard times; some observers attribute success to the role of charismatic leaders; others, to the quest for a better future; still others focus on the power of devotion to belief in a doctrine. One might also consider how these explanations differ from what attracts people to mainline denominations.

Whatever the proper mix to explain the Branch Davidians, the movement is not likely to vanish. Even if deprived of its property and leadership, the teaching will not die. Despite the fiasco of 1959, the old Davidians are stronger than ever. The Branch Davidians will also likely re-emerge. The critical question for them will be the modification of their millennial teaching which will in turn depend on the character of the prophetic figure who emerges to lead them.

Bill Pitts teaches the History of Religion at Baylor University. He served as Director of Graduate Studies in Religion at Baylor, 1988-1991.

Chapter 7

Reflections after Waco:
Millennialists and the State

Michael Barkun

Not since Jonestown has the public been so gripped by the conjunction of religion, violence and communal living as they have by the events at the Branch Davidians' compound. All that actually took place near Waco remains unknown or contested. Nonetheless, the information is sufficient to allow at least a preliminary examination of three questions: Why did it happen? Why didn't it happen earlier? Will it happen again?

As a *New York Times* editorialist put it, "The Koresh affair has been mishandled from beginning to end." The government's lapses, errors and misjudgments can be grouped into two main categories: issues of law-enforcement procedure and technique, with which I do not propose to deal; and larger issues of strategy and approach, which I will address.

The single most damaging mistake on the part of federal officials was their failure to take the Branch Davidians' religious beliefs seriously. Instead, David Koresh and his followers were viewed as being in the grip of delusions that prevented them from grasping reality. As bizarre and misguided as their beliefs might have seemed, it was necessary to grasp the role these beliefs played in their lives; these beliefs were the basis of *their* reality. The Branch Davidians clearly possessed an encompassing worldview

41

to which they attached ultimate significance. That they did so carried three implications. First, they could entertain no other set of beliefs. Indeed, all other views of the world, including those held by government negotiators, could only be regarded as erroneous. The lengthy and fruitless conversations between the two sides were, in effect, an interchange between different cultures—they talked past one another.

Second, since these beliefs were the basis of the Branch Davidians' sense of personal identity and meaning, they were nonnegotiable. The conventional conception of negotiation as agreement about some exchange or compromise between the parties was meaningless in this context. How could anything of ultimate significance be surrendered to an adversary steeped in evil and error? Finally, such a belief system implies a link between ideas and actions. It requires that we take seriously—as apparently the authorities did not—the fact that actions might be based on something other than obvious self-interest.

Conventional negotiation assumes that the parties think in terms of costs and benefits and will calculate an outcome that minimizes the former and maximizes the latter. In Waco, however, the government faced a group seemingly impervious to appeals based upon interests, even where the interests involved were their own life and liberty. Instead, they showed a willingness to take ideas to their logical end-points, with whatever sacrifice that might entail.

The Branch Davidians did indeed operate with a structure of beliefs whose authoritative interpreter was David Koresh. However absurd the system might seem to us, it does no good to dismiss it. Ideas that may appear absurd, erroneous or morally repugnant in the eyes of outsiders continue to drive believers' actions. Indeed, outsiders' rejection may lead some believers to hold their views all the more tenaciously as the group defines itself as an island of enlightenment in a sea of error. Rejection validates their sense of mission and their belief that they alone have access to true knowledge of God's will.

These dynamics assumed particular force in the case of the Branch Davidians because their belief system was so clearly millenarian. They anticipated, as historian Norman Cohn would put it, total, immediate, collective, imminent, terrestrial salvation. Such commitments are even less subject than others to compromise, since the logic of the system insists that transcendent forces are moving inexorably toward the fulfillment of history.

Federal authorities were clearly unfamiliar and uncomfortable with religion's ability to drive human behavior to the point of sacrificing all other loyalties. Consequently, officials reacted by trying to assimilate the Waco situation to more familiar and less threatening stereotypes, treating the Branch Davidians as they would hijackers and hostage-takers. This tactic accorded with the very human inclination to screen out disturbing events by pretending they are simply variations of what we already know. Further, to pretend that the novel is really familiar is itself reassuring, especially when the familiar has already provided opportunities for law-enforcement officials to demonstrate their control and mastery. The FBI has an admirable record of dealing effectively with hijackers and hostage-takers; therefore, acting as if Waco were such a case encouraged the belief that here too traditional techniques would work.

The perpetuation of such stereotypes at Waco, as well as the failure to fully approach the religious dimension of the situation, resulted in large measure from the "cult" concept. Both the authorities and the media referred endlessly to the Branch Davidians as a "cult" and Koresh as a "cult leader." The term "cult" is virtually meaningless. It tells us far more about those who use it than about those to whom it is applied. It has become little more than a label slapped on religious groups regarded as too exotic, marginal or dangerous.

As soon as a group achieves respectability by numbers or longevity, the label drops away. Thus books on "cults" published in the 1940s routinely applied the term to Christian Scientists, Jehovah's Witnesses, Mormons and Seventh-Day Adventists, none of whom are referred to in comparable terms today. "Cult" has become so clearly pejorative that to dub a group a "cult" is to associate it with irrationality and authoritarianism. Its leaders practice "mind control," its members have been "brainwashed" and its beliefs are "delusions." To be called a "cult" is to be linked not to religion but to psychopathology.

In the Waco case, the "cult" concept had two dangerous effects. First, because the word supplies a label, not an explanation, it hindered efforts to understand the movement from the participants' perspectives. The very act of classification itself seems to make further investigation unnecessary. To compound the problem, in this instance the classification imposed upon the group resulted from a negative evaluation by what appear to have been basically hostile observers. Second, since the proliferation of new religious groups in the 1960s, a network of so-called "cult experts" has arisen, drawn from the ranks of the academy, apostates from such religious groups, and members' relatives who have become estranged from their kin because of the "cult" affiliations. Like many other law-enforcement agencies, the FBI has relied heavily on this questionable and highly partisan expertise—with tragic consequences. It was tempting to do so since the hostility of those in the "anti-cult" movement mirrored the authorities' own anger and frustration.

These cascading misunderstandings resulted in violence because they produced erroneous views of the role force plays in dealing with armed millenarians. In such confrontations, dramatic demonstrations of force by the authorities provoke instead of intimidate. It is important to understand that millenarians possess a "script"—a conception of the sequence of events that must play out at the end of history. The vast majority of contemporary millenarians are satisfied to leave the details of this script in God's hands. Confrontation can occur, however, because groups often conceive of the script in terms of a climactic struggle between forces of good and evil.

How religious prophecy is interpreted is inseparable from how a person or a group connects events with the millenarian narrative. Because these believers' script emphasizes battle and resistance, it requires two players: the millenarians as God's instruments or representatives, and a failed but still resisting temporal order. By using massive force the Bureau of Alcohol, Tobacco, and Firearms on February 28, and the FBI on April 19, unwittingly conformed to Koresh's millenarian script. He wanted and needed their opposition, which they obligingly provided in the form of the initial assault, the nationally publicized siege, and the final tank and gas attack. When viewed from a millenarian perspective, these actions, intended as pressure, were the fulfillment of prophecy.

The government's actions almost certainly increased the resolve of those in the compound, subdued the doubters and raised Koresh's stature by in effect validating his predictions. Attempts after the February 28 assault to "increase the pressure" through such tactics as floodlights and sound bombardment now seem as pathetic as they were counterproductive. They reflect the flawed premise that the Branch Davidians were more interested in calculating costs and benefits than in taking deeply held beliefs to their logical conclusions. Since the government's own actions seemed to support Koresh's teachings, followers had little incentive to question them.

The final conflagration is even now the subject of dispute between the FBI, which insists that the blazes were set, and survivors who maintain that a tank overturned a lantern. In any case, even if the FBI's account proves correct, "suicide" seems an inadequate label for the group's fiery demise. Unlike Jonestown, where community members took their own lives in an isolated setting, the Waco deaths occurred in the midst of a violent confrontation. If the fires were indeed set, they may have been seen as a further working through of the script's implications. It would not have been the first time that vastly outnumbered millenarians engaged in self-destructive behavior in the conviction that God's will required it. In 1525, during the German Peasants' Revolt, Thomas Münzer led his forces into a battle so hopeless that five thousand of his troops perished, compared to six fatalities among their opponents.

Just as the authorities in Waco failed to understand the connections between religion and violence, so they failed to grasp the nature of charismatic leadership. Charisma, in its classic sociological sense, transcends law and custom. When a Dallas reporter asked Koresh whether he thought he was above the law, he responded: "I *am* the law." Given such self-perception, charismatic figures can be maddeningly erratic; they feel no obligation to remain consistent with pre-existing rules. Koresh's swings of mood and attitude seemed to have been a major factor in the FBI's growing frustration, yet they were wholly consistent with a charismatic style.

Nevertheless, charismatic leaders do confront limits. One is the body of doctrine to which he or she is committed. This limit is often overcome by the charismatic interpreter's ingenuity combined with the texts' ambiguity (Koresh, like so many millennialists, was drawn to the vivid yet famously obscure language of the Book of Revelation).

The other and more significant limit is imposed by the charismatic leader's need to validate his claim to leadership by his performance. Charismatic leadership is less a matter of inherent talents than it is a complex relational and situational matter between leader and followers. Since much depends on followers' granting that a leader possesses extraordinary gifts, the leader's claim is usually subject to repeated testing. A leader acknowledged at one time may be rejected at another. Here too the Waco incident provided an opportunity for the authorities inadvertently to meet millennialist needs. The protracted discussions with Koresh and his ability to tie down government resources gave the impression of a single individual toying with a powerful state. While to the outer world Koresh may have seemed besieged, to those in the community he may well have provided ample evidence of his power by immobilizing a veritable army of law-enforcement personnel and dominating the media.

Given the government's flawed approach, what ought to have been done? Clearly, we will never know what might have resulted from another strategy. Nonetheless, taking note of two principles might have led to a very different and less violent outcome. First, the government benefited more than Koresh from the passage of time. However ample the Branch Davidians' material stockpiles, these supplies were finite and diminishing. While their resolve was extraordinary, we do not know how it might have been tested by privation, boredom and the eventual movement of public and official attention to other matters. Further, the longer the time that elapsed, the greater the possibility that Koresh in his doctrinal maneuvering might have constructed a theological rationalization that would have permitted surrender. Messianic figures, even those cut from seemingly fanatic cloth, have occasionally exhibited unpredictable moments of prudential calculation and submission (one thinks, for example, of the sudden conversion to Islam of the seventeenth century Jewish false messiah Sabbatai Zevi). Time was a commodity the government could afford, more so than Koresh, particularly since a significant proportion of the community's members were almost certainly innocent of directly violating the law.

As important as patience, however, would have been the government's willingness to use restraint in both the application and the appearance of force. The ATF raid, with its miscalculations and loss of life, immediately converted a difficult situation into one fraught with danger. Yet further bloodshed might have been averted had authorities been willing both to wait and to avoid a dramatic show of force. Federal forces should have been rapidly drawn down to the lowest level necessary to prevent individuals from leaving the compound undetected. Those forces that remained should have been as inconspicuous as possible. The combination of a barely visible federal presence, together with a willingness to wait, would have accomplished two things: it would have avoided government actions that confirmed apocalyptic prophecies, and it would have deprived Koresh of his opportunity to validate his charismatic authority through the marathon negotiations that played as well-rehearsed millenarian theater. While there is no guarantee that these measures would have succeeded (events within the compound might still have forced the issue), they held a far better chance of succeeding than the confrontational tactics that were employed.

The events in Waco were not the first time in recent years that a confrontation between a communal group and government forces has ended in violence. Several years ago the Philadelphia police accidentally burned down an entire city block in their attempt to evict the MOVE sect from an urban commune. In 1985 surrender narrowly averted a bloody confrontation at Zarephath-Horeb, the heavily armed Christian Identity community in Missouri organized by the Covenant, Sword and Arm of the Lord. In August 1992 a federal raid on the Idaho mountaintop cabin of a Christian Identity family resulted in an eleven-day armed standoff and the deaths of a U.S. marshal and two family members. In this case, too, the aim was the arrest of an alleged violator of firearms law, Randy Weaver, whose eventual trial, ironically, took place even as the FBI prepared its final assault on the Branch Davidians. In retrospect, the Weaver affair was Waco in microcosm—one from which, apparently, the ATF learned little.

These cases, which should have been seen to signal new forms of religion-state conflict, were untypical of the relationships with government enjoyed by earlier communal societies. While a few such groups, notably the Mormons, were objects of intense violence, most were able to arrive at some way of living with the established order. Many, like the Shakers, were pacifists who had a principled opposition to violence. Some, like the German pietist sects, were primarily interested in preserving their cultural and religious distinctiveness; they only wanted to be left alone. Still others, such as the Oneida perfectionists, saw themselves as models of an ideal social order—exemplars who might tempt the larger society to reform. In all cases, an implied social contract operated in which toleration was granted in exchange for the community's restraint in testing the limits of societal acceptance. When external pressure mounted (as it did in response to the Oneida Community's practice of "complex marriage"), communitarians almost always backed down. They did so not because they lacked religious commitment, but because these communities placed such a high value on maintaining their separate identities and on convincing fellow citizens that their novel social arrangements had merit.

The Branch Davidians clearly were not similarly motivated, and it is no defense of the government's policy to acknowledge that Koresh and his followers would have sorely tested the patience of any state. Now that the events of Waco are over, can we say that the problem itself has disappeared? Are armed millenarians in America likely to be again drawn or provoked into violent conflict with the established order? The answer, unfortunately, is probably yes. For this reason Waco's lessons are more than merely historically interesting.

The universe of American communal groups is densely populated—they certainly number in the thousands—and it includes an enormous variety of ideological and religious persuasions. Some religious communities are millenarian, and of these some grow out of a "posttribulationist" theology. They believe, that is, that Armageddon and the Second Coming will be preceded by seven years of turmoil (the Tribulation), but they part company with the dominant strain of contemporary Protestant millennialism in the position they assign to the saved. The dominant millenarian current (dispensational premillennialism) assumes that a Rapture will lift the saved off the earth to join Christ before the tribulation begins, a position widely promulgated by such televangelists as Jerry Falwell. Posttribulationists, on the other hand, do not foresee such as rescue and insist that Christians must endure the tribulation's rigors, which include the reign of the Antichrist. Their emphasis upon chaos and persecution sometimes leads them toward a "survivalist" lifestyle—retreat into defendable, self-sufficient rural settlements where they can, they believe, wait out the coming upheavals.

Of all the posttribulationists, those most likely to ignite future Wacos are affiliated with the Christian Identity movement. These groups, on the outermost fringes of American religion, believe that white "Aryans" are the direct descendants of the tribes of Israel, while Jews are children of Satan. Not surprisingly, Identity has become highly influential in the white supremacist right. While its numbers are small (probably between 20,000 and 50,000), its penchant for survivalism and its hostility toward Jews and nonwhites renders the Christian Identity movement a likely candidate for future violent conflict with the state.

When millenarians retreat into communal settlements they create a complex tension between withdrawal and engagement. Many communal societies in the nineteenth century saw themselves as showcases for social experimentation—what historian Arthur Bestor has called "patent office models of society." But posttribulationist, survivalist groups are defensive communities designed to keep at bay a world they despise and fear. They often deny the legitimacy of government and other institutions. For some, the reign of Antichrist has already begun. To white supremacists, the state is ZOG—The Zionist Occupation Government. For them, no social contract can exist between themselves and the enemy—the state. Their sense of besiegement and their links to paramilitary subcultures virtually guarantee that, no matter how committed they may be to lives of isolation, they will inevitably run afoul of the law. The flash-point could involve firearms regulations, the tax system, or the treatment of children.

These and similar groups will receive a subtle but powerful cultural boost as we move toward the year 2000. Even secularists seem drawn, however irrationally, toward the symbolism of the millennial number. The decimal system invests such dates with a presumptive importance. We unthinkingly assume they are watersheds in time, points that divide historical epochs. If even irreligious persons pause in expectation before such a date, is it surprising that millennialists do so? As we move closer to the year 2000, therefore, millenarian date-setting and expectations of transformation will increase.

If this prognosis is valid, what should government policy be toward millennial groups? As I have suggested, government must take religious beliefs seriously. It must seek to understand the groups that hold these beliefs, rather than lumping the more marginal among them in a residual category of "cults." As Waco has shown, violence is a product of interaction and therefore may be partially controlled by the state. The state may not be able to change a group's doctrinal propensities, but it can control its own reactions, and in doing so may exert significant leverage over the outcome. The overt behavior of some millenarian groups will undoubtedly force state action, but the potential for violence can be mitigated if law-enforcement personnel avoid dramatic presentations of force. If, on the other hand, they naively become co-participants in millenarians' end-time scripts, future Wacos will be not merely probable; they will be inevitable. The government's inability to learn from episodes such as the Weaver affair in Idaho provides little cause for short-term optimism. The lesson the ATF apparently took from that event was that if substantial force produced loss of life, then in the next case even more force must be used. Waco was the result.

Admittedly, to ask the government to be more sensitive to religious beliefs in such cases is to raise problems as well as to solve them. It raises the possibility of significant new constitutional questions connected with the First Amendment's guarantee of the free exercise of religion. If the state is not to consign all new and unusual religious groups to the realm of outcast "cults," how is it to differentiate among them? Should the state monitor doctrine to distinguish those religious organizations that require particularly close observation? News reports suggest that Islamic groups may already by the subjects of such surveillance—a chilling and disturbing prospect. Who decides that a group is dangerous? By what criteria? If beliefs can lead to actions, if those actions violate the law, how should order and security be balanced against religious freedom? Can belief be taken into account without fatally compromising free exercise?

These are difficult questions for which American political practice and constitutional adjudication provide little guidance. They need to be addressed, and soon. In an era of religious ferment and millennial excitation, the problems posed by the Branch Davidians can only multiply.

Reprinted from the *Christian Century* (June 2-9, 1993) with permission of the Christian Century Foundation.

Michael Barkun is Professor of Political Science in the Maxwell School of Syracuse University. His book on the Christian Identity movement will be published by the University of North Carolina Press in 1994. He also serves as Editor of *Communal Societies,* the journal of the Communal Studies Association.

Chapter 8

The Millennial Dream

Jeffrey Kaplan

The ongoing standoff between federal agents and the Branch Davidian religious sect in Waco, Texas, has prompted a veritable flood of media interest in the otherwise arcane world of the study of apocalyptic sects and millennial religious movements. These questions boil down to two primary interests: Why do such movements turn to violence? And closely related, how do leaders who appear to outsiders to be mentally deranged manage to attract such fanatical loyalty that the members will follow them to the grave, if need be? While the scholarly "state of the art" is as yet unable to fully answer these questions—much less to predict the occurrence of such violent events—it is still possible to suggest some tentative explanations for such seemingly irrational phenomena.

The turn to violence by groups whose primary doctrine is the imminent end of days is an exceedingly rare event, but when it occurs, there does appear to be an underlying pattern. First, the group, having proclaimed its message and experienced considerable disappointment at the indifference or outright hostility of the community, will seek to withdraw from the dominant culture. This withdrawal may take a variety of forms, ranging from the selective, psychic withdrawal of urban religious sects who seek merely a unique sacred space while otherwise participating fully in the life of the community, to the extreme fringes of the survivalist movement scattered in the most rural reaches of the United States. Seldom, however, is this withdrawal total, with the move of Jim Jones's Peoples' Temple to the Guyanese jungles standing as primary contemporary example.

Whatever the degree of withdrawal, the next step appears to involve the leader, basing his or her teachings initially on an accepted sacred text, offering interpretations and prophesies which are increasingly at variance with the beliefs of the mainstream religious tradition. The very unacceptability of these teachings seem to be a primary factor not only in the further withdrawal of the movement from society, but—of greater importance—in inoculating the believers against the contamination of the outside world. Thus armored against the perceived snares of Satan who is posited in this Manichaean view as the true lord of this world, it is possible for trusted followers to work in the wider community without succumbing to its temptations.

All well and good, but then why, if the pattern of withdrawal is so common, do so few groups turn to violence in the face of the overwhelming rejection of their message? Here, the leadership variable appears to be the key factor. Faced with the rejection of his or her claims, and believing ever more firmly in the movement as the "righteous remnant" who alone will emerge in glory from the looming cataclysm to rule the post-apocalyptic paradise, a persecution scenario sets in which the leader sees the "elect" as beleaguered on all sides by immensely powerful "enemies." Often, confirmation of this belief is not long in coming. It may come in the form of defectors from the group who seek to call public attention to the leader's abuses. Or it may come in the form of the unwelcome attentions of "watchdog" groups seeking to expose the movement and "rescue" its adherents. Or ultimately, it may come in the form of government intervention: local or federal agencies seeking to enforce the law on such issues as taxes and building permits, the education and protection of children, the stockpiling of weapons, or outright calls for sedition.

Such violent scenarios, while rare, are not unknown in the contemporary United States. James Ellison's Christian Identity encampment, the Covenant, the Sword and the Arm of the Lord in Missouri was raided by a small army of FBI agents in 1985 on weapons charges. Michael Ryan's survivalist compound in Rulo, Nebraska, was similarly suppressed after reports of activities which included the murder of a five-year-old child. Violent confrontations with government authorities resulted in the deaths of right-wing religious zealots Gordon Kahl and Robert Matthews, founder of the revolutionary organization The Order. The activities in Waco are only the latest instance of the potential for violence of a movement which has withdrawn from the dominant culture, developed an increasingly idiosyncratic doctrine, and come to see itself as under siege.

More difficult than the question of why a millennial movement turns to violence is the mystery of why individuals would join and continue to support a movement whose leader appears to be growing increasingly unstable, and one in which the perception of persecution has become so strong that a hopeless battle against the powers-that-be is seen as inevitable? Simply put, why did so many at Jonestown willingly law down their lives in a mass suicide? Why do the adherents of the Branch Davidian sect hold out against an overwhelming force of federal agents?

Here too it is impossible, given the current state of scholarship, to answer with certainty. Instead, the reader is invited for a moment to try to see the world through the eyes of the believer. Given the opportunity, many of the least committed sectarians would indeed flee from the group when the time of testing arrives. For the core adherent, however, the available range of options are exceedingly dim. Should sect members choose to leave, what awaits them in the outside world? The knowledge that years of their lives have in essence been wasted? That their investment of faith and resources and, quite often, the severing of ties to family and friends were all in vain? That the vision of themselves as part of a world-changing movement, as members of a tiny elect of the faithful whose ultimate reward for perseverance is eternal life and ultimate power, was a lie? That the dream of being like unto the apostles of Jesus—or, in another cultural context, of being among the companions of the Prophet Muhammad of the tribe of Quraysh—was not to be?

And what does the world offer in exchange for the continual excitement, the constant adrenaline high, of being a part of such a movement? A return to the anonymous workaday world which the sectarian had found so devoid of meaning as to be open to the movement's appeal in the first place?

For this small core of the faithful it is far better to entertain the faith and to shut out any disconfirming evidence of the leader's claims! Better the sudden and heroic death of Masada than the shadow existence that for the true believer constitutes the world as you or I know it.

Jeffrey Kaplan, formerly a Lecturer and Researcher for the Committee on the History of Culture at the University of Chicago, is an Historian of the Arctic Sivunmun Illsaguik College in Barrow, Alaska, and is currently assisting in the organization of a project studying Iñupiac history, religion and culture.

Chapter 9

Varieties of Millennialism and the Issue of Authority

Catherine Wessinger

Although concrete data on David Koresh and his Branch Davidians is scarce at this writing in July 1993, I would like to reiterate[1] that the last decade of the twentieth century is an important time to study the varieties of millennialism. The loss of life on two separate occasions at the Branch Davidian compound near Waco, Texas, highlights the responsibility of scholars of religions to educate the public, the media, and governments on the types of millennialism and how to discern potentially dangerous situations and the best means to deal with them. In order to do this, scholars of religions need to educate *themselves* through research on the plethora of millennial groups. In distinguishing potentially volatile groups from benign groups, it is important to correctly understand a millennial group's worldview and especially its understanding of history—and the type of authority exercised by the leader(s).

Types of Millennial Groups

Firstly, it must be noted that there has been no consistent use of terminology among historians and sociologists who study what has variously been termed millenarianism, millenarism, or millennialism. The latter seems to have more current usage. A very general definition of millennialism is "any conception of a perfect age to come, or of a perfect land to be made accessible."[2] Christian thought concerning the perfect age to come is based on the New Testament book of Revelation and other Old Testament books such as Daniel and Isaiah. In Christian thought the perfect age is often described as lasting one thousand years, hence the term "millennium."

Scholarly studies of the various interpretations of the millennium have given rise to the terms "pre-millennialism" and "post-millennialism." Originally, these terms were applied to Christian conceptions of the millennium, but now they are generally used to denote two different views of history and time without necessary reference to Christian prophecy. Pre-millennialism denotes a pessimistic view of history. The world is evil and steadily becoming more corrupt every day. The millennium will be brought about in a catastrophic manner by supernatural or superhuman agents. Post-millennialism is an optimistic view of history that sees gradual improvement in conditions and continuity with the past. Human beings work to bring about the millennium, but they remain under the direction of a superhuman or divine agency.

Historians and sociologists have focused on the most well-known type of millennialism, known as pre-millennialism, since it is an easily identifiable pattern that is cross-cultural and is not limited to the Jewish and Christian religious traditions. Pre-millennial groups have also been termed "revitalization movements,"[3] that often arise in situations where a people's culture and religion has been disrupted by the colonializing incursions of a foreign people with more advanced technology.

Following the definitions of Norman Cohn and Yonina Talmon,[4] I define pre-millennialism as belief in a collective, terrestrial, and imminent salvation that will be accomplished by superhuman agents in a catastrophic manner.[5] Pre-millennialists believe that things are getting so bad that only catastrophic intervention by a superhuman agent can rectify the degraded human condition. Messianism is often but not necessarily a part of the pre-millennial pattern. Scholars have associated messianism with the pre-millennial belief in constant decline. A messiah is the superhuman agent who will bring redemption by mediating between the divine (or superhuman) and the human.[6]

Historians have tended to study post-millennialism more than sociologists. Post-millennialism sees history as consisting of constant progress, and the belief in progress was not prevalent in the West until the eighteenth and nineteenth centuries.[7] The events of the twentieth century have called into question the doctrine of progress, but it remains a widespread outlook. Following common scholarly usage, I define post-millennialism as a view of history that sees the collective and terrestrial salvation as being accomplished gradually by the effort of humans who are subject to the impelling force of some superhuman agency.[8]

In my study of Annie Besant's millennialism, I found that the two categories of pre-millennialism and post-millennialism were not sufficient to address Besant's millennial thought. Annie Besant combined a progressive evolutionary view of history with the urgent message that the messiah's appearance was imminent. Previously, scholars associated messianism only with the pre-millennial view of the constant decline in history and humankind. Upon further observation of the contemporary New Age movement, I determined that a third descriptive category was needed, which I term "progressive messianism."

Progressive messianism, like post-millennialism, entails a progressive and evolutionary view of history. It sees human beings as being guided by superhuman agents to accomplish the goal of creating a heaven on earth. However, unlike post-millennialism, and like pre-millennialism, progressive messianism involves the view that the terrestrial salvation will be accomplished imminently by a messiah who will enter the historical process to effect a radical but non-catastrophic change. This salvation is collective, but not exclusivistic as in the pre-millennial view that only the "elect" will be saved. Thus progressive messianism combines an optimistic and evolutionary view of history with messianism.

More detailed study of late-twentieth-century millennial movements will determine if progressive messianism as a category usefully describes certain phenomena. I anticipate that additional nuances and categories will be needed to enhance understanding of the varieties of millennialism.

The Issue of Authority in Millennial Groups

My understanding of the issue of authority in millennial groups has been greatly influenced by the work of sociologist Margrit Eichler.[9] Eichler suggests that if the leader/prophet/messiah possesses charismatic authority that is not accessible to other members of the group, which she terms closed access (CA) authority, then the door is open for that charismatic leader to assert totalitarian control over the followers.

Charisma takes a variety of forms in the religions, but I have found it useful to distinguish between "ordinary charisma" and "extraordinary charisma." I define ordinary charisma as the direct experience of what is considered sacred or superhuman, which is accessible to any and all members of the group.[10] I define extraordinary charisma as being any sort of direct revelation understood to be available only to the leader and not generally accessible to other members of the group. This is the type of charisma that Eichler designates as CA authority.

It is possible that totalitarian control over the followers may not be exercised by a leader with extraordinary charisma (CA), but there is nothing to prevent the totalitarian control since that leader "claims and is believed to possess a monopoly of access to the legitimating source."[11]   The benchmark of totalitarian control is the restructuring of family and marital relationships, that is the CA leader's meddling in the most intimate aspects of the followers' lives, their sex and family lives.[12]   If the news reports are accurate, David Koresh was a CA leader with extraordinary charisma, who was able to restructure the sex lives of his group.

Using the phrase coined by Joseph Nyomarkay,[13] Eichler terms those prophets or leaders who do not exercise totalitarian control over their followers, and who do not claim to have sole access to the source of legitimation, "ideological leaders" who exercise open access (OA) authority. In a millennial movement with ideological or OA leadership, the secondary leaders and other followers have access to the legitimating source of the ideology.   The source of authority is open to all who participate in the movement.   According to Eichler, the ideological leader must demonstrate how his or her teachings represent a correct interpretation of the ideology of the group.   If the source of authority is not a preserved body of teachings, but direct experience of the sacred or superhuman, OA authority constitutes what I term "ordinary" or "democratic" charisma.

Finally, it needs to be noted that a millennial group will probably manifest different types of leadership.   A prophet or messiah with charismatic authority (either CA or OA) may not necessarily possess organizational abilities, so another person (or persons) takes on this task.

Post-millennialism with its test in gradual improvement and the efficacy of human effort does not encourage CA authority with totalitarian control over the followers.   My studies of Annie Besant and Theosophical millennialism suggests that post-millennialism, as well as progressive messianism, encourage respect for diversity of views and individual effort.[14] It appears likely that the exercise of authority in post-millennial and progressive messianic movements is for the most part benign.   Members of a post-millennial or progressive messianic movement will resort to social work—not violence—to achieve the millennium.

The pre-millennial pattern contains greater possibility for CA authoritarianism.   In a pre-millennial movement, the prophet or messiah may, but not necessarily, claim sole access to the source of legitimation of his or her authority.   Additionally, in pre-millennial movements, there is the expectation that the collective terrestrial salvation will be accomplished in a catastrophic manner.   When the millennial expectation is frustrated, there is the temptation for the believers to resort to violence to bring about the millennium.   Eichler cites the Anabaptists at Münster and Nazism as examples of violent pre-millennial movements in which the leaders possessed CA authority of extraordinary charisma.   Whereas pre-millennial movements do not necessarily become violent, the combination of an authoritarian leader possessing extraordinary charisma with the means to enforce the leader's authority (i.e., arms) presents a potentially volatile situation.

David Koresh and His Branch Davidians
    I wish to stress that I am not suggesting that *all* pre-millennial religions result in violence. Tragically, however, the events of April 19, 1993, near Waco, Texas, bear out my earlier observation that a potentially volatile situation can be discerned in a religion that has: (1) a pre-millennial expectation of a catastrophic end that will be orchestrated by a superhuman or divine agency; (2) a leader/prophet/messiah who has divine authority that is not accessible to anyone else and who exercises totalitarian control over the followers; and (3) arms. The news media accounts of David Koresh's restructuring of his followers' sex lives suggest that he utilized his extraordinary charisma (CA authority), which in part rested on his ability to interpret the Bible better than anyone else, to exercise totalitarian control over his followers. This totalitarian control extended even to the diet of his followers in the Waco compound.
    If a pre-millennial group is armed, there appears to be two possible scenarios. The first, evident in revitalization movements in various cultures, occurs when the pre-millennial group uses its arms to attempt to accomplish the catastrophic end of the current order so that the millennial condition can be created on earth. Or, the pre-millennial group may arm themselves for protection during the catastrophic end-times, thus marking the shading of pre-millennialism into survivalism. Since pre-millennial movements and their leaders (as prophets or messiahs) are often viewed as challenges to the temporal government, the temporal authorities may attempt to take action against the leader and/or the group. If the pre-millennial group is armed and resists, the second possible scenario will result—a siege. At this writing, the evidence is mixed about the extent to which the Branch Davidians resisted the initial ATF assault. Nevertheless, it is certain that the fact that David Koresh and his Branch Davidians possessed arms created a situation which attracted the attention of the ATF—the potentially volatile situation referred to above.
    In the case of a siege, certain factors are not conducive to a peaceful resolution: the leader's reluctance to give up divine or superhuman status commensurate with possession of extraordinary charisma (CA authority); the pre-millennial group's dualistic cosmology that views the forces of evil as battling it out with God's forces; and the pre-millennial expectation of a catastrophic end to the currently evil world. As is evident in the Branch Davidian case, aggression on the part of the government will only be viewed by pre-millennialists as satanic attacks on their godly community.
    In a religion in which access to the source of authority is closed (CA) to all but the leader, the actions of the leader cannot easily be questioned by

followers, since no one else has access to the source of the revelation. Persons unwilling to acknowledge the total authority of such a leader will simply leave the group. The type of person who relishes total control over followers, and who enjoys an exalted status within the group, is not likely to voluntarily give it all up for the ignominy of handcuffs, shackles, and prosecution. The Branch Davidians could see on television that this fate awaited all who came out. David Koresh's expressed fear of being raped in prison seems to be an indication that he realized that he would lose control over even his own person if he exited the compound. Koresh's exercise of totalitarian control within his little world may have been his way of compensating for lack of self-esteem that seems likely given his illegitimate birth, his poor performance in school, and his slight build. David Koresh's personal history, and how he gained control of the Branch Davidians near Waco, taught him that he could gain totalitarian authority over the group through his unique ability to interpret the Bible, and his use of sex and arms.

At this writing, it is not clear if David Koresh ordered the fire to be set, as asserted by the government, or if the FBI either intentionally or unintentionally caused the fire. Let me suggest that even if a leader with extraordinary charisma (CA authority) does not want to commit suicide, he or she may see no other choice when confronted with the imminent destruction of the insular godly community by the forces of evil. *If* David Koresh caused the fire, it indicates that such a CA leader will not give up total authority.

It is clear that less confrontational methods need to be utilized in dealing with armed and authoritarian pre-millennial groups. After the gun battle with agents of the Bureau of Alcohol, Tobacco, and Firearms on February 28, 1993, it should have been obvious to the governmental authorities that they were not dealing with ordinary criminals. That the FBI "didn't get it," even after speaking with David Koresh and other members of his group for fifty-one days, highlights the need to educate government agents about the varieties of millennialism and the issues of authority in these groups. This cannot be left to the many "highly respected cult experts" who leap to the task to further their own anti-cult agenda. As we approach the next millennium, scholars of the religions must further their own *and* the public's understanding of the many permutations of millennialism.

Notes:

[1]The points made in this chapter have previously been published in Catherine Lowman Wessinger, *Annie Besant and Progressive Messianism* (Lewiston, NY: The Edwin Millen Press, 1988); "Annie Besant and the World Teacher: Progressive Messianism for the New Age," *The Quest* 2/1 (Spring 1989): 60-69; and "Annie Besant's Millennial Movement: Its History, Impact, and Implications Concerning Authority," with "Epilogue on David Koresh and the Branch Davidians," *Syzygy: Journal of Alternative Religion and Culture* 2/1-2 (Winter/ Spring, 1993):55-70.

[2]Sylvia L. Thrupp, ed., *Millennial Dreams in Action: Essays in Comparative Study*, Comparative Studies in Society and History, Supplement II (The Hague: Mouton & Co., 1962), 12.

[3]Anthony F. C. Wallace, "Revitalization Movements," in *Reader in Comparative Religion: An Anthropological Approach*, edited by William A. Lessa and Evon Z. Vogt, 4th ed. (New York: Harper & Row, 1979).

[4]Norman Cohn, "Medieval Millennialism: Its Bearing on the Comparative Study of Millenarian Movements," in *Millennial Dreams in Action*, edited by Sylvia L. Thrupp, 31; Yonina Talmon, "Millenarian Movements,"*Archieves Europeenes de Sociologie* 7 (1966):159.

[5]Following evidence provided by Margrit Eichler, I prefer to stipulate superhuman forces rather than supernatural forces as Cohn's definition stipulates. See Wessinger,*Annie Besant and Progressive Messianism*, 22-23; and Margrit Eichler, "Charismatic and Ideological Leadership in Secular and Religious Millenarian Movements: A Sociological Study" (Ph.D. diss. Duke University, 1971). Understanding millennialism to rely on superhuman forces, rather than supernatural, allows for the study of UFO millennial groups that anticipate the imminent intervention of aliens from other planets.

[6]Yonina Talmon, "Pursuit of the Millennium: The Relation Between Religious and Social Change," *Archieves Europeenes de Sociologie* 3 (1962):133.

[7]J. B. Bury, *The Idea of Progress: An Inquiry into Its Origin and Growth* (London: Macmillan and Co., Limited, 1921); Ernest Lee Tuveson, *Millennium and Utopia: A Study in the Background of the Idea of Progress* (Berkeley: University of California Press, 1949); Theodore Olson,*Millennialism, Utopianism, and Progress* (Toronto: University of Toronto Press, 1982).

[8]W. H. Oliver, *Prophets and Millennialists: The Uses of Biblical Prophecy in England from the 1790s to the 1840s* (N.p.: Auckland University Press, 1978), 20-23; J. F. C. Harrison, *The Second Coming: Popular Millenarianism 1780-1850* (New Brunswick, NJ: Rutgers University, 1979), 7.

[9]Eichler, Charismatic and Ideological Leadership"; and Margrit Eichler, "Leadership in Social Movements," in *Leadership and Social Change*, edited by William R. Lassey and Marshall Sashkin (San Diego: University Associates, 1983), 286-305.

[10]See endnote 12 in Catherine Wessinger, "Going Beyond and Retaining Charisma: Women's Leadership in Marginal Religions," in *Women's Leadership in Marginal Religions: Explorations Outside the Mainstream*, edited by Catherine Wessinger (Urbana, IL: University of Illinois Press, 1993), 1-19.

[11]Eichler, "Charismatic and Ideological Leadership," 79.
[12]Ibid., 114, 212.
[13]Joseph Nyomarkay, *Charisma and Factionalism in the Nazi Party* (Minneapolis: University of Minnesota Press, 1967).
[14]This perspective is expressed over and over in lectures delivered by the current president of the Theosophical Society, Radha Burnier, recorded in *Human Regeneration: Lectures and Discussions* (Amsterdam: Uitgeverij der Theosofische in Nederland, 1990). Annie Besant promulgated her millennial views while serving as the second president of the Theosophical Society.

Catherine Wessinger is Associate Professor of the History of Religions at Loyola University, New Orleans. She holds a Ph.D. in the history of religions from the University of Iowa. She is the author of *Annie Besant and Progressive Messianism* (1988), and is the editor of *Women's Leadership in Marginal Religions* (1993).

Chapter 10

Cult Label Made Waco Violence Inevitable

Robert D. Hicks

[This wire service item was issued Friday, March 12, 1993, almost four weeks *prior* to the final FBI assault on the Branch Davidian community.]

Ever since the Bureau of Alcohol, Tobacco, and Firearms (ATF) laid siege on February 28 to the Branch Davidian compound in Waco, Texas, observers—including some law enforcement leaders—have questioned the assault. Other than suspecting that the Branch Davidians were violating federal firearms laws, the ATF has offered no explanation for the raid. What did the ATF think was going on?

The strongest hint of the ATF's rationale lies in their language—labeling the Branch Davidians as a "cult" and their leader David Koresh as a "self-proclaimed messiah." By labeling the Branch Davidians a cult, the ATF—and the news media which have followed its lead—has branded the group's motivations as criminal and even evil.

Talk of cults abounds these days. The Matamoros killings in Mexico in 1989 were attributed by newspaper reports to a witchcraft cult. Muslims everywhere, it seems, can't escape the cult description since they are led by "fanatical extremists." And our TV sets regularly treat us to middle-aged white women claiming to have had babies in satanic cults.

The allure of the word "cult" in the popular mind lies in its vague meaning; it sets people with apparently odd beliefs apart from the rest of "us" who are, by definition, moral. The word allows us to create a "them" and distance ourselves from it. We have religion; they have a cult.

Law enforcement officers have been quick to label as cults religions that involve animal sacrifice and spirit worship. The Matamoros killings in Mexico, for example, were followed by sensational publicity that played up the ties of those involved with Afro-Caribbean religions such as Palo Mayombe and Santeria.

Santeria is a legal religion in the United States practiced by Cuban immigrants from New York to Miami. Yet, according to ex-cop and "cult consultant" Dale Griffis, it has become the religion of choice for drug smugglers. The implication is that adherents to Santeria have *a priori* criminal proclivities, rather than that some adherents—as in all religions—commit crimes. Griffis is typical of law enforcement officials who use the word "cult" to denote anything not mainstream.

For law enforcement officials, the cult model does indeed have menacing attributes that go way beyond a messianic leader who dominates his followers. The descriptions one finds in law enforcement training seminars are replete with references to a "charismatic, controlling leader" who proselytizes through "mind control."

A three-part series in the influential FBI *Law Enforcement Bulletin* from 1982, examining cults and their "sometimes detrimental effects," goes beyond mind control to churn up a discussion of brainwashing. And brainwashing not with a religious purpose, either, but to inculcate loyalty to a cult leader who believes himself above the law.

The articles portray cult members as "childlike" in their docility and conclude that law enforcers "must be responsible enough to avoid interfering with religious beliefs; [but] . . . certain cult behavior (i.e., fraud, violence, deceptive practices) appears to result in substantial harm to society and this outweighs their First Amendment protection. Moreover, some cult recruitment methods and behavior-control techniques indicate that decisions to join and remain in the cult often are not freely and voluntarily made."

Contrary to the FBI's assertion, sociologists of religion have demonstrated that most religious groups' adherents come and go; people's participation in cults is largely voluntary. Law enforcement's contention that cults cloak their true nature under the Constitution—thereby justifying the setting aside of First Amendment protections—is a dangerous Catch-22.

Once the police feel that the First Amendment shelters criminal religious groups, they will feel less constrained by the same Bill of Rights in their zeal to protect us. The First Amendment has never protected those who commit crimes. And people do conspire to commit crime, sometimes in furtherance of religion. But when one is deploying a hundred officers to charge a compound of well-armed people, one needs to be certain that real criminal acts have been committed or are being planned.

Most of our knowledge of small religious groups comes from apostates or defectors, whose information must be checked against independent sources. And incidents of cult violence, coercion, or the gloss of "destructive behavior" do not support the "false conclusion suggested by many cult critics that cult life is inherently dangerous or threatening," according to Dr. Gordon Melton, possibly our pre-eminent authority on "alternative religions."

We know precious little about Branch Davidians. We don't know why the ATF began a shoot-out. But if ATF and other government authorities simply adopted cultspeak to define the menacing "them," then a shoddy linguistic grid filtered their perceptions and determined their actions. And at the moment, the Waco stand-off shows little hope of a peaceful resolution.

Reproduced, with permission, from *Pacific News Service,* March 12, 1993.

Robert D. Hicks, a former police officer, is a Law Enforcement Specialist with the Virginia Department of Criminal Justice Services and author of *In Pursuit of Satan: The Police and the Occult* (1991).

Chapter 11

What Went Wrong in Waco?
Poor Planning, Bad Tactics Result in Botched Raid

Col. Charlie Beckwith

It needs to be made clear from the outset that this examination will not focus on the individual performances of the four brave men of the Bureau of Alcohol, Tobacco, and Firearms (ATF) who were killed on the morning of 28 February 1993 east of Waco, Texas, nor on the sixteen ATF agents who were wounded at the same time. Nor should we cast stones at those ATF agents who were ordered to take part in the unsuccessful assault on the Branch Davidians' compound.

This examination will focus on ATF's assault plan, the execution of the plan and the leadership of the ATF responsible for the conduct of the entire assault effort and failure to accomplish the mission on 28 February. As a "self-appointed expert," to quote ATF Director Stephen Higgins, this writer believes it's prudent and most fitting to hold school on Higgins and his lieutenants for the gross lack of leadership they exercised during the planning and preparation phase, and in the assault phase.

It is apparent that Higgins and his lieutenants have never busted a cap nor smelled the smoke from gunpowder during a conflict with an armed adversary. If they have combat experience, they forgot everything they learned. ATF's failure to accomplish its mission, coupled with the loss of four ATF agents, rests squarely on Higgins's shoulders and he should be held accountable. Had a similar event taken place in the U.S. Army, the responsible party would now be serving time in the correctional facility at Fort Leavenworth, Kansas.

Every principle involved in mounting and conducting a successful raid/assault operation was violated by the leadership of the ATF. The principle *objective* was not obtainable from the outset. Warrants to arrest certain cult members (David Koresh) and to search for and seize illegal weapons and explosive devices inside the compound were never served. I regret to say it, but there are those on the street who believe that the ATF's objective on the morning of 28 February was to impress the new secretary of the Treasury Department, to pave part of the way for a larger annual budget.

Building Takedown 101

Anyway you cut it, the ATF failed to accomplish its objective. In addition, *Command, Control, Communications and Intelligence* (commonly referred to as "C³I") are vital to all operations. The commander of the assault force made numerous mistakes in judgment; however, the most blatant one was his inability to examine the assault from start through finish to determine two important factors:

- *The risk to human life within the assault force and to the cult group inside the compound.*
- *Assessment of the assault's probability of success.*

Any commander who is unable to honestly perform the above examination has no business in command. Additionally, any director of a U.S. government agency similar to the ATF should ensure that both the risk and probability of success have been carefully and realistically hammered out. The decision to undertake any assault is based on these two factors.

Of course, there must be a clear understanding of the capabilities of any adversary in order to weld together a viable plan. Intelligence along with intelligence gathering about all aspects of the adversary provide the framework to determine capabilities. A careful examination of capabilities considering weather conditions, training of your own forces, time of the planned assault and security measures are all part of what is called *mission planning*.

ATF needs to adopt a new motto, "P-P-P-P-P-P-P (Prudent Prior Planning Prevents Piss-Poor Performance)." Had ATF leadership carefully undertaken the steps outlined above, they would not have attempted the assault on 28 February. Also, no commander can be successful if he or she works in a vacuum. He must talk to his subordinate commanders and make sure that every individual involved in the assault understands his task and the tasks of those on his left and right.

Unfortunately this was not the case with the commander of the ATF assault force. A short time before the actual assault, while in the staging area, the commander was made aware of the fact that he had lost the *element of surprise.*

I laugh every time I hear Higgins or one of his lieutenants say, "*We lost the element of surprise,*" and, "*Someone informed the cult we were coming.*" Has Director Higgins never heard of contingency planning? I recall a time in South Vietnam when a group of Special Forces soldiers was only seconds away from assaulting its target; then one of them tripped on a vine and accidentally discharged his weapon. We immediately went to Plan B, a contingency plan, accomplishing our mission without a single casualty.

I cried when I heard that four ATF agents had been killed and sixteen wounded in the wake of this poorly thought-out attack and became very angry when I learned that there was no, repeat *no*, medical team or doctor attached to the assault force. It took more than three hours to evacuate personnel.

OPSEC a Joke

Operations Security (OPSEC) can make or break a combat operation. The lack of OPSEC hit the ATF assault force squarely on the ass. The first violation was to conduct a rehearsal at Fort Hood, Texas. Fort Hood is too close to the actual target site. Also, the rehearsal area was not carefully policed nor swept before the assault force departed the area.

The Dallas ATF office invited the media to the Branch Davidian compound, allowing reporters to tag along on the assault and remain in the target area. It was not until the FBI arrived on 29 February that the media was put under control and moved outside the target area.

The decision to base the ATF assault force out of Waco prior to the actual assault was totally obtuse. ATF might just as well have run a flag up telling everyone something was about to happen. Also, motel and restaurant employees have big ears. It would have been prudent to base out of Dallas/Fort Worth or even Austin instead of Waco. Waco was much too close to the target area.

Economy of force: The ATF apparently did not take into consideration this principle. The number of personnel involved in the assault force was adequate to storm the compound, had the leadership used different tactics, equipment and not violated basic tactical principles. With respect to *security* and *speed*, the ATF assault force ignored the principle of security and attempted to capitalize on the principle of speed in order to reach and take down the compound.

Of course, the selection of the time for the assault was another gross error in judgment (0900). Successful assault operations are conducted during the hours of darkness or a few minutes before first light.

Personnel within the compound and inside the two-story tower building dominated the entire area, providing excellent fields of fire outside the compound. The ATF were sitting ducks in open terrain with no cover. I am surprised that more agents were not killed and wounded.

I mentioned earlier the principle of *surprise*. This vital principle is normally strengthened and made workable through supportive deceptive measures. There was no deceptive plan in support of the assault force at the time the force conducted its attack on the compound. There are those who are surprised that the secretary of the Treasury has not placed Higgins and his lieutenants on administrative, leave pending the outcome of future investigations.

In summary, the terrible fire which destroyed the Branch Davidians' compound on 19 April would have never happened had the ATF served its warrants and not undertaken an assault which was far beyond the agency's scope.

Some folks are saying the ATF needs to go. They believe the ATF's current functions should be divided between the FBI and the Secret Service. I disagree with this concept and believe we need a viable ATF. On the other hand, I further believe that the current leadership in the ATF must go. The ATF is in serious need of strong, experienced and effective leadership to foster unity among all its agents and to totally reorganize training objectives and operating procedures throughout the entire agency.

Repr. with permission from *Soldier of Fortune* magazine, July 1993.

Retired U.S. Army Colonel Charlie Beckwith is founder of America's elite Delta Force, and a noted authority on raid and assault planning.

Chapter 12

Killed by Semantics:
Or Was It a Keystone Kop Kaleidoscope Kaper?

Moorman Oliver, Jr.

There is no intention in this essay to focus reproach toward the BATF agents who were ordered, by their *superiors,* to take part in the failed assault on the compound at Mt. Carmel near Waco, Texas, on the momentous morning of February 28, 1993. They were, unknowingly, following seriously flawed orders that killed four of their valiant fellow agents and wounded sixteen others. Nor is the following meant as a defense of David Koresh, his beliefs, his followers nor their version of the Davidian religion. This is intended primarily as a review of the *planning,* and the discharge of the plan by inept *strategists,* that led to what appeared, in the end, to be the calculated and deliberate destruction of the Constitution of the United States of America.

No one disputes that Koresh was strange. He was conceivably a megalomaniac—so the government claims—whom his devotees followed blindly like sheep. Impersonating a messiah is not illegal in any state. He was accused of child abuse and sex perversion, but child abuse and sex perversion falls under state jurisdiction, not federal. Koresh was accused of having sex with "many women" but, unless the sex was by force, sexual multiplicity is not illegal anywhere in America. Allegations of sex with underage girls had already been put to rest by the local authorities. The

71

"illegal weapons" were found by looking through BATF records and were therefore, apparently, legal. The Branch Davidians were ultimately accused of being a "cult." The mere fact of being a "cult" is not against any criminal statute. The term "cult" is also greatly overused and almost always misused.

Guilty? Maybe. Maybe not. If guilty, who, and of what? Guilty of being different, certainly. But whether singularly or as a group, there is nothing the Davidians could have done to deserve such extreme violation of their constitutional rights and the macabre inferno that followed, perpetrated by "religious thought police" and officials within our own government.

In 1988, a sheriff and his deputies confiscated weapons, made seven arrests, with the Davidians cooperating. There were no injuries and no deaths. In 1992, three Child Protective Services (CPS) workers and two sheriff's deputies were in and out of the compound over a two-month period, investigating child abuse and sex perversion. There were no injuries and no deaths.

On February 28, 1993, more than one hundred BATF agents and other assorted law enforcement, several National Guard helicopters, (and, later, several tanks and armored combat engineer vehicles) moving on unsubstantiated and questionable information, attempted to storm in a military, Ramboesque manner the "heavily" defended religious compound of untrained religious zealots. End results: nearly one hundred dead, including law enforcement officers, children, expectant mothers, devoted followers, and a messiah who was reputed to be "crazy." There were believed to have been fewer followers at the compound during the BATF raid than at either of the other two prior contacts by local officials.

The beginning of this fiasco had its roots in distorted information and the labeling of the Davidians as "cultists" by a group of self-appointed religion police that goes by the name "Cult Awareness Network" (CAN). The first mistake by BATF planners was to give excessive weight to questionable and prejudiced information they received from CAN members who have an axe to grind against all others who dare to be different.

Phony Davidian ex-members (BATF knew, or should have known, they were phony) and CAN had targeted the Davidians with the same charges as in the past, but those charges had been investigated by local Texas authorities and the case was closed without any criminal filing. In 1992, two local sheriff's deputies and three Child Protective Services workers were in and out of the compound over a period of two months. Children were examined and Koresh, with his wife, even went to the CPS office for interviews. Examinations of the children showed no evidence of psychological, physical or sexual abuse. No one was injured and no one killed.

Not satisfied with the local investigation, it appears the same information, with some embellishments, was then passed on to the BATF.

Soon after, according to BATF's own timetable statements, the agency began an investigation of its own. BATF covered the same information investigated by the local officials as well. Again, law enforcement should know that all information from any self-appointed cult watch group or individuals with an axe to grind should be examined thoroughly before being acted upon. Either the information from CAN was not scrutinized enough, or it met some clandestine criteria of BATF. There is some evidence which points to the latter.

The crux of the problem lies with the discrepancies that, as more evidence comes to light, appear to be high-level recklessness and irresponsibility if not outright deliberate distortion (also known as lying). The apparent deceptions in this debacle have played a major part in the lack of confidence of the BATF and the FBI, so much so that many question whether or not the agencies are capable of investigating what went wrong. Even some of the agents involved in the first day's raid spoke of their disgust at their superiors' attitudes and disregard of human life. One even mentioned violations of the Constitution.

There appears to have been "dishonesty and misrepresentation" (another way to say "lies") even before the raid. The Texas governor said BATF agents told state officials the Davidians were "involved in drug trafficking." This is one of the conditions to meet Texas requirements to lend Texas National Guard aircraft to federal agencies. IRS agents were dragged along for the appearance of legitimacy, because of "money laundering" associated with drug trafficking. After the raid, BATF spokesman David Troy publicly stated twice that there was "no suspicion of illegal drug activity" at the Davidian compound.

In late March, after the Texas governor revealed and complained about the deceptions, BATF spokesman David Troy went before television cameras and alleged that the agency had discovered "evidence" of a methamphetamine lab "late" in the investigation. The evidence?? "... a prior infrared overflight had revealed the presence of a 'meth lab.'" Remember, however, that Agent Robert Rodriguez had been in the compound for a considerable length of time and had said nothing about drugs or a "meth lab." The "overflight" was allegedly made by a "British military aircraft brought over from England." Is it legal to have foreign troops acting against U.S. citizens on American soil?

James L. Pate, a freelance reporter and author, was told by one of his sources in the BATF that the allegation regarding the drug lab "was made up. . . .[It was] a complete fabrication" to avoid further criticism by Texas officials. If there were an overflight using infrared, it would have shown stoves and lanterns the Davidians were using for light and cooking after the feds turned off all their power to the compound.

The planners have also been criticized for a raid of such proportion. Was this particular military-style raid necessary? In 1988, McLennan County Sheriff Jack Harwell and his deputies served warrants on David Koresh and his followers. Weapons were confiscated and Koresh along with six of his followers were arrested on charges far more serious than those listed by BATF. No one was injured and no one killed. Why? "Because we treated them like human beings, rather than storm-trooping the place," said former District Attorney Vic Feazell, who had prosecuted the case. "They were extremely polite," he added. The weapons were returned after Koresh and his followers were found innocent and the weapons found to be legal.

Why a military-type assault to begin with? Why not remove Koresh as the focal point by arresting or detaining him on one of his many forays into Waco and then serve the search warrant? BATF claims that they had not seen Koresh outside the compound for as long as eight months, leading most to believe they had him under surveillance for that entire time. However, videotapes show him watching a band performance in December in Waco. A Waco doctor said that he had treated Koresh in December for a back pain that was stress-related. Brent Moore, the manager of the Chelsea Street Pub in Waco, said that Koresh had been in the pub once a week for lunch from late January through February to a week before the raid, and that he had been accompanied by another man and woman. The *Waco Tribune-Herald* confirmed that Koresh had been in Waco at least as late as February 22. There was no reason to believe he would not have come out of the compound again.

The entire plan for the assault was built around secrecy, surprise and a covert signal from an agent inside that the Davidians weapons would be locked up when the offensive began, according to the BATF. They first stated there were undercover operatives inside the compound "for as long as nine months," then "for eight months," later "for several weeks" and other miscellaneous lengths of time. This and similar deceptive discrepancies given to the public, through a news press willing to overlook such discrepancies, gives the impression of subterfuge. BATF Agent Robert Rodriguez was in fact inside, but the Davidians had suspected him as being an agent from the start. Still, the Davidians did not throw the agent out, and even allowed him to leave safely after they found out about the imminent attack.

BATF's David Troy originally said Agent Rodriguez had advised that all was well and left the compound an hour before the raid was to begin. But all was not well. Agent Rodriguez actually told his superiors that Koresh had been warned and was ready. The warning went unheeded by the planners and they ordered the raid to continue. The agents went in expecting to surprise the Davidians, but were instead surprised themselves. It should be pointed out that military planners have said the location and layout of the compound precluded secrecy under any circumstances, during daylight specifically and probably even at night. No contingency plans had been made in case surprise was lost. No contingency was made for heavily armed resistance.

Diverse speculations have been made regarding how Koresh found out about the raid. David M. Jones, a mail carrier and brother-in-law to Koresh, supposedly learned of the impending attack when he was either asked directions to the compound or warned to stay clear of the area by a TV cameraman. The government is trying to tie the local Waco TV station to this, one of the wounded agents even filing a lawsuit against the station. But, how is it that one of the TV crews waiting at the scene was from *Oklahoma?*

Obviously, as more information comes to light, it is increasingly clear that BATF agents themselves alerted the news media because they thought they were going to have an easy walk-through. They thought they would be able to crash through the doors unchallenged, put everyone on the floor like we see every day on the TV cop shows, and that would be the end of it. This was also about the time they were trying to convince Congress they needed more money and would be able to say to Congress, "See what terrible people we have to deal with."

Nor did BATF think much of secrecy in town. Many Waco citizens saw numerous BATF agents, dressed in black and "camo" SWAT-type gear scurrying around various hotel lobbies early that fateful morning (BATF uniforms are royal blue, but are so dark they appear to be black and will be referred to as black throughout). The news media listened to scanner traffic on unsecured portable radios and cellular phones, talking about the raid. Before and during the raid, the agents were heard, on scanners, trying to make contact with other agents and talking about regularly searching mail and UPS packages addressed to the compound. Secrecy and surprise was non-existent. Another question here is, Were there warrants that covered opening the Davidians mail and packages?

Who fired the first shot? Even before the agents on the ground arrived, the Davidians claim they were fired on from above by agents in the helicopters that preceded the ground assault. BATF claimed their helicopters were fired on from within the compound. On the ground, BATF vacillatingly insisted that the Davidians fired first, then later the agency said an agent tripped and "accidentally" fired the first shot. Audio tapes of various conversations during the fifty-one days later surfaced, and tend to support the Davidian version.

Evolving evidence tends to indicate that Koresh came out the front door to meet the agents on the ground, where he was shot twice, first by a sound suppressed (silenced) H&K MP-5 SD submachine gun, fired by an agent who was allegedly "assigned to take Koresh out if necessary." This agent is believed to have been one of the agents killed in the return fire from the compound.

While retreating, the wounded Koresh was shot again by a second agent. Another agent told reporters that he had seen Koresh shot twice, proving that Koresh was at least outside and in plain sight at the very beginning. It was during the initial exchange of gunfire that a small daughter of Koresh was said to have been killed. Why was no attempt made to talk to Koresh as he walked out the door? When Koresh first came out to meet the agents was the time to talk and negotiate. After he was shot, it was past the talking stage.

The planners expressed concern about the children and other innocents inside, but they used armor-piercing bullets that are manufactured specifically for and only available to law enforcement and the military. They claim good "intelligence," but in spite of having an agent on the inside, they had to ask one of the first Davidians (an elderly woman) who came out to draw them a floor plan of the compound.

Later, after the tragedy had ended, BATF officials claimed that the Davidians had used grenades against them on the first day. However, the "pineapple" type BATF claimed the Davidians used would be distinctively different from the "stun" type news media showed being used by BATF. If the Davidians used grenades, why did the feds wait so long after the end of the conflagration to make such a claim? The answer is simple: they didn't and the government spokesmen again had to back off from another fake claim.

Inconsistencies grew and multiplied. BATF originally denied the use of stun grenades as a diversion at the beginning of the raid; however, several different views on television show that stun grenades were in fact used by the agents. The agents were clearly seen throwing grenades through windows. Reports from inside the compound during the standoff indicate that at least one and maybe more Davidians were killed by BATF grenades, one of them a child. It is also believed that some of the agents' wounds were caused by these very same stun grenades, as well as from friendly fire.

The execution of the plan was an effort in futility and the attempt at a cover-up that followed, with the aid of a willing news media, was pathetic. It may be more aptly described as a Keystone Kop Kaleidoscope Kaper. Many of the teams were not able to communicate with each other due to the lack of sufficient equipment as well as widely diverse equipment. The entry into a second-story window that BATF believed led to the Davidians' weapons cache proved deadly.

Three agents, after getting in, came under fire, possibly from their fellow agent still outside the window. The agent outside was observed, in newscasts, throwing a grenade and then twice firing his MP-5 (a fully automatic weapon) through the window that his three fellow agents had entered only moments before. It is believed that the agents inside, thinking they were being attacked by Davidians, returned the fire. It is thought that it was their rounds that were seen coming through the wall, and that struck the helmet of the agent outside, sending him retreating, uninjured, down the ladder. His retreat was later cut from the news, leaving viewers to believe he had been seriously wounded.

The three agents the media showed going through the window were killed while inside, and several other agents who entered elsewhere were wounded and/or captured. Two agents were alleged to have been killed inside by two "grandmotherly" Davidians when the agents threw their grenades into the nursery and entered shooting. Several more children were said to have been killed at that time also, one child by a grenade, others by BATF gunfire. So much for the claims of concern for the children.

Another agent was said to have wounded himself in the leg during the initial assault, but first reports tried to make it seem that he was shot by the Davidians. It rapidly went downhill from there. There has been some talk, that as many as half (or more) of the BATF casualties were from friendly fire. Former McLennan Country District Attorney Vic Feazell was very critical of the "vulgar display of power on the part of the feds," and said the feds were "being met with fear and paranoia on the part of the Davidians."

BATF spokesmen claim that they were under very intense gunfire. But if it was so heavy, how did they get their ladders up against the buildings and their agents onto the roof? They claim that their policy is not to fire unless "there is a clear sight pattern," but TV broadcasts showed some agents firing weapons, including fully automatic weapons, without sighting, across the hoods of the vehicles. These same broadcasts do not show any bullets striking the ground or the vehicles near the agents. At first the BATF claimed that the Davidian gunfire was so heavy that some of the agents never got to fire a shot (the film footage shows differently), but there are some reports that say agents retreated with only about forty rounds of ammunition left between all of them.

The first day, February 28, 1993, four brave agents were killed, sixteen (later revised to seventeen) wounded, and an unknown number captured. A reputed megalomaniac messiah was wounded and his two-year-old daughter killed along with as many as six others inside, because of poor law enforcement leadership. No matter, all but a few still inside would be dead in fifty-one days.

One of the Davidians, Mike Schroeder, had left for work before the raid. Around five p.m., he, along with two other Davidians, tried to return to his family within the compound. While trying to skirt the agents' lines, he was killed, shot once through the eye and then in the back multiple times. One of the other two Davidians, though severely wounded, made it into the compound. The third, Delroy Nash, was captured and arrested. Schroeder was left hanging across a fence for five days before the feds used a helicopter with grappling hooks to retrieve his body, which by that time had been mutilated by wild animals and birds. The feds at first said the three were "trying to shoot their way out of the compound" and were armed, but these assertions were later proved false.

Later, on that first Sunday, there was a cease fire, permitting BATF to retrieve their dead, wounded and captured agents. They then pulled back, in disarray. There were no ambulances immediately at the scene, so the dead and wounded had to be moved on truck beds and hoods of vehicles. Even news vans were called upon to assist in an evacuation that took more than three hours. Ambulance and helicopter medivac, having been called by a reporter from a news van, arrived only after a long delay. There were no medical personnel available at the scene. The lack of proper planning for such possible emergencies is amazing!

The FBI arrived on the scene four days later. That should have been the end of the bumbling double-talk, but it wasn't. Negotiations were begun, and the question many are now asking is, Were those negotiations in good faith? Koresh was ridiculed and mocked repeatedly by FBI Agent Jeffrey Jamar. Jamar joked about the sanity of Koresh, his religious zeal and his followers. The press joked back. The Davidians were picking this up inside. Any officer should know one negotiates with a "crazy" person (if, in fact, Koresh was "crazy") by treating them softly, not with arrogant, heavy-handed demands.

FBI Agent Bob Ricks reported many times about the "broken promises of Koresh," but information that came out during early hearings on Capital Hill tended to confirm allegations that the federal negotiators were only baiting Koresh. Tape recordings released to the media, tending to show Koresh as unbalanced, were later proved to have been heavily edited, and did not show what was really happening. This despite a federal judge's order for the federal authorities not to tamper with any video or audio recordings. This would seem to be an obvious contempt-of-court violation.

These edited tapes were intended to be entered as evidence for the Grand Jury in Waco. They were also presented to the Senate committees, but their edited state was noticed by a communications specialist for Waco's local law enforcement. Preparing and presenting false evidence is also a criminal offense. Regardless of the federal government agent's claims, they were not negotiating. Instead, they were deliberately pushing Koresh into a corner.

During the standoff, Ron Engleman, a Dallas talk show host, arranged to have two volunteer doctors tend to the wounded Koresh and his followers, but federal authorities refused to allow the doctors past the first checkpoint. The Davidians were denied doctors for their sick and wounded for the entire period of the standoff. Doesn't this seem like a human rights violation? Koresh told the feds that if Engleman was allowed to come in and remove the wounded Davidians, he would come out and give up. His offer was refused. On March 2, former McLennan County District Attorney Vic

Feazell, in a *Houston Chronicle* report, predicted, "The feds are preparing to kill them. That way they can bury their mistakes."

In early April, two well-known Second Amendment law activists, Linda Thompson and John Baird, who are partners in an Indiana law firm, arrived. They came, however, as journalists with valid press credentials. They were treated as the other reporters until agents found out who they were. They were then illegally detained, searched, threatened and maligned by agents sworn to uphold the Constitution. Thompson surreptitiously took photos of BATF agents threatening them with their weapons.

At no time were Thompson and Baird placed under arrest, but agents told other news media they had been arrested. Two unknown persons being placed into a paddy wagon were falsely identified as Thompson and Baird to discredit them. Their credentials were taken from them and never returned. It was during this illegal detention that Thompson discovered agents posing as reporters mingling with the press. Other reporters questioned the "official" version at the staged news briefings. These reporters also claim to have been harassed and denied access to further briefings.

Linda Thompson and her husband attempted to deliver baby food and other children's supplies to the Davidian compound on April 3 and 4. They were detained, questioned and turned back. Thompson questioned FBI spokesmen at the field headquarters, "Has it come to this? Does the U.S. government want babies to starve to death?" According to Thompson, the verbatim answer was, "Yes." Two others, including a man named Gary Spaulding, attempting to take baby supplies to the compound on the Friday before the conflagration were arrested and charged with "obstructing." Spaulding was told by the arresting agent, "I can assure you that I speak for high command when I say that this food is not going in to those babies."

Towards the fateful fifty-first day, after days of tiring on-again, off-again negotiations, it began to be apparent that the law officers' patience was wearing thin. It could be heard in their statements, particularly revealed when an FBI agent said, "We are on our own time schedule, not that of Koresh," or ". . . submit to proper authorities . . . [or face a gas attack]." Janet Reno also contended that the FBI team "was tiring and irreplaceable."

Yard-high, razor-sharp, concertina wire had been strung around the compound to prevent anyone from entering or leaving the compound. The feds were using loudspeakers to blare tapes of the negotiations, dentists' drills, locomotives and tortured animal screams at the compound. Electrical power had been cut off. Powerful and brilliant spotlights were played across the compound at night. No way to act toward reputed psychopaths, unless the intent is to make them more psychotic.

An FBI spokesman at first said that they feared the Davidians would attempt an armed breakout, possibly using children as shields. They then contradicted themselves by saying they had expected that, when the gas was pumped in, the Davidians would rush out and surrender for the sake of the children. They also claimed the already poor conditions were getting so bad inside that they could wait no longer.

Government spokesmen claimed to have "continuing evidence" that the children were being constantly abused because of electronic "bugs" sent in with milk for the children and other items requested by the Davidians. But the Davidians found the bugs and destroyed them as fast as they came in. Later, the feds withdrew the allegations of "continuing evidence of child abuse." Some of the survivors claim that not only were there "bugs" with the milk, but possibly poison, because some of the children became sick, one of them dying, after drinking the milk. The agents did finally set "spike optical devices" through the walls of the compound that transmitted pictures, as well as dropping transmitters down air shafts for sound.

Spokesmen maintained they had evidence the Davidians were planning mass suicide à la Jonestown. The possibility of suicide was raised early in the siege by federal agents, apparently to justify their failed raid, but that fear was based on little more than rumor and opinion provided by the likes of Cult Awareness Network. However, it provided good fodder for the media. The attorney general later refuted the claim of impending mass suicides.

Planners claimed they had thought of using a water cannon, but rejected the idea because the strength of the water stream might cause the building to collapse on the children inside as well as destroy evidence. They didn't seem to think about the possibility of crushing a few children by ramming the buildings with tanks and armored vehicles to insert the gas. Even when whole sections of walls slammed down or sections of the roof collapsed, the ramming continued.

Various command officers of the agencies as well as Janet Reno claimed the purpose of the gas and tanks were "just to rachet up the pressure" on those in the compound. "Today was not meant to be the day . . . ." Reno continued. But people living around the area were told by FBI that "it was going to end today." Paul C. Roberts wrote in the *Washington Times*, comparing the assault to the Rodney King case, "If a billy club is excessive force, what is a tank?"

FBI spokesman Bob Ricks asserted that, after exploring many different options, they finally decided on a "non-pyrotechnic" tear gas. But by tearing gaping holes in the building, in combination with thirty-plus miles per hour winds, they should have known the effectiveness of the gas would at least be greatly diminished, if not quickly dissipated. A source well acquainted with both the FBI and BATF told James Pate, ". . . every time they want to hurt somebody, they use tear gas. They use pyrotechnic burning devices. They do it intentionally. I've been there when they did it." This statement seemed to be confirmed by news media reports of agents referring to additional tear gas "canisters" being inserted "when it became evident the Davidians weren't coming out." Tear gas "canisters" are generally pyrotechnic. The "non-pyrotechnic" tear gas sprayed from the tanks was *CS gas*. CS is a solid and is normally mixed with various other liquids which are combustible to form the gas. The only liquid CS could be mixed with to be non-flammable is water, and this mixture produces a narcotic-like gas. The U.S. government, along with 120 other nations at the Paris Chemical Weapons Convention, signed an agreement that they would not use CS gas on other nations. It is incomprehensible that our government could use a gas on its own citizens that it would not use on its enemies.

Several military experts questioned why snipers were not used to "remove Koresh as the problem." The feds claimed that it was against federal policy to use snipers to take out someone like Koresh, but the government did have several snipers present (called "sharp-shooters" by the press). BATF had ECTs ("Entry Control Teams") at the Davidian compound from day one. ECTs always have one or more sniper teams in their make-up. Like many law enforcement special weapons teams, they wear camouflage and/or black uniforms. The presence of ECTs usually indicate the intent to serve a "no-knock" warrant (forced entry before knocking and identifying). But the warrant they were trying to serve was not a no-knock warrant.

There is mounting evidence that in the beginning planners had, in fact, made arrangements "to take Koresh out." They certainly used snipers in the August 1992, Randy Weaver case in Idaho, where an unarmed mother holding her ten-month-old baby and two other children standing by her side was shot in the head by a federal sniper while federal agents were attempting to arrest her husband. Official explanation was that it was an accident (sound familiar?).

The feds claim to have "seen a black-uniformed cult member wearing a gas mask and kneeling with his hands cupped" start the fire in front of a window, but all of the windows were covered with black-out cloth. They later backed off from the claim of "seeing" a cult member start the fire. Could it be that such black-uniformed persons with gas masks may actually have been federal agents? News footage showed a black-uniformed figure jumping from the compound roof near a fire outbreak and leisurely strolling away. News footage at another location show a black-uniformed figure leave through a hole in the building and climb into an armored vehicle just before fire erupted at that location. The Davidians didn't have armored vehicles.

Other inconsistencies are the claims that the fire began "hours" or "long" after tanks had rammed the buildings, and claims that the fires were started where there were no tanks. However, several different views on various televised newscasts show a tank ramming the building and, as it is backing up and turning away, flames and black billowing smoke begin coming from an adjacent corner window. Moments later, fire and smoke come from the hole punched by the tank. Another media view showed a tank smash into a wall twice in the same place, and, each time it backed out, it appeared as if flame was coming from the barrel. One military observer claimed the tank in question "is a Dragon Tank," used for delivering "liquid fire."

The *New York Times* reported, "A vehicle rammed the upper story on the northeast side of the building to insert more tear gas. A few minutes later, from the same section of the building, a flicker of orange could be seen." Later, the feds issued a statement that, "A flammable liquid, probably lantern fluid, is believed to be the accelerant." Well, that's no surprise as all power to the compound was shut off after the first day. The Davidians, for the preceding fifty days, had been using propane camp-style stoves and lanterns that use inflammable liquids. But don't forget the "additional tear gas canisters," or the black-uniformed figure "kneeling with his hands cupped," or the flames that appeared to be coming from the tank's barrel.

Most law enforcement know that one does not make gaping holes in buildings which one wants to saturate with gas. Holes such as those made by the tanks would cause the gas to dissipate and escape. The feds claimed the reason they made the holes was for the Davidians to escape, but that excuse rings hollow. The only reason for the holes, by any rationale, would be to make sure the structure, built in 1941 of white pine and tar paper, was well ventilated so that fire would quickly spread. The first strikes by the tanks were in the areas of stairs and are believed to have collapsed the stairs, preventing anyone from descending to escape. One corner of the compound, directly over the tunnel to the bunkers, was knocked off its foundation. One film shot shows a black-uniformed figure climbing back into an armored vehicle just before smoke is seen coming from the bunker area.

"This is not an assault," they cried as they tore into the compound with tanks. "Do not shoot. We are not entering your compound," they shouted through bull-horns as tanks punched through walls and roofs sagged. "You are responsible for your own actions," agents shouted. Why should the Davidians believe the agents when they shot their "messiah" on the first day? Why should they believe the agents who had negotiated falsely with them for over a month? "Armageddon" had obviously been the agenda from day one—but by whom?

Whether Koresh was right or wrong, he had been pushed into a corner. All cops know that one just doesn't "corner" someone who is supposed to be a psychopath—and these were supposed to be "expert" negotiators! Those still inside had seen their fellow Davidians, who surrendered earlier, arrested. They knew they would be charged with murder, and in their minds they had only defended themselves; their friends were the ones who had been murdered by the government. Who would possibly believe, with tanks smashing through their home, that "this is not an assault"?

The BATF and FBI insist that the tanks, like the helicopters, were Texas National Guard, but the tanks came from Fort Hood, an Army base just south of Waco. The U.S. Government Code 32, Section 1835, commonly known as the Posse Comitatus Act, forbids the use of military troops against U.S. citizens. There were other military vehicles on the scene also, towing the various pieces of equipment used, such as the stadium lights and sound equipment. National Guard or U.S. Army? The unmarked black helicopters seen on occasion, besides the National Guard helicopters, are said to be used as part of a "multi-jurisdictional" task force, and their storage locations are a secret. Why secret? Why unmarked? Intimidation?

There are more questions to be raised about the validity of evidence gathered by these federal agencies that are already at the center of so many questions. Mistakes were made, big mistakes. Discrepancies so glaring that many have called for con-gressional investigations. But the best evidence, the burned compound itself, was ordered bulldozed for "health reasons" by the very agencies to be investigated. Will the bullets and shrapnel taken from the victims, agents and Davidians alike, be the same bullets that get to the labs or the courts? If a rocket launcher suddenly shows up, the question, "Was it planted?" will certainly be raised. Can any of the evidence controlled by the agencies under question, the BATF or FBI, be reliable?

On May 28, 1993, the FBI admitted in court that some of the photo evidence used in the 1992 Randy Weaver case in Idaho was staged. Will the evidence in the present case be staged? After the holocaust in Waco, a retired military officer, well known to federal agencies, stated that he was told by a disgruntled BATF agent that weapons, which he termed "throw-aways," confiscated in other raids were flown into a closed airport near Waco. Were these throw-aways meant for the burned compound as planted evidence? It's happened before in other agencies.

According to several attorneys across the United States, who obtained copies of the documents, the affidavits and warrants used to justify this fiasco were packed with errors, innuendoes, insinuations, distortions, wrong U.S. Code sections and they totally lacked probable cause. The Davidians were suspected of possessing illegal weapons—that is, "machine guns"—but at least one member, Paul Fatta, was a legal federally licensed Class III gun dealer and could legally own and sell a machine gun by paying a $200 tax and filling out a federal form for that purpose. The "illegal weapons cache" indicated in the warrant affidavits was found by checking through BATF's registration records. However, if the weapons are legally registered, then the weapons are legal.

The BATF implied that the Davidians could (and implied they were) converting AR-15s to fully automatic by use of "EZ Kits." There is no such thing as an "EZ Kit," but the Davidians did have what is called "E2 Kits" which contain parts such as pistol grips, rounded foregrips and heavy barrels.

There is no way anyone can convert an AR-15 to fully automatic with an E2 Kit. So far, there has been no evidence at any time of illegal conversions.

Much was made about explosives and the "inert grenades" and the possibility the grenades could be made active. However, it was known by many in the area that the Davidians were mounting the legally purchased inert grenades on presentation plaques and selling them at Texas gun shows as novelties. The dynamite they bought openly and legally for breaking through bedrock for expanding the compound, which included a swimming pool still under construction at the time of the raid.

The so-called BATF "experts" refer to "upper and lower receivers for AK-47s," yet AK-47s do not have upper and lower receivers, but a solid block receiver. The *Shotgun News* is sold openly on newsstands nationwide, not "clandestinely" as stated in the affidavit (many law enforcement personnel subscribe to it). Other errors are dates and time frames that are days and even weeks out of sequence. It is no crime to lie to the news media, but it is a felony to lie on a sworn warrant affidavit. The second search warrant, issued April 13, six days before the inferno, made no mention of drugs. This is a glaring omission, since it was well after BATF's David Troy made his "meth lab" claim, which was a bone of contention regarding the acquisition of Texas National Guard equipment.

Many people, including some in the U.S. Congress, believed a cover-up was taking place. The narrow and indignant stands of President Clinton and Attorney General Janet Reno only added fuel to the controversy. President Clinton and Reno both claimed the main reason for the decision to approve the plan was that there was "mounting evidence of the children being continually abused." But FBI Director William Sessions stated two days later that there was "no evidence of continuing abuse." Reno said, at first, that the siege had to end, but "we were prepared to carry it out tomorrow and the next day [and longer]" Now, that's inconsistency all the way to the top.

Inconsistency isn't the only, nor the largest, problem at the top. Federal agents, in an order from Washington on March 15, were forbidden to discuss the raid publicly, with the order implying that they could be punished, fired and prosecuted for any such discussion. That sounds ominously like a whitewash, if not an outright cover-up, in progress.

President Clinton remained defiant, blindly declaring there were no government mistakes, and that the only parties at fault were the Davidians, even after mounting evidence showed otherwise. Not many were aware that Clinton was emotionally involved. Three of the agents killed on the first botched day had been his body-guards during the previous presidential campaign, and he had gotten to know them well.

President Clinton continued, saying there is ". . . a rise in this sort of religious fanaticism all across the world. We may have to confront it again." He has thus, officially and publicly, put his stamp of approval on using

military tactics against civilian U. S. citizens in cases of religious difference—
a very real threat to many of the smaller religions across the nation, and
certainly to anyone who would dare to be "different."

Reno fiercely defended her decision, saying, "It was my call, and I made
it the best way I knew how." She said that her call was based on the
information she received from "experts." These "experts" were the so-called
cult watchers. It's obvious that she listened to biased experts who had axes
to grind, knew less than they claimed, and she trusted their expertise too
much. Reno herself was well known for her tenacity regarding "satanic cults"
while she was a prosecutor in Florida. Reno, like the president, warned that
situations like the Waco disaster "probably could occur again."

Question should arise about more than just experts and tactics; questions
should also be asked about judgments and leadership, legality and
Constitutionality. Whatever hearings *are* being held, they are not being
reported as meticulously as was the fifty-one days of infamy. We never learn
from our history. The liberal press was fed tidbits of news in the fashion that
the FBI and BATF planners wanted, and the media reported it faithfully as
told. Those who questioned FBI and BATF actions were intimidated,
threatened and falsely arrested. News from Waco during the Davidian
disaster was outrageously controlled to hide mistakes that needlessly cost
human lives.

In the past, the government has proved itself all too willing to lie to
cover up its mistakes and debacles, and the news media has proved all to
willing to print these lies and distortions as truth, then cover up the matter
when found out. The "rights" enumerated in our Constitution are a two-
sided coin. On one side are our *rights* and on the other are our
responsibilities. The news media is fast to hide behind "their rights" as set
forth in the First Amendment, but they absolutely fail in accepting their
responsibilities. News is knowingly and willingly manipulated and twisted for
sensationalism, at the expense of the truth and even at the expense of life.
Today is no different from yesterday; but if that right is ever lost, the media
can only blame themselves.

There is no doubt that the majority of agents in both the FBI and BATF
are fine dedicated men and women. Neither is there any doubt that a debt
of gratitude is owed to these fine agents who put their lives on the line daily.
I have worked with many of them; they are my friends and I ache at their
losses. There can be no question that there is a real need for both of these
agencies. But the Waco tragedy shows the need for a thorough "house
cleaning" of "rogue agents" and incompetent leaders and planners who have
no qualms harming others. Secret units, with such code-names as
"Wolfgang," formed for the purpose of illegal, immoral or questionable
activities must not be allowed. There is no need for black-painted
helicopters with no markings. Such equipment can only be intended for

intimidation. (Besides, the lack of markings is a Federal Aviation Administration violation.) Cover-ups will only help those who wish to weaken or disband these distinguished agencies. Their leaders must be replaced with people who know the legalities and are responsible and ethical—not just administrators appointed as political favor.

Interestingly, the Waco tragedy was the fiftiethth anniversary of another holocaust, the Nazi assault on the Jewish ghetto in Warsaw, Poland. It was also the anniversary of the ride of Paul Revere. One a shame and one a pride. Today we seem to have another shame.

Detective Moorman Oliver, Jr., is a retired criminal investigator with the Santa Barbara Sheriff's Office. He served as his department's specialist on gangs and cults. He currently serves as Law Enforcement Consultant for the Association of World Academics for Religious Education (AWARE).

Chapter 13

Showdown at the Waco Corral:
ATF Cowboys Shoot Themselves in the Foot

James R. Lewis

> Prior to Feb. 27, 1993, the followers of David Koresh were citizens that to my knowledge had caused no problems of any kind in their community. On Feb. 28, 1993, following what appeared to be a staged for TV assault by BATF on the compound they were living in, they all became heinous criminals.
>
> ——Rep. Harold Volkmer, D-Mo.

The "revenuers" of cartoon fame who traded shots with Snuffy Smith and Li'l Abner were agents of the Bureau of Alcohol, Tobacco, and Firearms (ATF), a branch of the U.S. Treasury Department. The least well-trained and least professional of all federal cops, a North Carolina lawyer once described them as "bottom-feeders in the evolutionary scale of Federal law enforcement." The rationale for the continued existence of the ATF as a distinct entity has often been called into question, and the agency had to defend itself against the Reagan administration's attempts to abolish the agency (former President Reagan went so far as to describe the ATF as a "rogue agency") and transfer its functions to the Customs Service and the Secret Service.

Perhaps as a holdover from the days when its primary enforcement activity was busting up stills in rural Appalachia, the ATF has a marked propensity for breaking down doors and roughing up suspects (even other law enforcement agencies describe ATF agents as "cowboys"). To maintain the impression of an active, important agency, the ATF routinely engages in "sting" operations that trick otherwise law-abiding citizens into breaking the law (certainly easier and less risky than pursuing real criminals). For example, a favorite ATF trick has been to sell illegal weapons (or to sell otherwise legal weapons in a non-legal manner) to unsuspecting individuals (usually minorities) in less well-to-do areas, and then arrest them when a purchase is attempted. It has been estimated that as many as seventy-five percent of all ATF arrests involve such entrapment tactics.

Quite recently, the ATF has been investigated for discriminating against minorities in its hiring and promotional practices. The agency has also been accused of turning a blind eye to sexual harassment charges within its ranks. As reported in *U.S. News and World Report,* the prospect of overcoming this tarnished image probably "influenced the decision to proceed with the high-profile raid" of the Branch Davidian community outside of Waco, Texas.

It has also been suggested that ATF began searching for such a high-profile operation soon after it became apparent that Bill Clinton would become the next president of the United States. Clinton had been broadcasting a strong anti-gun message, and certain ATF officials perceived an opportunity to expand the scope and powers of their agency within the new president's anti-gun agenda. The Waco attack, if this suggestion is correct, was designed to attract positive attention to the ATF in a highly publicized raid. The raid was apparently planned with an eye to the Senate Appropriations Subcommittee on Treasury, Postal Service, and General Government that was slated to meet in early March.

Another factor playing into the Branch Davidian fiasco was the ATF's well-deserved reputation for initiating dramatic raids on the basis of ill-founded rumors. The Johnnie Lawmaster incident is a case in point. This is an interesting incident, worth recounting for the light it throws on the ATF assault on the Branch Davidians.

On December 16, 1991—the first day of the third century of the Bill of Rights—agents from the Bureau of Alcohol, Tobacco, and Firearms forced their way into the house of Johnnie Lawmaster. ATF was acting on a *rumor* that Lawmaster had illegally modified a semi-automatic rifle to fire in full automatic mode. Although he would have been happy to have let them in, the ATF busted into Lawmaster's house, kicked down the door and cut the locks off of his gun safe. Federal agents chose to show up while Lawmaster was away from home, and used his absence as a pretext to ransack the premises.

Despite the fact that he had never been guilty of anything more serious than a traffic violation, ATF and local police assaulted Lawmaster's home with a total of sixty law enforcement officers. According to an account published in the *American Hunter:*

They cordoned off the street; took station with weapons drawn in the back yard; used a battering ram to break through the front door; kicked in the back door; broke into his gun safe; threw personal papers around the house; spilled boxes of ammunition on the floor; broke into a small, locked box that contained precious coins; and stood on a table to peer through the ceiling tiles, breaking the table in the process. Then, they left. The doors were closed but not latched, much less locked. The ammo and guns were left unsecured.

As Lawmaster later remarked, "Anybody could have waltzed in there and stolen everything I own. A child could have taken a gun. The guns, the safe—everything was open and laying around."

When he returned home after the raid, Lawmaster felt he had walked into a nightmare. He was still standing around in shock when the gas, electric and water companies showed up to turn everything off. They informed Lawmaster that they had been told to shut things down. He then discovered a brief note: "Nothing found—ATF." In Lawmaster's words, "They didn't make any attempt to notify me. I've lived in Tulsa all my life and never got more than a traffic ticket. How come they can't look that up, realize I've been law-abiding my whole life, then come to the door when I'm home? They didn't leave someone here to watch over my private property. They didn't even come by to explain what happened. They just raided my home, ransacked it, left it wide open and left."

The parallels between the Lawmaster case and the assault on the Branch Davidians are both illuminating and disturbing. This case was, however, only the most recent in a long series of abusive raids on the homes of law-abiding citizens. Considering what happened to Kenyon Ballew some twenty years earlier, Lawmaster should regard himself as *fortunate* that he was away from home when the ATF arrived.

On June 7, 1971, Kenyon F. Ballew, a former Air Policeman, was dozing in the bathtub of his Silver Spring, Maryland, home. He was awakened by the sounds of his wife screaming and the front door being broken down. Neither fully clothed nor fully awake, Ballew jumped out of the tub and grabbed the first weapon he could lay his hands on—an antique 1847 cap-and-ball revolver. Rushing out into the hall to defend his family, he was cut down by a barrage of gunfire. One of the bullets lodged in his brain, destroying most of the tissues that controlled his right arm and leg. A total of four bullets hit him, several after he had already fallen to the floor unconscious. He was permanently crippled.

ATF agents, acting on a *rumor* (third-hand information from an anonymous tipster) that Ballew had created live grenades out of empty grenade shells (similar to the rumor about the Branch Davidians), chose to burst into a law-abiding citizen's home instead of politely coming to the door with a search warrant and peaceably examining the premises. If the intruders had even as much as yelled "Police!" Ballew did not hear them. In a show of bravado, one of the agents even fired bullets into the ceiling as he stepped into the apartment—a stunt worthy of a B-grade movie actor. None of the grenade shells contained explosives, and Ballew was not charged. He was, however, left a penniless cripple, getting by as best as he could on welfare.

Rep. Gilbert Gude, in whose district Ballew was shot, later urged a thorough investigation. His ringing indictment of the ATF, as recorded in the *Congressional Record,* included such statements as:

> I am thoroughly appalled by this revelation of the reckless, brutal, and inept methods employed by the Alcohol, Tobacco, and Firearms Division . . . in executing search warrants in private homes. This kind of storm-trooper exercise may have been commendable in Nazi Germany, but it must be made unmistakably clear to the ATFD that it is intolerable here . . . . In my opinion, the manner in which this search was conducted was not only unreasonable, it was high-handed and incredibly stupid, if not criminal.

In words that seem prophetic in light of what later happened at the Branch Davidian community, Gude went on to say:

> When police are permitted to barge into people's homes . . . they are just inviting violent resistance. The present deplorable tactics of the ATFD demonstrate nothing less than a callous disregard for the probable and predictable consequences.

Framing the Branch Davidians

The overriding motivation for the February 28 attack was the desire to attract favorable publicity to the ATF, as well as to attract increased funding. The Davidians were, however, such a poor choice for this raid that agency officials had to manufacture evidence to support a warrant: The Branch Davidians were, in other words, *framed* by the ATF. Initially hidden from public view, cries of cover-up eventually forced the ATF to release the original warrant and its supporting affidavit. The misinformation contained in the affidavit documents a fantastic abuse of power exercised by ATF officials in their frame-up of the Branch Davidians.

A close examination of the affidavit, nominally authored by Davy Aguilera, a relatively inexperienced special agent, reveals that it failed to establish the "probable cause" necessary to justify a search warrant. Certain assertions in the Aguilera report are straightforward lies. For example, in an unsettling commentary published in the *Washington Times* (June 1, 1993), Thomas Fiddleman and David Kopel point out:

> Some parts of the affidavit were plainly false. For example, Agent Aguilera told the federal magistrate that Mr. Koresh had possession of a "clandestine" firearms publication. The "clandestine" publication was *Shotgun News,* a

national newspaper that carries want-ads by gun retailers and wholesalers. The newspaper is sold at newsstands all over the country, and to tens of thousands of subscribers. With a circulation of more than 150,000, it's no more clandestine than the *New Republic.*

Certain other parts of the affidavit misrepresented the situation by excluding key information. For instance, Fiddleman and Kopel point out:

> Mr. Aguilera asserted that a neighbor heard machine-gun fire, but Mr. Aguilera failed to tell the magistrate that the same neighbor had previously reported the noise to the sheriff, who investigated the noise. The sheriff found Mr. Koresh had a lawful item called a "hell fire device" which simulates the sound of machine-gun fire but does not turn a regular gun into a machine gun.

Other information in this document reflects an ignorance about firearms that Aguilera and the U.S. magistrate, Judge Dennis G. Green, apparently shared. For example, the affidavit noted that Koresh had obtained the "upper and lower receivers" (a receiver contains the inner mechanism of a firearm) of an AK-47 rifle—an observation implying that the Davidians were modifying the inner workings so the AK would fire in full automatic mode. This observation is, however, inaccurate because the AK-47, as well as its legal, semi-automatic versions (the type of firearms possessed by the Davidians), have a solid receiver that cannot be broken into upper and lower halves.

Perhaps the most peculiar section of this strange and twisted document was the report of a conversation of Agent Carlos Torres with Joyce Sparks of the Texas Department of Human Services. Sparks was the official who investigated the Davidians on charges of child abuse. During her second visit to Mt. Carmel on April 6, 1992, she had a conversation with David Koresh in which, according to Aquilera:

> Koresh told her that he was the "Messenger" from God, that the world was coming to an end, and that when he "reveals" himself the riots in Los Angeles would pale in comparison to what was going to happen in Waco, Texas. Koresh stated that it would be a "military type operation" and that all the "non-believers" would have to suffer.

This information was widely repeated by the media, helping to shape the public image of Koresh as a violent, dangerous fanatic. The LA riots did not, however, begin until April 30—twenty-four days following the supposed conversation between Sparks and the Davidian leader. Clearly, either Koresh had *truly* prophetic gifts, or someone fabricated the conversation for the purpose of further demonizing the Davidians. In either case, neither Green nor Aquilera noticed this peculiar discrepancy.

Many other discrepancies and bits of odd, irrelevant information pepper the document. On pages fourteen and fifteen, for example, Aquilera asserts that Koresh stated to an ATF undercover agent that he "did not pay [federal] taxes or local taxes because he felt he did not have to." However, this assertion flies in the face of the statement on page three of the affidavit that "The taxes owed on the Mt. Carmel Center have been paid by Howell's [Koresh's] group." Again, neither Green nor Aquilera noticed the discrepancy.

Aquilera also often repeats the accusations about Koresh being a child molester who beat the children excessively. At points, he seems to go on and on about this, as well as about various sundry sexual accusations. As an example of the later, on page eleven he relates:

> Both interviews with Poia Vaega revealed a false imprisonment for a term of three and one half months . . . and physical and sexual abuse of one of Mrs. Vaega's sisters, Doreen Saipaia . . . . The physical and sexual abuse was done by Vernon Wayne Howell and Stanley Sylvia . . . . According to Mrs. Vaega, all the girls and women at the compound were exclusively reserved for Howell.

The problem with repeating these kinds of accusations is that they are totally irrelevant to the case at hand. ATF's responsibility lies in the enforcement of firearms laws; the other matters mentioned in the affidavit are the responsibility of the state. To repeat these unsubstantiated rumors merely to stress to the judge that "we're dealing with evil people" shows either a lack of understanding or a lack of professionalism.

Showdown at the Waco Corral

On February 27, 1993, Sharon Wheeler, a secretary working for the Bureau of Alcohol, Tobacco, and Firearms in Dallas, called various news media, some from as far away as Oklahoma: would they be interested in reporting a weapons raid against a local "cult"? (Wheeler later denied being this specific; rather, she claimed, she had just informed them that "something big" was going to happen.) The ATF initially denied contacting the media—more clumsy prevarication. Uncovered by the congressional committee investigating the Waco fiasco, this phone call was but one manifestation of the increasingly ghoulish pact between media and law enforcement: you give me free publicity; I'll give you newsworthy violence. This ill-considered bid for the media spotlight, sanctioned and initiated by senior ATF officials, set the stage for the tragic fiasco at the Mt. Carmel headquarters of the Branch Davidian Seventh-Day Adventists.

The Davidians learned of the raid at least forty-five minutes—some sources say two hours—beforehand. When news of the tip-off became public, the ATF immediately fingered the media as the responsible party.

If this attribution is correct, it means the agency, which contacted the press the preceding day, has only itself to blame for the deaths of its agents. The ATF also denied knowing that they had lost the element of surprise, but, once again, this denial was a lie. Surviving Branch Davidians assert that the raid began when the helicopters controlling the mission fired on Mt. Carmel. In response, a few shots were fired back from the community. The ATF officers in the air, Ted Royster and Phil Chojnacki, then ordered the ground troops in without informing them that the helicopters had already taken fire.

One of the Branch Davidians I interviewed had been with Koresh for over ten years. An important piece of the puzzle I received from this Davidian was the explanation for the large store of guns and ammunition at Mt. Carmel: one of Koresh's followers, Paul Fatta, was a gun dealer, and his merchandise was stored in the community. I also learned that, contrary to the NBC docudrama *Ambush at Waco,* most community members were *not* trained to use weapons—my contact person had fired a gun twice in the ten years he was with David Koresh. The ATF knew all of this, which is why they felt safe to go ahead and attack Mt. Carmel even after they knew they had lost the element of surprise. Some of the young men, however, took guns from Fatta's stock (Fatta was at a gun show on the morning of the raid) and prepared to fight off attackers.

Ninety-one heavily armed ATF agents drove up to Mt. Carmel—almost as many agents as community members. They were hidden in cattle trailers—like lambs to the slaughter—but the Davidians knew who their visitors were. The agency claimed that the Davidians fired first. However, given ATF's track record of one falsehood after another, as well as Koresh's history of peaceful cooperation with law enforcement officials, David's assertion that he just opened the door and was shot seems far more believable than the agency account. To a religious group nourished on apocalyptic images from the Book of Revelation, the assault must have seemed like the first skirmish in Armageddon.

Not long after the initial raid, *Newsweek* issued a hotly contested report that, after the gunfight was in full swing, some of the agents were gunned down by "friendly fire." Some of the early reports mentioned that an agent fell off a ladder, shot himself in the foot, and started yelling, "I'm hit! I'm hit!" While these episodes may be apocryphal, they are emblematic of the lack of professionalism with which the whole operation was carried out. What we do know with certainty is that irresponsibly fired ATF bullets killed one of Koresh's young daughters and several other innocents at Mt. Carmel.

ATF has repeatedly asserted that they had been practicing the assault for months, at least some of the agents involved were not briefed until the preceding day, and were never told that they would be facing high-power, assault-type weapons. Incredibly, the ATF did not even bring a doctor along to treat wounded agents—a standard practice of more professional agencies

94

From the Ashes

like the FBI. These inept, Keystone Cop antics of the ATF are difficult to understand unless we suppose that agency officials simply assumed that the Davidians would give up at the first sign of a superior force—a fatal assumption that would have been immediately rejected by anyone who had researched survivalist religious groups.

The mythic imaginations of the Davidians were shaped by biblical narratives. But what about the ATF? The imaginative fantasies of ATF officials seem to have been programmed by late night action-adventure movies. Their fatal decision to invite the media to what should have been a private party appears to have been an attempt to cast themselves in the role of the rescuing heroes—kind of a real-life "Rambo IV." Clearly the ATF saw itself as staging a rescue operation—rescuing not only hostages, but also ATF's status as an independent agency—a cause noble enough to legitimate an aggressive assault.

The pretext for the ATF raid was that the Davidians were illegally modifying their firearms to fire in full automatic mode. The gunfire recorded by TV cameras on the day of the assault, however, was that of *completely legal, semi*-automatic assault rifles. There is thus room to question both the ATF's tactics as well as the information on which the ATF chose to act. The Waco raid may have been another Johnnie Lawmaster fiasco—an expensive, time-consuming raid undertaken against someone who was not actually violating the law. Given the thoroughness of the final, fiery holocaust, we will probably never know if Koresh and company were actually violating federal gun laws. Had there been any evidence to the contrary, it was conveniently covered up with the collusion of ATF.

Paul Gray, head of the team of "independent arson investigators" who let the FBI off the hook by reconstructing a scenario in which only the Davidians could have started the fire, had worked with the ATF in the past. His wife was also an ATF employee. On the pretext that the charred remains constituted a "health hazard," Mt. Carmel was bulldozed almost as soon as the ashes cooled—thus destroying evidence that a truly independent investigator might have utilized in constructing an alternative scenario.

However dubious the victory, ATF was not above celebrating its grim final triumph by raising the ATF flag over the ashes of the Davidian community. One reporter reacted with the comment, "I don't think any flag should be raised over the bodies of dead children."

James R. Lewis is Academic Director of the Association of World Academics for Religious Education (AWARE), an information center set up to propagate objective information about non-traditional religions. An extensively published scholar with specialized interest in new religious movements, Native American religions, and the Sikh tradition, he is also the Editor of *Syzygy: Journal of Alternative Religion and Culture*, the only academic periodical devoted entirely to non-traditional religions.

Chapter 14

Misguided Tactics Contributed to Apocalypse in Waco

Stuart A. Wright

One day after the conflagration in Waco, President Clinton asked, in a press conference, several piercing questions. "Is there something else we should have done?" "Is there some other question we should have asked?" "Can I say for sure . . . we could have done nothing else to make the outcome different?" In the order in which they were asked, the answers to those questions are yes, yes, and yes.

Events during the spring of 1993 in Waco, Texas, strongly suggest that the FBI and ATF failed to understand how to deal effectively with sect leader David Koresh or the Branch Davidians. From the outset, the federal authorities appeared confused, unprepared and misdirected. According to one report, FBI spokesperson Jack Killorin was quoted as saying, "I think everybody involved would have to say we're chartering new ground. This one is not one where you can say, 'Gee, you're not going by the book'" (*Houston Chronicle*, "Cult Guidelines Become Urgent Need," April 25, 1993, p. 15 A). Well, perhaps Mr. Killorin is reading the wrong book.

The culmination of efforts ending in the tragic act of mass immolation should not have surprised anyone, given the questionable tactics and strategies employed. These tactics clearly *contributed* to the apocalyptic finale and these federal agencies must account for some serious mismanagement of the whole affair. If some of these tactics were derived from advice from behavioral science experts, as Attorney General Janet Reno suggested in statements made on the Larry King talk show, the "experts" in Quantico ought to be fired. Consider the following facts.

1. The ATF engineered a Rambo-like siege on the Davidian compound in order to serve a search warrant (not an arrest warrant). Some of my criminal justice colleagues inform me that had the agents simply waited until Mr. Koresh was alone, perhaps when he left the compound to run an errand, they could have served the warrant and probably avoided any violence. Federal agents had information obtained from surveillance for at least a year preceding the siege that Koresh was a jogger. Why not serve the warrant when he was outside the compound during a morning jog? Was it really that difficult to secure Koresh alone given the time-frame? What was the rationale of the siege strategy?

2. The FBI deployed the dubious method of "psychological warfare" to pressure members into surrendering. Flood lights beamed down on the Davidian compound at night to prevent sleep (sleep-deprivation?), loud music piped in at painful volumes to annoy and agitate members, recordings of repetitive chanting played to irritate the faithful, electricity cut off to reduce any remaining comforts. But why this tactic? What is the rationale of psychological warfare in this particular context? One has to question the wisdom of a strategy designed to heighten or amplify already abnormal levels of apprehension, fear, shared anxiety and even paranoia. According to numerous reports, both the FBI and ATF were aware that mass suicide was a possibility. Why, then, would the bureau institute a tactic of deliberate provocation or harassment that would increase the probability of an apocalyptic outcome—one which they claimed they wanted to avoid?

3. FBI spokespersons Ricks, Swensen and others repeatedly ridiculed Koresh in public to the media, often immediately following negotiations with the sect leader. According to reports, Koresh was variously depicted as a deluded messiah, a fraud, a lunatic, and a liar. While the agents may have held these attitudes in private, it is quite another matter to go on public record with such epithets and characterizations. They were fully aware that Koresh had access to radio coverage of the negotiations. What did this do to the agency's credibility in these negotiations? How sincere did Koresh feel they were in making any promises?

I have approximately fourteen years' experience studying religious cults and I simply fail to see the logic of the government agencies' actions in light of any empirical research. There are volumes of social scientific research on new religions or cults. Did anyone at Quantico bother to refer to this body of data, or inquire of those who have spent their careers in this field of study? My guess is that the "experts" on specific forms of criminality made the erroneous assumption that their expertise could be transferred to the area of cults. Thus the psychological warfare tactic, successful in apprehending Noriega, was assumed to be an effective weapon against Koresh. Would research on sectarian, charismatic leaders support such a comparison? Not likely. Charismatic leaders may exhibit authoritarian characteristics, but they do not tend to cave in to the demands of political authority or the State if it represents a moral conflict of loyalty. Moreover, they and their followers are not afraid to die for their beliefs, convinced that their acts of religious conviction can be defined as martyrdom, earning them spiritual rewards in the afterlife. Communal groups, by definition, have separated from mainstream society to build a distinct lifestyle and moral order. They have already made a statement about their disapproval of conventional norms and values. Their very purpose in life is epitomized in this existence, and becomes meaningless if co-opted or destroyed by the surrounding society.

There are a number of other questions that need to be answered as well. Was the perceived threat presented by Branch Davidians exaggerated? Were reports of alleged plans to attack Waco credible? Personal collections of arsenals in rural Texas are probably more common than people realize. This is NRA territory. Reports of the weapons do indicate substantial violations of the law. But with that in mind, how much more should caution and patience have been the guiding principles? It is a bitter irony that we were able to successfully negotiate an end to the prison riot in Ohio in the spring of 1993, but failed so miserably in Waco.

The U.S. attorney general suggested that the siege was made imperative by growing concerns of child abuse. But was the assault by armored tanks and tear gas a method designed explicitly to secure the release or safety of the children? By what logic? Surely, this line of reasoning suffers from the same flaws as the psychological warfare mentality. Moreover, the accusations of child abuse have been factually contested. If the allegations of abuse were true, why didn't investigations by local child-welfare authorities in 1992 turn up sufficient evidence to substantiate these allegations? The Department of Health and Human Services made at least three visits to the compound in that year.

What was the actual threat this group presented? Polygyny? There are numerous Mormon polygynist sects scattered throughout Utah, Idaho, Nevada, and New Mexico. Should they be alerted?

Koresh is no hero, and I'm not suggesting that we make him a martyr. But the government's feverish reaction to this sect troubles me deeply. The apocalypse in Waco was not necessary, no one needed to die, and the federal authorities must account for their role in contributing to a self-fulfilling prophecy.

Stuart A. Wright is Associate Professor of Sociology at Lamar University in Beaumont, Texas. He holds a Ph.D. in Sociology from the University of Connecticut and is the former recipient of an NIMH Research Fellowship at Yale University to study the social and psychological effects of cult involvement among former members. Dr. Wright has published a book entitled *Leaving Cults: The Dynamics of Defection* (1987), as well as numerous journal articles and book chapters in edited volumes on this controversial topic.

Chapter 15

Excavating Waco

Susan J. Palmer

The tale of the Branch Davidians in Waco has turned out to be a most unsatisfying narrative with many enigmatic features. As a story it combines elements from John Wayne westerns with mediaeval sieges in European history with media stereotypes of the "cult," in an incongruous sequence. Most unsatisfying of all is the generally agreed-upon verdict of "suicide" to explain the Branch Davidians' tragic ending. While sources quoted in newspaper stories are nameless, and evidence is being withheld or is difficult to verify, common sense and a study of historical precedents tell us that the Waco tragedy does not *smell* like a religious suicide. As for the protagonist, David Koresh, there has been no character development. What he thought or felt is a mystery. Faced with the greatest challenge to his religious leadership, his strategy (being a charismatic prophet) was to await God's instructions. We will never know if they came or not, and the scope of his religious talent will never be revealed. In the popular press he is reduced to a bleached clone of Jim Jones. Koresh the man and future prophet remains an unknown quantity.

The purpose of this study is to review three famous religious mass suicides in history in order to demonstrate how Waco does *not* fit into this category of religious phenomenon, and finally, to reflect upon the ways in which the voices in our culture (and religious subcultures) have chosen to interpret an unconventional religion—and have contributed to its deviant status.

Shapes of Religious Suicide
Jonestown

Chidester (1988) presents us with a typology of religious suicide in his study of the 1978 Jonestown tragedy in Guyana, and he argues that the mass suicide of the Peoples Temple included characteristics of all four types. *Ritual* suicide was enacted in suicide rehearsals that served to reinforce the purity of the community in relation to the defilement represented by the outside world. *Release* suicide offered Jones's followers an escape from a world of suffering; "an intolerable world of capitalist sin, fascist dictatorships, and other unbearable conditions by simply stepping over into the quiet rest of socialist death." *Revenge* suicide was involved in their perception of chosen death as a means of discrediting the U.S. government, news media and traitors to the movement (Chidester, 1988:137). Finally, the people of Jonestown expected to achieve immortality in history by committing a *revolutionary* suicide to protest the conditions of an inhuman world.

From what we know of the Branch Davidians, at least two of these types of religious suicide do not apply. There have been neither rumors nor concrete evidence that this community held ritual rehearsals for suicide— Koreshian versions of Jones's "white nights." Koresh was not a Marxist revolutionary interested in educating the American public through dramatic demonstrations of dissent. While the *release* and *revenge* type of suicide might appear appropriate for the occasion, we have no recorded speeches nor letters of Koresh recommending this drastic solution. The main reason in the public mind for believing the FBI's statement that the Branch Davidians' death was voluntary and religiously motivated resides in the powerful label "cult" and the inevitable association that four-letter word now has with Jonestown; for the anti-cult movement tells us that people in "cults" get "brainwashed"—into heading for the purple Kool-Aid—or the nearest equivalent—if you don't stop them in time!

Masada

The most striking parallel which springs to mind is not Jonestown, but Masada. It is remarkable that Masada and Koresh's "compounds" were destroyed in the same sequence—first by a siege, then a battering ram, then a massive fire. Although these events occurred almost nineteen centuries apart, they took place in the same month, the Roman month of Xanthicus (April). What is so satisfying about Masada is that *everyone agrees on the facts* and, moreover, everyone agrees on their interpretation. All parties, whether Jewish, Gentile, ancient or contemporary, concur that when the defeated Zealots made the same choice as the Peoples Temple, "avoiding a subhuman status through the single, superhuman act " (Chidester, 1988: 138)—that theirs was a *noble* choice. There is no muttering about their leader Eleazar ben Ya'ir "brainwashing" his "cult members." When we read Josephus' account of how the martyrs of Masada put their (possibly polygamous) families to the sword before surrendering to their mutually chosen executioner, no one brings up the murky issues of child abuse or the subjugation of women. How was this consensus achieved?

The first to tell the tale were two Zealot women and five children who chose to live by hiding in the water conduits beneath the city of Masada. They emerged the morning after the terrible event when they heard the Roman army wandering through the burning rubble and "related the truth to the Romans as it really happened." The Roman general in turn told Josephus, the Jewish-turned-Roman historian, and Josephus recorded the event in rich and moving detail—not hesitating to place a stirring speech in the mouth of Eleazar ben Ya'ir, as was the custom among Roman historians. Centuries later, in the 1960s an international team of archaeologists unearthed evidence of this religious mass suicide committed in A.D. 72, and *The Zealots of Masada: Story of a Dig* (Pearlman, 1967) tells the story of how they excavated the charred piles of personal belongings meant to demonstrate to the Roman besiegers that the burning of Masada was not accidental, but their defiant and deliberate choice. When eleven *ostraca* (pieces of inscribed pottery) were dug up, the archaeologists recalled Eleazar's historic address to his doomed companions after they had dispatched their wives and children; and, in Josephus' account:

> ... they cast lots for the selection of ten men of their number to destroy the rest. These being chosen, the devoted victims embraced the bodies of their deceased families, and . . . resigned themselves to the hands of the executioners. When these ten men had discharged their disagreeable task, they again cast lots as to which of the ten should kill the other nine, and last of all himself. (Pearlman, 1967:28-29)

The eleven *ostraca* were inscribed with names, seemingly by the same hand, one bearing the name, "Ben Ya'ir." While the archaeologists cautiously stated, "there can never be any certainty that these were the actual lots by which the grim choice was made" (Pearlman, 1967:168), they nevertheless noted that these "touching finds . . . brought to life for the twentieth century diggers the dramatic scene and mood of that last tragic night." Ancient Roman soldiers, Jews and modern archaeologists—separated by almost two thousand years—appear to be moved by Josephus's picture of the 960 Zealots of Masada huddled around their leader, Eleazar ben Ya'ir, moved by his powerful arguments to choose death rather than submission to the dishonoring of their wives, the enslavement of their children and the inevitable torture for themslves.

The "religious mass suicide" in Waco, Texas, happened only months ago, and yet the public is not at all clear about what took place. The seige at Waco was the fifty-one-day focus of international journalists dedicated to gathering accurate, objective information. Hundreds of people witnessed the tragedy (or selected parts of it) and the final pillar of smoke. Arson investigators sifted through the ashes as soon as they cooled. More survivors escaped from Waco than Masada to tell their tale. Even so, none of the different interest groups agree upon the set of events that began and ended the siege.

Münster

This siege lasted six months at the fortified town of Münster in Westphalia in 1535, which had become a refuge for Anabaptists. It began with the theocratic rule of Anabaptist prophets Jan Matthys and Jan Bockelson who took over Münster in 1534, expelled all "misbelievers" and set up a New Jerusalem with a new government based on ancient Israel. Presiding over the twelve elders was Bockelson who proclaimed himself Messiah of Last Days, the heir of the sceptre and throne of his forefather King David. Strict discipline was enforced inside the town and dissidents were ruthlessly shot or beheaded. Sexual mores in King David's realm were initially puritanical, but in response to new revelations, polygamy and community of goods were instituted, in emulation of the patriarchs of Israel. Bockelson established his own court of fifteen extravagantly dressed wives. The town was initially besieged by the Catholic bishop's troops, reinforced by allies and mercenaries. Bockelson proved to be a good military organizer; when the town was bombarded in preparation for a morning attack, the women worked all night to repair the damaged walls, which the Anabaptists proceeded to defend with cannon shot, boiling water, and flaming pitch. The major blockade commenced in January 1535, after the Imperial Diet at Worms decreed that all the states of the empire contribute funds for the prosecution of the siege. Münster was encircled by trenches, blockhouses and a double line of infantry and cavalry and the population slowly starved to death. The besiegers fired leaflets into town offering amnesty and safe conduct, but town defectors found themselves restrained within the double line where they died of starvation. When the last two or three hundred Anabaptists accepted their besiegers' offer of safe conduct, and laid down their arms, they were killed by the penetrating army in a massacre which lasted several days. Bockelson was led about on a chain like a performing bear, then publicly tortured to death with two of his elders, and their bodies exhibited in cages suspended from the church tower. Münster became once more a Catholic town, and its fortifications were razed to the ground (Cohn, 1972:271-80).

The Waco situation is anachronistic in that it shares some of the characteristics of the renaissance siege at Münster. Both "fortresses" celebrated an initial victory over their besiegers, but suffered through the slow depradations of hunger and wounds, and the bodies of the dead were subjected to what Chidester (1988) terms "rites of exclusion." When Branch Davidian Mike Schroeder attempted to climb the fence to rejoin his family inside the "compound," he was shot in the back and his body hung there for several days until it was removed by a helicopter's grappling hook and dropped in a nearby field. Remniscent of the Münster cage exhibit, another member's body was left up on the water tower for days (Thompson, May 19, 1993). Bockelson and Koresh resemble each other in their charismatic claims and their mission to restore the lost lineage of King David through polygamy—a pattern that has of course been repeated many times in the American history of heresy. Harold Bloom, commenting on what he perceives as the quintessentially American religion of Mormonism, observes, "To myself, culturally an American Jewish intellectual . . . nothing about our country seems so marvellously strange, so terrible and so wonderful as its weird identification with ancient Israelite religion" (Bloom 1992:81). While the Anabaptists at Münster did not enact a *ritual* suicide, they were religious martyrs who died for their faith and sought *release*. The story of these Germanic "Israelites" fails to evoke the noble sentiments associated with Masada, but at least historians agree upon the events.

Within their surrounding cultures, these religious sieges raise different issues. No one worries about alternative authoritative forms of baptism in the Branch Davidians. Instead, we focus on the oppression of women and children, as demonstrated by such articles as "One Lived, One Died: Two Canadian Women and Their Tortured Links to David Koresh" (*Maclean's,* May 3, 1993:16-23) and "Cult Children Face a New World" (*Ottawa Citizen,* April 27, 1993:A2). Koresh is not denounced as a heretic or a blasphemer, but is charged with the standard, politically incorrect abuses of patriarchy. The Zealot patriarchs stabbed their wives and children to death in preparation for their own collective suicide. Bockelson slaughtered townspeople, broke up families and married polygamously. None of their contemporaries bothered to record how this was affecting the children. Considering that previous investigations into allegations of child abuse in the "compound" had proved fruitless, and that Koresh's sex life pales in comparison with other rock musicians, why are we so concerned with these issues? Very little concern is expressed over the unnecessary deaths of eighty-five people. The media focuses on the "growing menace" of armed "apocalyptic cults" and the abuse of women and children in the power of charismatic "cult leaders"—red herrings which are no more or less relevant to the real-life situation than the Nation of Islam's racialist response:

> The FBI waited fifty-one whole days because they *knew* those folks in there were *white* folks. When they surrounded our brothers in Philadelphia, they knew they were dealing with *black* folks, so do you think they waited one minute before opening fire? (Minister Khalim Muhammad, Concordia University lecture, Montreal, May 3 1993)

Newsweek treats the American public to salacious thrills in describing the intimate details of Koresh's "repeatedly committed statutory rape" (May 17, 1993:49): "when Koresh took up with one girl he 'was having trouble penetrating her, because she was so young and little. He told her to start using tampons, the kind you insert in, to make herself larger.'" While ostensibly expressing a righteous concern for the children's welfare, this kind of journalism contributes to what Erving Goffman (1963) called "stigma"— the spoiling of social identities.

Perhaps a key to this enigma—this obsessive, unwarranted concern with "children of the cult," whether they reside in Island Pond, Rajneeshpuram in Oregon, Children of God communes or Waco where "corporal punishment is the rule" *(Newsweek,* May 17, 1993:49), is found in a statement Harold Bloom made about American religion:

> America had started European and venerable, then grew back to become new and youthful . . . . Other religions have promised us Eternity; only the American religion promises us what Freud tells us we cannot have: "an improved infancy," as Hart Crane calls it. (Bloom, 1992:31)

Manslaughter, Murder, or Suicide?

The Waco siege resembles the Japanese film *Roshomon* insofar as there are at least three versions of reality: the *manslaughter* version, the *murder* version, and the *suicide* version. Let us review the main arguments for each position:

The Manslaughter Argument

First, there is the testimony of the nine followers of Koresh who escaped the flames, and they insist that there *was* no suicide pact. They claim that the fire started when armored vehicles knocked over a propane tank and several kerosene lanterns while battering the walls of the compound and spraying "non-lethal" tear gas *(The Gazette,* Montreal, April 21, 1993:A11).

Supporting this notion of death by clumsiness and stupidity are many indications of bureaucratic bungling on the part of the FBI and the ATF. The more outstanding examples are the following:

The Sunday Raid
The initial ATF attack was made on a Sunday because undercover agents who had infiltrated the group months before reported that Sundays would be the safest time to seize weapons and arrest the cult leader: during Sunday morning prayer service the men would be separated from the women and children and from a cache of weapons. The *New York Times* (National, March 3,1993:A11) notes, "But something clearly went awry because the cult members were clearly anticipating the raid and took the agents by surprise." "Awry" understates the situation, since any undergraduate major in religion could have told them that Seventh-Day Adventists worship on the Sabbath, meaning the *seventh day* or Saturday.

Inappropriate Experts
The so-called "experts" chosen for consultation did not have the necessary expertise to offer useful advice. The right wing of the anti-cult

movement is apparently ten years out of date in Texas, since their "deprogrammers" haven't learned to call themselves "exit counsellors" yet, and are still spouting discarded pseudo-scientific terms like "snapping" and "cult mind control." Theologians consulted were competent in measuring the degree of Koresh's departure from orthodoxy in biblical exigeses, but not in analyzing the social dynamics involved in the negotiation. Those consultants in techniques of psychological warfare were apparently reviving the archaic theories of *ethos* in music recommended in Aristotle for the art of kings. One recalls tales in Nichomachus of rampaging youths deflected from crimes of gang rape and vandalism by the soothing strains of a mixolydian mode on the lyre. So why did these experts recommend "Achy Breaky Heart" and "These Boots Are Made for Walking"—all tunes in military or erotic modes rather than on more philosophical, healing Phrygian modes? It is obvious the experts who should have been consulted were sociologists of religion, or historians of utopian communes.

Ignoring the Relatives

Relatives were phoning the FBI daily, begging to be put in touch with their loved ones inside the compound. Their messages were recorded by an answering service, but no one called them back. There seems to have been the assumption that the followers were all too far gone to be swayed by their families, so why bother? Presumably, the members experienced different kinds of relationships with Koresh and their kin, representing many degrees of alienation or closeness. Moreover, previous studies of the charismatic relationship indicate a dynamic "give and take" pattern, for leaders wishing to retain their followers must be sensitive to their needs. Many varying and unique combinations of tyranny, democracy and oligarchy are found in communal utopias. So, why did the FBI assume that all the Branch Davidians couldn't think for themselves, influence Koresh, or respond to the love of their relatives?

The Absence of Fire Engines

Where were the fire engines? Authorities who had ordered the compound's electricity cut off might have considered the possibility of fire as they rammed into the wooden building lit by kerosene lanterns and insulated by bales of hay. They claimed it would be irresponsible to order firemen to go into a burning arsenal of weapons. Then, why did they bother to call the fire trucks at all, and why did it take fire fighters half an hour to arrive on the scene? Why did they not have them standing by, ready in case they were needed?

The Murder Argument

The line between manslaughter and murder begins to attenuate when we consider that some of this "bungling" might have been deliberate. It is impossible for an outsider to understand the process of decision-making in the ATF and the FBI, and the complexities of the power relationship between these two agencies; but if one considers that four ATF agents had been killed, one might presume that there is an unwritten code among police officers which would automatically rule out decisions which decreased the opportunity to avenge the death of their comrades. Decisions which endangered the lives of Branch Davidians would therefore tend to be favored.

The *New Yorker* magazine (May 3, 1993: 4-6) suggests that the U.S. government contributed to and collaborated in the Waco mass suicide, and bears some responsibility for the deaths of eighty-five people. According to this analysis, Koresh preached that the destiny of the Branch Davidians was to perish in a fiery Armageddon, and "the government was accommodating enough to play out the role that Koresh assigned it." The FBI is criticized for allowing itself to be "duped and goaded into helping create the inferno that Koresh had prophetically called into being."

The most extreme position is taken by R.W. Bradford, writing for *Liberty* (June, 1993), who writes, "Janet Reno, the nation's top law enforcement agent is a mass murderer." He accuses Janet Reno of making sure a fire would start in order to flush out the "compound," and of ensuring that no firefighting equipment was available—without realizing it would flare up so quickly and consume so many people.

The Suicide Argument

The FBI claimed that "cult members set fires in three places, and fuel sprinkled throughout the compound spread the flames." They also found "new evidence" a few days later: fuel cannisters used in the "mass act of immolation ordered by the cult leader" *(The Gazette,* April 23, 1993:A8). This claim was supported by an "independent arson investigator," Paul Gray of the Houston Fire Department, who reported, "The team believes the fire was deliberately set." *Time* magazine (May 3, 1993:18) mentions that journalists spotted a mysterious "man in a gas mask" cupping his hands as though lighting something"—the implication being that he was following Koresh's orders.

The fact that Paul Gray's wife works for the ATF makes us wonder about the "independence" of this arson investigator, but the main objection to this version of events is that, from what we know about Koresh and the Branch Davidians, suicide was out of character. Koresh was described throughout the negotiations as projecting a defiant, bellicose stance towards the outside world. The *Guardian Weekly* (March 14, 1993:9-10) quotes FBI negotiator Bob Ricks, who characterized Koresh as warlike rather than as self-destructive: "Our great fear is that he intends to provoke a situation where our people are fired upon and we will have to fire back. He does not want to fulfill his prophecies by taking his own life. He expects to die in a firefight." Ricks saw Branch Davidians assuming firing positions at the windows, presumably in the hope of provoking a shootout, and he quoted one of Koresh's more aggressive statements: "Your talk is all in vain. I am giving you the opportunity to save yourselves before you get blown away!"

Ex-members reported Koresh's taste for war movies like *Platoon, Full Metal Jacket* and *Hamburger Hill,* which they claimed he watched many times. "He would say the Bible prophecies war. We were being toughed" *(New York Times,* National, March 5, 1993:A16 L.)

In contrast to these concrete expressions of battle lust, predictions of suicide seem to be based on vague and unreliable sources:

> [A] federal official, speaking on condition of anonymity, said agents raided the compound after receiving information the group was contemplating mass suicide . . . . The report raised fears of a repeat of a 1978 Guyana tragedy. *(Ottawa Citizen,* Thursday, March 4. 1993:A9)

The same report mentions Koresh's denial: "The head of a religious cult trapped in a six-day standoff . . . told negotiators he has no plans to lead more than 100 followers in a mass suicide, the FBI said."

After studying Chidester's models and examples in history, common sense tells us that the behavior of this religious community during its final hours does not conform to what we know about apocalyptic expectation or religious mass suicide. Unlike Jonestown, there were no "white nights" rehearsals, nor did the Branch Davidian families gather to die in circles or huddled embrace. We have no record of a speech by Koresh exhorting martyrdom. Would not Koresh have wanted this as a defiant demonstration for posterity? Insiders' descriptions of how Koresh and his flock spent their final hours are distinctly mundane, lacking that stylized, timeless quality of religious ritual:

> Koresh left his apartment . . . and stalked through the halls. "Get your gas masks on," he told them . . . . Once equipped, people went about their chores, women did the laundry, cleaned or read the Bible in their rooms, even as a tank crashed through the front door, past the piano, the potato sacks and the propane tank barricaded against it. *(Time* May 3, 1993:18)

Another account reads as follows:

> As tanks battered the compound early Monday . . . the Davidians kept to their routines. Women in gas masks did laundry. Other cultists read Bibles in their rooms. The 17 children, all under 10, were on the second floor with their mothers . . . . Scattered through the house, the Davidians made no effort to gather together . . . . The fire erupted too fast for fire extinguishers to be pulled from the walls, the survivors said . . . . In 45 minutes the compound was gone, with as many as 86 lives. *(The Gazette,* Montreal, April 23, 1993:A8)

If these reports are accurate, there was no time to get into the mood for suicide, and no speeches could be made through gas masks. It appears reasonable to assume that there was no unanimously agreed-upon suicide, nor carefully articulated spiritual rationale for self-destruction, and that most of the eighty-five communards had no idea they were about to die. Even if Koresh had imposed a frantic, last-minute suicide on his followers, the assumption in the press appears to be that they willingly participated in his fiery holocaust—as if they were mindless extensions of their messiah's will, somehow psychically connected to his decision-making behind their gas masks.

The Case for "Deviance Amplification"

We may never know who or what started the fire, but the most relevant model for understanding the escalating hostilities, the breakdown in communication and the spoiling of social identities that took place in Waco is called "deviance amplification."

Roy Wallis (1976: 206-8)) first applied the deviance amplification model to the behavior of new religious movements (NRMs) in his study of Scientology. He notes that this model was originally elaborated by Leslie Wilkins (1964) to account for gang delinquency. In its most primitive form this model relates the following story:

1. Initial deviation from valued norms, leading to . . .
2. Punitive reaction, which leads to . . .
3. Further alienation of the deviants, leading to . . .
4. Further deviation, which leads to . . .
5. Increased punitive reaction, leading to no. 3 and so on, in an amplifying spiral.

This interpretation of the dynamic and worsening relationship between Koresh's community and the secular authorities seems to apply, when we consider that the incident began with a rumors of illegal firearms and unsubstantiated allegations of child abuse. The ATF shot first, causing the Branch Davidians to retaliate and kill four of their men. Koresh was labeled a "psychopath," a "cult leader," child-abuser and spoiler of underage virgins. As Lemert (1951:2) states:

> . . . older sociology tended to rest heavily upon the idea that deviance leads to social control. I have come to believe that the reverse idea, i.e. social control leads to deviance, is equally tenable and the potentially richer premise for studying deviance in modern society.

From the beginning of the siege, Koresh was crammed into the standard stereotyped portrait of the cult leader—the iron-willed, patriarchal dictator who exacts unquestioning obedience from his zombie-like followers:

> Koresh was a type well-known to students of cult practices: the charismatic leader with a pathological edge. Psychologists are inclined to classify Koresh as a psychopath. *(Time,* May 3, 1993:22)

Photographs like the "Tragedy in Waco" cover of *Time* show him tossing his head in ungodly ecstasy, and focus on his unshaven neck and chin, so that his bristles become ominous portents of social disorder. The press exhibits a strange fascination with his sexual prowess. One apostate complains of his puritanical stance towards sex, his condemnation of masturbation, his insistence on celibacy for male followers—and yet, paradoxically, criticized him for "using every gutter word and teenage word you could think of in front of this mixed group" *(Newsweek,* May 17, 1993:48). Koresh is portrayed in the media as a rampaging sex maniac preying voraciously upon prepubescent girls and their aging mothers, when he isn't beating up small toddlers and throwing tantrums in rehearsals with his rock band. One wonders how such a man could ever find the time to direct and administer his community, let alone prepare and preach his sermons, give Bible classes or receive revelations from above!

The Branch Davidians' response to external persecution resulted in a severe sense of alienation from the surrounding society and the development of new norms conceived to be essential for their survival in defensive or retaliatory measures, which were construed by the media and FBI as further evidence of deviance. Koresh himself was wounded and watched his daughter die from gunshot wounds. He heard himself ridiculed and stigmatized on the radio by those very officials who were respectfully seeking to negotiate his surrender. It is highly likely, under these circumstances, that Koresh's community experienced increased feelings of alienation and imminent threat. It is possible that Koresh expressed these feelings by tightening internal measures of control and by encouraging a more sectarian attitude among his flock. If Koresh did in fact impose a "suicide" upon his followers, it was the final result of his mutually hostile relationship with the FBI and the amplifying spiral of deviance amplification. If he did not, the fact that the slaughter of the Branch Davidians is dismissed as a "cult suicide" can also be understood as the final stage in the deviance amplification process.

The media frenzy of stigmatizing Koresh and spoiling the identity of his dead and living devotees obfuscates the real issue: we still don't know why eighty-five people had to die. Common sense tells us that the FBI was at least partially responsible—if only because the targets of its armored battering rams and tear gas just happened to die *on the very same day* they were attacked. Backing off from accepting responsibility, the authorities and the media "otherize" Koresh and his flock so that we will not feel any dignity in their dying, nor experience their deaths as fully human.

References

Bloom, Harold (1992) *The American Religion: The Emergence of the Post-Christian Nation.* New York: Simon & Schuster.

Bradford, R.W. (June 1993) "Mass Murder, American Style," *Liberty,* Vol. 6: No. 5:21-54.

Chidester, David (1988) *Salvation and Suicide: An Interpretation of Jim Jones, the Peoples Temple and Jonestown*. Indianapolis: Indiana University Press.

"Children of the Cult," *Newsweek*, May 17, 1993:48-51.

Cohn, Norman (1972) *The Pursuit of the Millennium* New York: Oxford University Press.

"Cult Children Face a New World," *The Ottawa Citizen*, Tuesday April 27, 1993:A2.

"Cult Leader Wants God's Orders Before Ending Siege," *The Ottawa Citizen*, Thursday, March 4, 1993:A9.

Dublin, L. (1963) *Suicide: A Sociological and Statistical Study*. New York: The Ronald Press Company.

Eliade, Mircea (1987) *The Encyclopaedia of Religion*. New York: MacMillan, Vol.14.

"FBI Says Negotiations with Cultists Are Stalled," *The Gazette*, Montreal, March 8, 1993.

Fogarty, Robert S. (April 12, 1993) "Cults, Guns and the Kingdom," *The Nation:* 485-87.

"Freed Cult Members, U.S. Agents Depict Scene in Compound," *Washington Post*, Thursday, March 4, 1993:A11.

"'God' Warns FBI of Fire and Destruction," *The Ottawa Citizen*, Tuesday, April 13, 1993.

Goffman, Erving (1963) *Stigma: Notes on the Management of Spoiled Identity*. Englewood Cliffs, New Jersey: Prentice Hall.

"It's Got a Beat and You Can Surrender to It," *The Globe and Mail*, April 1, 1993.

Josephus, Flavius (1981) *The Complete Works of Josephus*. Edinburgh, Scotland: William P. Nimmo.

Lemert, Edwin M. (1951) *Social Pathology*. New York: McGraw-Hill.

"No Evidence of Any Gunshot Wounds in Victims: Medical Examiner," *The Gazette*, Montreal, Friday, April 23, 1993: A8.

"One Lived, One Died: Two Canadian Women and Their Tortured Links to David Koresh," *Maclean's*, May 3, 1993:16-23.

Pearlman, Moshe (1967) *The Zealots of Masada: Story of a Dig*. New York: Charles Scribners.

"Promise of the Millennium Has Long Driven Cults," *The New York Times*, National, Wednesday, March 3, 1993:A11.

"Prophet's Fulfillment," *The New Yorker*, May 3, 1993:4-6.

"Spectre of Koresh Haunts Adventists' Reunion Plans," *The Gazette*, Montreal, May 8, 1993:J4

"Survivors of Waco Fire Recount the Final Hours inside Sect's Compound," *The Gazette*, April 23, 1993:A1-8.

"Texas Cult Leader Is Ready for War," *Guardian Weekly*, March 14, 1993.

Thompson, Linda (May 19, 1993) "Waco, Another Perspective." Posted on Fidonet, AREA: AEN NEWS.

"Tragedy in Waco" (Special Report) *Time*, May 3, 1993:16-31.

Wallis, Roy (1976) *The Road to Total Freedom: A Sociological Analysis of Scientology*. London: Heinemann Educational Books Ltd.

Wilkins, Leslie T. (1964) *Social Deviance*. London, Tavistock Press.

Susan J. Palmer received her Ph.D. from Concordia University in Montreal, Quebec, where she worked on a research project involving new religions, directed by Frederick Bird. She is co-author (with Arvind Sharma) of *The Rajneesh Papers*, 1993) and has published articles on various movements—including the Raelian Movement, ISKCON, the Unification Church, I AM, La Mission de l'Esprit Saint, the IDHHB, Friends of Osho—which have appeared (or will appear) in anthologies and journals.

Chapter 16

Who Started the Fires?
Mass Murder, American-style

R. W. Bradford

Who started the fires? There are three plausible possibilities.

1. It was mass suicide.

Supporting evidence: The FBI says that Koresh planned a mass suicide from the start. FBI spokesman Jeff Jamar said, "This was his plan from the beginning. It's clear to us it would have happened thirty days ago if we had gone in there." The day of the assault, FBI spokesman Bob Ricks said, "An FBI hostage rescue team member observed a subject through a window in the second floor, wearing a black uniform and a gas mask, undergoing a throwing motion. The person was knelt down with his hands cupped from which a flame erupted."*

The FBI said that those who escaped the flames said that Koresh and other Davidians had started the fire. When asked what that "very specific evidence" was, Jeff Jamar replied:

> At least three people observed a person spreading something out in this motion [bends over and holds his hands together]. This was reported

111

yesterday, bent down with a cupped hand, and then was a flash of fire. We have aerial observations of multiple fires. So the person saying that there was one instance of where the CEVs may have bopped something—this is not so. We have another person telling us the [inaudible] was reported to you yesterday that the fire was started with lantern fuel. There has been fuel containers found at the scene. There's no question in our mind that that's how the fire started.

Evidence against: Immediately after the conflagration, FBI spokesmen said that the fire was a complete surprise to them, and they had no indication that Koresh or the Davidians might commit mass suicide. The escapees all denied having said that Koresh or other Davidians started the fire, and all claimed the FBI had started it by knocking over lanterns within the compound.

Other information: In addition, a team headed by Paul Gray, an arson investigator from Houston, concluded that the fires were set in "at least two different locations." Gray said that all the investigators "were independent of any federal law enforcement agency." However, the Bureau of Alcohol, Tobacco, and Firearms confirmed that Gray had worked as part of a federal task force with ATF and that Gray's wife was an employee of ATF.

2.   The fire started by accident, when the FBI knocked over lanterns inside the compound.

Evidence for: The survivors of the fire have stated at every opportunity that this is how the fire was ignited, and that it spread quickly, thanks to the flammability of the building and its contents, the high winds, and the fact that the FBI had knocked holes in the walls. This hypothesis is consistent with the fact that the buildings were illuminated with lanterns, since the FBI had turned off the electrical power to the compound.

Evidence against: The FBI claimed shortly after arrest of the survivors that the survivors stated that the fires were ignited by members of the group.

3.   The FBI started the fire, intentionally or quasi-intentionally.

Evidence for: The FBI took numerous actions that insured that a fire would spread very quickly and could not be stopped once it started. It chose a dry day with high winds for its attack—conditions that are terrible for flushing out people with tear gas but excellent for burning down a building. It cut off water that might be used to put out fires. It did not have fire-fighting equipment on hand. It kept fire fighters away from the scene, and delayed their arrival once they had been called: "The reason the fire trucks were not allowed to go in immediately was the fireman's safety. It's that simple.

There were people there with automatic weapons ready to fire." Jamar did not explain why, despite ample opportunity, the Davidians never used the automatic weapons whose possession rendered the situation too dangerous for fire fighters. Nor did he explain why the FBI allowed the press within 1.5 miles of the assault, but kept fire fighters and their equipment miles away in Waco. Nor did he explain why the sophisticated aerial fire-fighting techniques of the military were neither employed nor ready for use, or why the FBI intercepted and halted fire fighters and equipment who were coming to the scene.

The FBI was frustrated at the inability to flush out the members of the community with tear gas. FBI spokesman Jeff Jamar told reporters the next day that at the time of the fire, "we were of the opinion that deep inside the compound—you've seen your pictures where there's a concrete structure standing there—we were of the opinion that they were inside that structure and that they were able to survive in there even with the gas because maybe it would protect them from the gas, maybe it was sealed. " Presumably, if the FBI's tank and tear gas assault failed, the FBI would be even more embarrassed.

Furthermore, the mass annihilation of the Davidians could serve as an object lesson to other individuals and groups who might attempt to defy the federal authorities. As President Clinton said during his press conference on April 23, "I hope very much that others who will be tempted to join cults and to become involved with people like David Koresh will be deterred by the horrible scenes they have seen."

Evidence against: The FBI are good guys, who would never do anything bad.

But whether the truth will ever come out is dubious. There will certainly be investigations. Even President Clinton has sanctioned them: "That's up to the Congress, they can do whatever they want . . . . If any congressional committees want to look in it we will fully cooperate. There's nothing to hide here, uh, this was probably the most well-covered operation of its kind in the history of the country." Of course, the superb coverage the president spoke about took place from a mile and a half away, and consisted mostly of news spoon-fed by FBI spokespeople, substantial portions of whose statements were obviously contradictory and patently false.

Note

* The "hostage rescue team member" was in fact an FBI sniper viewing the compound through the telescopic sight of a high powered rifle. Although the FBI called its squad of agents a "Hostage Rescue Team," all available evidence is that the compound held neither "hostages" nor anyone who wanted to be "rescued," except possibly from the threat posed by the FBI.

Reprinted with permission from *Liberty,* June 1993, Vol. 6, No. 5.

R. W. Bradford is the editor of *Liberty* magazine, a classical liberal/libertarian review of thought, culture and politics. His writing has also appeared in *Barron's, Reason, Free Inquiry* and other publications.

Chapter 17

Fanning the Flames of Suspicion:
The Case against Mass Suicide at Waco

James R. Lewis

> Any time you start the day by gassing women and children, you have to expect it to end badly.
> — Wesley Pruden, *Washington Times*

On April 19, 1993, the FBI's workday began somewhat prior to the gas attack. As reported by a nurse who was interviewed on two different radio programs—one in Laport and the other in Waco—the FBI had dropped by the local hospital at 5:00 a.m. Monday morning to find out how it was equipped to handle burn victims. This incident indicates that the FBI fully *expected* Mt. Carmel (the Davidians' name for their "compound") to catch fire, and stands in sharp contrast to the agency's *apparent* lack of preparedness for the final fiery holocaust. The nurse's radio interview is, however, only the most glaring item of information in a rather lengthy laundry list of suspicious events and situations—bits of information that, while insignificant in isolation, together appear to indicate that the Mt. Carmel fire was intentionally set by government officials.

Consider, for example, that, tactically, the best times for tear gas attacks are days on which the wind is still, allowing the gas will hang in the air around its target rather than being blown away. Instead of waiting for such

115

conditions, the feds chose to move on a day when the wind was blowing at a brisk thirty miles per hour. On top of that, they called the Davidians at 5:50 a.m., and casually informed them, "Well, we got tired of waiting, so we decided we were going to gas you instead," (or words to that effect). Now, it doesn't take a genius to figure out that the people inside the community would respond by opening up the windows and doors, so as to allow the wind simply to blow the gas through the building and out the other end. This would have created a wind-tunnel effect—an effect *increased* by the large, gaping holes the tanks created as they ripped into the building. Clearly these were *poor* conditions for a tear gas attack, but *ideal* for setting fire to a wood frame structure.

The potential for Mt. Carmel to go up in flames should have been readily apparent. Electricity had been cut off on March 12, compelling the community to use gasoline-powered generators, propane, and kerosene lamps. The building itself was a crudely built firetrap, constructed from plywood, used as well as new lumber, and tacked together with tar paper. Bales of hay had been pushed against windows to help stop bullets.

On April 26, a team of "independent" arson investigators led by Paul Gray, assistant chief investigator for the Houston Fire Department who had confidently asserted that his group of experts was "independent of any federal law enforcement agency," issued their report. Gray and his team concluded that the blaze must have been initiated by people inside the building in two or more different locations at about the same time. (Defending the scenario of several simultaneous starting points was an important point in eliminating the possibility that one of the tanks tipped over a lamp that set the building on fire—the Davidian version of the story.) However, other authoritative sources assert that flames broke out at different points *within 50 to 120 seconds* of each other—not exactly "simultaneous" when we take into consideration a thirty mile per hour wind in a firetrap that burnt to the ground in less than forty-five minutes.

Suspicions were also raised on April 28 when *CBS News* correspondent Sarah Hughes broadcast the information that the "independent" arson team had "close ties with the FBI." It was also discovered that the wife of arson team leader Paul Gray was an employee of the ATF. Gray responded indignantly to these revelations with the assertion that to "even suggest that any information we may be getting from the FBI is somehow tainted is absolutely ridiculous." However, on *Nightline* that same evening, lawyer Jack Zimmermann posed the question, "Why in the world did they bring in, as chief of this investigating team looking into the fire, a fellow who had been on an ATF joint task force for eight to ten years, out of the Houston office of the ATF, the office that planned and executed the raid?"

In a situation already reeking with the stench of dissimulation and cover-up, choosing an individual with close personal ties to the very agencies he was hired to exonerate could only have had the opposite effect of increasing rather than decreasing widely-held suspicions. As if to *further* confirm critics' suspicions, the burned-out remains of Mt. Carmel—along with any remaining evidence—were bulldozed on May 12. This action, which assured that no *truly* independent arson investigator would be able to sift through the charred remains and construct an alternative scenario to the official version, was justified on the pretext of safety and health concerns—filling holes, burying trash, and so on.

The government's interpretation assumes that, like Jonestown, the Davidians had actually planned a mass suicide. Given this assumption, it is plausible that they set fire to Mt. Carmel rather than surrender to government forces. Otherwise, the contention that Koresh's followers torched their community is implausible. The only sources for asserting that Mt. Carmel was another Jonestown were Mark Breault (a rival prophet who claimed to be a disenchanted defector) and individuals associated with the Cult Awareness Network—neither reliable sources of information. There is far more evidence to support the alternative contention, namely that the Davidians were not suicidal, and that Koresh and company were planning on living into the future.

From as authoritative a source as William Sessions, then director of the FBI, we learn that the agency had concluded before the April 19 assault that Koresh was not suicidal. On April 20, during the *MacNeil/Lehrer* news program, Sessions noted that "every single analysis made of his writing, of what he had said, of what he had said to his lawyers, of what the behavioral science people said, what the psychologists thought, the psycholinguist thought, what the psychiatrists believed, was that this man was not suicidal, that he would not take his life."

On April 29, Dr. Murray Miron, one of the psychologists consulted by the FBI, informed newsman Tom Brokaw that, with respect to the letters authored by Koresh that he had been asked to analyze, "All of his communications were future oriented. He claimed to be working on a manuscript. He was talking about the publication rights to that manuscript through his lawyer. He was intent upon furthering his cause." Koresh even went so far as to retain literary attorney Ken Burrows to handle his story. He also requested another attorney to prepare a will that would protect Davidian property rights, as well as establish a trust for his children to safeguard any future income from books or movies.

Beyond Koresh himself, there are many indications that the other Davidians were not suicidal. For example, despite claims by the FBI that the community had not tried to save its children during the final fire, a May 14 report issued by the Associated Press revealed that "most of the children were found huddled in the concrete bunker, enveloped in the protective embraces of their mothers," in what had clearly been an attempt to avoid the

flames. These and many other particulars that could be cited indicate that
the Davidians were not planning mass suicide.

Yet other kinds of questions are raised by the FBI's choice of tear gas.
The gas used in the attack—a white, crystalline powder called CS (O-
chlorobenzylidene malonitrile)—causes nausea, disorientation, dizziness,
shortness of breath, tightness in the chest, burning of the skin, intense
tearing, coughing, and vomiting. It is so inhumane that in January 1993, the
United States and 130 other nations signed the Chemical Weapons
Convention agreement banning CS gas. This treaty does not, however, cover
internal uses, such as quelling domestic disturbances.

On April 23, 1993, Benjamin C. Garrett, director of the Chemical and
Biological Arms Control Institute in Alexandria, Virginia, was quoted in the
Washington Times as saying that CS gas would have had the greatest impact
on the children at Mt. Carmel. "The reaction would have intensified for the
children," Garrett said, because "the smaller you are, the sooner you would
feel response." According to the FBI, the anticipated scenario was that
mothers, in an effort to protect their children, would leave the building with
their offspring after the gas had thoroughly saturated it. White House
spokesman George Stephanopoulos, speaking at a news conference, was
unwilling (or unable) to account for why such a deadly form of tear gas—
one that temporarily blinds and disables people—was selected over other
possibilities.

Given the deadly choice of tear gas, the question of how the fires started
on the plains of east Texas that fateful day becomes all the more intriguing.
All of the survivors, despite FBI claims to the contrary, denied that
Davidians had started the fire. Instead, they asserted that the tanks had
knocked over lanterns, which set the blaze. The Davidians were, however,
more generous to the FBI than the evidence indicates. As we have already
noted, it seems that the FBI took steps to guarantee that flames would
spread quickly, and could not be stopped once started. A dry, windy day
was chosen for the assault—a day that, as we pointed out earlier, would
have been terrible for a tear gas attack, but perfect for incinerating a
building.

Despite the obvious risk of a fire, fire trucks were nowhere near the
attack scene when the assault began. When smoke began to appear, the FBI
waited at least ten minutes before calling 911 to request fire fighters from
Waco be dispatched. The McLennan County Sheriff's Department relayed
the request to the fire station:

Dispatcher: "Sheriff's office dispatch."
Fireman: "Yes."
Dispatcher: "Is this Hawthorne?"
Fireman: "Yeah, it is."

Dispatcher: "They've got a fire at the compound."
Fireman: "Tell me!"
Dispatcher: "Are y'all en route?"
Fireman: "No, we're looking at it. Just waitin' for you to call."
Dispatcher: "Okay, take off then."

Clearly, stopping the fire was not a high priority on anyone's list. When fire trucks finally arrived, they were held at the checkpoint *under FBI order* for another sixteen minutes—more than enough time to guarantee that Mt. Carmel would be reduced to a pile of embers before a drop of water touched the flames. The FBI's explanation? "The reason the fire trucks were not allowed to go in immediately was the fireman's safety. It's that simple. There were people there with automatic weapons ready to fire." How individuals dying in the inferno could have posed a risk to firemen was not explained.

What does all of this indicate? Given the FBI's visit to the local hospital early that morning to inquire about burn facilities, given that the conditions were less than ideal for a tear gas attack, given the inadequate preparations for the possibility of a fire, et cetera, et cetera, we get the following as a possible scenario:

For whatever reason, the FBI had become impatient and decided that they were going to end the siege once and for all on April 19. They planned a two-stage assault. In stage one, they would pump Mt. Carmel full of tear gas—the worst possible, non-lethal gas they could find—and hope the Davidians, or at least the mothers and children, would be forced out of the building. If by noontime the tear gas attack failed—and, given the determination displayed by the Davidians up to that point, it is unlikely that they would have backed down from their resolve—the FBI would avoid embarrassment by setting the place on fire. Most of David Koresh's people would then vacate the building to save themselves and their children. The agency's intentional igniting of Mt. Carmel would effectively be disguised by the tear gas attack, and afterwards they could claim either that the Davidians had set the blaze, or that the fires had started accidently.

The plan went terribly wrong, however, when the Davidians failed to run out, and the FBI has since been trying to hide any evidence of wrongdoing. Hiring an arson investigator with close links to the agency, and bulldozing the site to destroy evidence, were clumsy cover-up efforts, unworthy of the FBI. If the fires were indeed set intentionally, the stupidity characterizing the cover-up indicates that the deaths of most community members had not been the anticipated result of the assault. While it is difficult to contemplate that an agency with the reputation of the FBI could have perpetrated the Mt. Carmel fire, it is a far more likely explanation—given the information currently available to us—than the notion that the Davidians committed mass suicide. The same conclusion was expressed in the final stanzas of a poem composed by some of the children who were released before the FBI attack, and whose father perished in the blaze:

Deep down inside your heart, you know the truth;
you cannot hide.
Christians who believe in God don't contemplate suicide.

The day will come we'll all be judged
as we stand before the Lord.
Koresh may have thought himself as Christ
But you thought yourself as God.

James R. Lewis is Academic Director of the Association of World Academics for Religious Education (AWARE), an information center set up to propagate objective information about non-traditional religions. An extensively published scholar with specialized interest in new religious movements, Native American religions, and the Sikh tradition, he is also the Editor of *Syzygy: Journal of Alternative Religion and Culture,* the only academic periodical devoted entirely to non-traditional religions.

Chapter 18

The Mythology of Cults

David G. Bromley

The presence of cults among us has been a recurrent theme of American life. The Branch Davidian tragedy has concentrated our attention on them with a vengeance. It's time we stopped and thought a bit about cults. What are cults and how serious are the dangers they present?

The word *cult* is obviously the nucleus of the word *culture*. It has been used in the past by anthropologists and religious scholars to mean an organized set of beliefs and rituals surrounding some object of worship. Thus, within modern Roman Catholicism there exists a cult of the Virgin Mary (referred to as Mariolatry, the purpose of which is to venerate her role in Christianity) just as in ancient Egypt certain gods, such as Isis and Osiris, were singled out for particular adoration. Outside of religion, similar cultlike followings surround Elvis Presley, the Beatles and the television series *Star Trek*.

However, the most consistent use of the term by modern scholars, in particular sociologists, is organizational. Sociologically, a cult is the starting point of every religion. Its organization is extremely simple. There is no bureaucracy or priesthood. There is barely any structure at all except for the single charismatic leader and his or her small band of devoted followers. Jesus and his twelve disciples offer a classic example of a cult. Nor are there scriptures, not only because the cult rejects all or part of society's dominant religious traditions but also because it is simultaneously engaged in the act of creating its own traditions out of which later generations will record "gospel" truth. The cult is thus nonconformist for two reasons. First, it struggles to start a radically new religious tradition; and second, it exists in tension and conflict with what it regards as a corrupt, troubled world.

Anti-cult mythology has created the impression that cults are a new and unprecedented menace to American society. However, the new religious groups that have become the focus of this controversy are neither unique nor as new to American society as their opponents contend. In fact, new religious groups, far from being new to the American social landscape, have been one of its most perennial features. The best available data indicate that currently in the United States there are some nine hundred churches deriving from the Western Christian heritage and another six hundred religious groups from a variety of other traditions. Religious diversity and the flowering of new religious groups are actually hallmarks of American history.

The most recent cohort of new religious groups did not simply burst onto the American scene. Most had existed for some time and experienced growth only when socio-cultural conditions in the 1970s became more favorable. For example, the Children of God was simply one offshoot of the vital and diverse Jesus Movement of the late 1960s. The Unification Church was established in Korea in 1954 and reached the United States in 1959, only to languish in relative obscurity until the early 1970s, and the Church of Scientology was founded in 1955 but did not experience rapid growth until some years later. Several Eastern groups, such as Hare Krishna and the Divine Light Mission, arrived in this country in the late 1960s and early 1970s. But the catalyst for this Eastern transplantation was a combination of unrelated social factors, such as the widespread attraction to Eastern philosophy and religion beginning in the 1950s, the repeal of the Oriental Exclusion Act in 1965, a flow of war refugees from Southeast Asia, and conversions and marriages by servicemen during tours of duty in the Far East during the 1960s.

How much control these groups exert over members' lives varies. The members of such groups as Transcendental Meditation and Scientology live conventional lives and devote no more time to religious practice than do many other pious Americans. On the other hand, the members of high-demand groups such as The Family and the International Society for Krishna Consciousness live communally and devote full time to the group and its practices. In some cases, too, structural characteristics have changed over time. Lifestyles within the Divine Light Mission, for example, have varied from a relatively conventional individual household style, to traditional communalism, to quasi-communal living arrangements that permit outside employment.

There are a number of public perceptions about the American "cults":

• That many of these groups possess tens of thousands of members, with the total number of persons involved in the hundreds of thousands or even millions. In fact, most of these groups are quite small and have never achieved substantial size.

• That the charismatic leaders have accumulated substantial personal wealth. In truth, many religious leaders, not just cult leaders, around the world live in a lavish style that their followers consider commensurate with their perceived spiritual status. The extent of wealth and the purposes to which it is put vary and seem to be related to the overall goals of the group. For example, Prabhurpada, the spiritual leader of Hare Krishna, lived out his life as an ascetic monk. By contrast, Sun Myung Moon possesses considerable personal wealth. Still, Moon appears to be willing to use—and risk—it all to underwrite the Unification Church's religious agenda.

• That leaders use brainwashing (coercive mind-control techniques) to recruit and retain their members. But there is much *prima facie* evidence against the brainwashing allegation.

Anti-cultists have drawn heavily on the experience of American POWs in Korea and China, where the concept of brainwashing was born. But actual results of techniques used on American POWs belie claims of extraordinary capabilities to destroy or alter personalities. Some thirty-five hundred Americans were held prisoner in north Korea and China during the Korean War and were frequently confined under the harshest and most totalitarian conditions. Despite this, of the thirty-five hundred Americans imprisoned, only fifty made pro-communist statements under duress and only twenty-five refused repatriation at the end of the war. This is hardly impressive evidence of an extraordinary capacity for influence.

If cults have access to esoteric mind-control techniques, their success in recruitment should be relatively high. Virtually all empirical research on the subject reveals the contrary: despite intense proselytization by some of these groups, conversion rates are modest at best.

Defection rates should be low, but again the evidence shows precisely the opposite. Defections begin soon after recruitment, and most members have left after two or three years. It appears that defection rates are on the order of at least 20 percent per year, a figure consistent with the reported record of communal groups in general.

• That cult leaders manipulate their followers to create docile compliance. The record reveals otherwise. Close observers of all the major new religious groups report that conflict and schism are endemic to these groups, despite the best attempt of leaders to keep their followers in line.

Several unfortunate consequences have resulted from the creation of the myths about all cults. First, the myths deflect attention away from the real socio-cultural factors that make alternative realities and alternative social arrangements attractive. Youthful adherents were drawn to, not coerced by, these alternatives. Substituting the subversion theory for concrete social analysis too conveniently obscures this fact. Second, the metaphors supporting the mythology have been too easily reified. After all, brains have not been washed. Rather, individuals have adopted new symbolic contexts within which to relate to themselves and to others. In most cases, malevolent gurus have not conspired against us. Instead, inadequacies in conventional socially constructed reality have provoked the alternatives of the new religious groups.

Finally, even though the Davidian group was led into horrifying tragedy, the lure and power of the new religious groups have been exaggerated. The most telling critique of these groups is not that they capture and enslave innocent youth but that they ultimately have not been able to provide the answers they had hoped for and that they are failing to produce meaningful social change, either by their own standards or those of conventional society. Some adherents may have carved out meaningful lives for themselves in these groups, but this is not the kind of dream likely to draw the aspiration and commitment of American youth.

Reprinted with permission from *Style Weekly*, May 11, 1993.

David G. Bromley is a Professor in the Department of Sociology and Anthropology at Virginia Commonwealth University. He has studied and written extensively about cults in America. Among his books is *Strange Gods* (1982) written with Anson D. Shupe Jr.

Chapter 19

"Cults," "Mind Control," and the State

Thomas Robbins and Dick Anthony

"Cults"

"Cults" are back. The events in early 1993 in Waco, Texas, involving members of a heavily armed apocalyptic religious sect besieged by federal agents—with four of the latter slain—and then subsequently immolated, has put a media spotlight on a topic which had seemed to fade in recent years. As the Waco tragedy unfolded, all sorts of deprogrammers, "exit counselors" and "cult experts" were explaining to television audiences about the sinister menace of cultist "mind control." The latter supposedly overpowers the free will of converts and imprisons them, even without the use of overt physical constraint, in dangerous and destructive groups. There are a number of implications of this notion, including, ironically, the ostensible innocence of devotees who, as "cult victims," are said not to be responsible for unconventional and/or criminal acts which their leaders "psychologically coerced" them into perpetrating.

Most of the media experts do not deal regularly with the small minority of very violent groups such as the Branch Davidians in Waco led by David Koresh. They are more generally concerned with the "usual suspects" such as Scientology and other "therapy cults," the Unification Church and various eccentric movements on the fringes of pentecostal and fundamentalist revival. Professional anti-cult activists seem to eagerly seize upon the occasional bloody disaster such as Waco or the much greater 1978 Jonestown holocaust to disseminate "cult awareness" and encourage hostility to unconventional spiritual groups. Over the past decade the Cult Awareness Network (CAN) has consolidated a media hegemony in the sense that reporters and editors seem to view its spokespersons as the premier source of expertise on "cults." Periodic catastrophes such as the Waco events tend to reinforce this hegemony.

To judge from the comments of the deprogrammers and "counselors" sounding off in the media in early 1993, the archetypal mind-controlling cult is "the Moonies." One deprogrammer related how he seeks to convince a deprogrammee that his group is a sinister cult by pointing out its similarities to Reverend Moon's operation. Certainly the extreme right-wing Unification Church of Reverend Sun Myung Moon has some objectionable elements, including a former deceptive foot-in-the-door ploy in which young persons would be invited to seminars (e.g., "Ethical Issues in the 80s") without being told that the event would take place under the auspices of Unificationist recruiters or had any connection with the movement. Yet in its heyday from the mid-1970s through the early 1980s the movement was actually a revolving door with a continual influx and exodus of temporary participants, the vast majority of whom made their exit without the assistance of abductors.[1] To mention the Unification Church in the same breath as the violent Waco Davidians or Jonestown, as occurred frequently in the media in the spring of 1993, seems farfetched.

Although occasionally some media reporter slips and refers to the Davidians as a "sect," the label "cult" for Koresh's group and for other violent and excoriated religious movements has now become almost ubiquitous in popular reporting on the topic. In the sociology of religion, the cult term refers most clearly to groups which are not part of an existing religious tradition and which have mystical theologies and a loose organizational style. In current popular usage, however, the term is applied to a disparate array of groups and has no clear and consensual denotation. It does, however, have the sensational *connotation* of an authoritarian, mind-controlling movement in which convert-victims are mentally enslaved and can be made to perpetrate violence and crime as ordained by a charismatic prophet or guru. A label possessing an unclear denotation but a sharp negative connotation becomes primarily an emotive vehicle for conferring a stigma.[2]

The cult term thrives because there may possibly be as yet no fully adequate alternative. "Sect" is a term which is more appropriate than "cult" from a scientific standpoint.[3] Sects traditionally tend toward apocalypticism, fervent claims of uniquely correct theologies, and tightly controlled organizations—qualities which anti-cult critics find problematic in current groups. However, many of these groups are novel, at least in the American context, and therefore do not fit the criterion of the meaning of "sect," which confines the term to offshoots of traditional religions. Some sociologists of religion prefer the term "new religion." Yet some groups viewed as problematic, such as the Lyndon LaRouche movement, do not even claim religious status. Indeed the appeal of "cult" lies partly in its capacity to embody the valid perception that some powerful movements cut across received compartmentalizations of "religious," "political" and "therapeutic" groups; for example, the Moonies and the LaRoucheies may share some (putatively sinister) traits. In *Cults: Faith, Healing and Coercion,* psychiatrist Marc Galanter appears to use "cult" interchangeably with "charismatic group," but the latter term implies that the group is organized around a central leader, a property that not all groups viewed as problematic have.[4] Perhaps the term "millenarian movement" would be most useful. It could correctly be used to refer to the several types of groups which are viewed as controversial, that is, those which are novel, those which are schismatic offshoots of traditional religions, and those which are not explicitly religious. Moreover, it is the apocalyptic or millenarian properties of these movements which appear to give them the heightened fervor and tightly controlled organizations which create the controversy surrounding them. (Even controversial therapy groups, which may lack explicit millennial doctrines, nevertheless tend to embody utopian or apocalyptic moods and motivations.)

"Mind Control"
The label "cult" is now inseparable from the notion of "mind control." At best, "mind control" is a kind of shorthand verbal symbol for various (allegedly manipulative) procedures and group pressures for conformity, which are hyped as an irresistibly "coercive" psychotechnology. Often such procedures simply build upon the general tendency for many of us to adopt the views of those who appear to be giving us social support. In a CNN segment an ex-Moonie and ex-deprogrammer, who is currently a lawyer specializing in suing cults, explained how when he tried to convince his sister to leave the Moonies, the group seduced him by singing songs about how much they loved him—a variant of the infamous Moonie "love bombing" technique! Yet the brainwashing concept that is used to refer to such arguably manipulative procedures is often reified into an irresistible force. Thus reified, the brainwashing term does not simply represent certain procedures (which if scrutinized too closely might appear mundane or inane) but rather is treated in discourse as a kind of "thing," a concrete object such as an incapacitating drug, whose presence automatically neutralizes participants' free will.[5]

The mind control construct also provides a self-deceptive excuse for former converts, who can deny responsibility for ideological commitments they made to unpopular groups and the consequences which ensued. Becoming a devotee of some guru is not treated as something that you have done and becomes instead something someone has done to you. It has even been argued in court that cult followers who participated in crimes should be excused from responsibility or have their penalties substantially mitigated on the grounds that they were victims of mind control and thus were not truly "willing" perpetrators.[6] Recently in a number of prosecutions involving crimes ranging from homicide and mail fraud, defendants' alleged experience of traumatic mind control in unconventional or therapeutic groups has been the basis for pleas of insanity or diminished capacity. (Frequently the criminal acts involved were not even encouraged by the stigmatized group.) So if one has transgressed and just happens to have previously participated in a marginal religious, therapy or political group, this experience could prove helpful on the legal front.

The mind control or "brainwashing" defense has actually produced rather mixed results. It did not work for Patty Hearst when she was tried for the Hibernia Bank robbery in the mid-1970s, although it is worth noting that her primary defense was actually that she participated in the armed theft under physical duress; mind control was brought in to explain the incriminating post-Hibernia "Tania" tapes in which Ms. Hearst declared solidarity with her "terrorist abductors."[7] Since then there have been cases in which allegations of mind control have been used to generalize to the leader all responsibility for an act perpetrated by members of a sect (such as parents injuriously spanking a child), thus mitigating the penalty for the immediate perpetrators. Brainwashing claims also have been successfully employed in defense of deprogrammers accused of kidnapping devotees and have been featured in civil actions against religious and therapeutic movements for fraud, negligence, false imprisonment and intentional infliction of emotional distress.[8] There have been some multimillion-dollar jury awards in such suits, which have tended to be reduced (but have not always been eliminated) by appellate courts. At present an adult heir to the DuPont fortune has most of his trust money withheld from him through a conservatorship designed to prevent him from granting excessive largesse to the movement led by imprisoned felon Lyndon LaRouche, under whose mental domination the heir is said to languish.[9]

There has recently been some dispute over whether methods of mind control (variously termed "brainwashing," "coercive persuasion" or "thought reform") actually destroy converts' mental capacity to exercise free will, particularly given an absence of overt physical coercion and threat. Theories of mind control derive originally from studies of POW camps, forced confessions and re-education programs transpiring within brutal totalitarian regimes.[10] Can such models be fruitfully applied to formally voluntary movements which do not physically threaten or confine recruits? If there are some elements of thought reform or coercive persuasion that *do* fit the latter groups, do they really imply extenuation of the personal responsibility of indoctrinees? Testifying in the Hearst trial, psychiatrist Robert Lifton noted that Ms. Hearst was subject at the hands of her captors to an extreme mode of thought reform which involved direct physical threats to her very existence. In court cases involving cults and mind control, both sides tend to cite Lifton's early research on Chinese thought reform and more recent essays. His well-known complex of eight social psychological elements (milieu control, mystical manipulation, sacred science, cult of confession, etc.) has been defined by Lifton as "ideological totalism," a construct which Dr. Lifton in recent decades has applied not only to "cults" but also to fundamentalism[11] and "nuclearism," the latter being the absolutist ideology said to transfix the minds of enthusiasts for atomic weapons. Yet we generally do not think of fundamentalists or rabid nuclearists as being bereft of free will and personal responsibility. Courts are unlikely to indulge a deprogrammed ex-nuclearist who wants to sue Ronald Reagan for deceptively brainwashing him about the "peacekeeper missile."

The view taken here is that in terms of our concerns there are two types of mind control models.[12] Models which embody what has been called "hard determinism" definitely affirm that victims actually *lose their capacity for voluntary social action* under the impact of mental conditioning regimens variously termed brainwashing, menticide, the "Dependency, Dread and Debility" ("3-D") syndrome, etc. Included here are early lurid formulations such as those of Edward Hunter, a publicist for the CIA who popularized the term "brainwashing" and who wrote of persons being transformed into "robots" and "puppets."[13] The problem with these models, which are potentially legally powerful because they do indeed affirm a stringent socially induced incapacity, is that research has shown them to be stigmatizing myths rather than credible scientific accounts. Insofar as science has been able to determine, there are no specialized techniques of social influence which are capable of overwhelming free will.

In contrast to such science fiction versions of the thought reform concept, there are more sophisticated thought reform models which are based upon actual research on totalitarian methods of indoctrination and which may have some relevance to conversions to new religions. Such models do not interpret communist methods as distinctive in terms of their techniques of influence or in being capable of overcoming an individual's practical reasoning ability. Totalitarian influence involves socialization into an arguably undesirable view of the world, a property which it shares with the influence of dysfunctional families, adolescent gangs, and other problematic social groups. Philosophers refer to scientific accounts of such undesirable influence as involving "soft" rather than "hard" determinism, in that they do not involve assertions that free will has been lost in any legally or ethically extenuating way. It may be regrettable when the individual succumbs to softly deterministic social influence, but he or she remains legally and morally responsible for his or her actions.[14]

Thus, softly deterministic models of totalitarian indoctrination, which are scientifically credible, are not relevant to the legal causes of action based upon brainwashing testimony because they are so widely applicable that they do not demonstrate coercive social influence in any legally distinctive way. Models which embody hard determinism and which would be legally relevant because they assert distinctively coercive influence, on the other hand, are inadmissible because of their lack of scientific support. It is our perception that the more sophisticated of those social scientists who testify in court about how sinister cultic mind control renders victims helpless tend, perhaps inadvertently, to shift back and forth between sophisticated "soft" and cruder "hard" models depending upon whether they are expressing their views to a scholarly audience or to a trial court.[15]

A significant case transpired in 1990 when Steven Fishman, an ex-Scientologist, was tried for mail fraud in federal court. His lawyers sought to develop a diminished capacity defense based on his alleged experience of disorienting mind control in the Scientology "cult." District Judge Jensen declared expert defense testimony on thought reform and coercive persuasion inadmissible under the element of the federal Frye standard which requires that expert testimony be "generally acceptable" within the scientific community as well as "more probative than prejudicial." There is not a consensus within the scientific community, noted Jensen, of the anti-cult brainwashing theory that individuals lose their free will as a result of cultic influence.[16] Judge Jensen appeared to accept the argument of sworn declarations to the court submitted by one of the present writers (Anthony), a consultant to the prosecution, that if physical force is rejected as a boundary condition, there is no natural or objective cutting point as to when coercive persuasion is powerful enough to overbear free will. Evidence was also presented to indicate that the American Psychological Association had rejected the views of the defense "experts." Fishman subsequently plea-bargained and went to prison. Since the *Fishman* decision, several similar procedural rulings including testimony on mind control have been made by federal or state courts.[17]

Coincidentally the legitimacy of the judge-made Frye standard came before the Supreme Court in 1992-93 in a case which did not directly involve religious movements or mind control. There was some expectation that a conservative court would uphold or even tighten the standard in response to loud complaints from corporations that they have been victims of irresponsible damage awards assessed by judges and jurors who have been influenced by "junk science" peddled by experts who are either incompetent or disposed to make claims before lay jurors which they would not make in scholarly venues.[18] The issue of the admissibility of mind control expertise in court was thus implicitly joined with the more general question of the degree to which judges should serve as gatekeepers screening "scientific" expertise offered to a jury, to keep the latter from being swayed by glib or prejudicial pseudoscience. Arguably the case for judicial gatekeeping is especially salient when stigmatized groups such as putatively sinister "cults" are involved in litigation, and particularly in situations in which the role of prejudice may be magnified by the intrinsic subjectivity of claims of "coercion" which are not based on tangible physical actions but on verbal communications expressive of religious beliefs.[19]

As it transpired, the Supreme Court, in *Daubert v. Merrell Dow* (1993), declared that the Frye Rule had been superseded by the Federal Rules of Evidence passed by Congress in 1975. The Frye standard was declared to be too "austere" to be relied on exclusively, although the consensual acceptability of proffered expert testimony and analyses to scientific peers may be taken into account. Although in *Daubert* the Court acceded to the plaintiffs' view that the Frye standard has been superseded, it clearly did not indulge their preference for sharply curbing the authority of judges to withhold evidence from juries. Rather, this authority actually appears to have been augmented by Justice Blackman's majority opinion in *Daubert*.[20] It therefore seems likely that judges will continue to exclude cultic brainwashing arguments that embody hard determinism, because these arguments have little if any scientific support.

The Limits of State Control

The legal and other issues which arise from claims about mind control, its efficacy, effects and the appropriate counterresponses, are complex and difficult. Marginal religious movements lack a sufficient population base to permit conventional "churchly" funding via a multitude of small lay donations. To survive they must intensify solidarity, commitment and discipline such that the membership crystallizes into a kind of Gideon's army of highly committed devotees who will make large donations (tithe or better) and/or donate non-remunerated labor in commercial and other enterprises operated by the group. The actual cultivation of the requisite morale may be somewhat manipulative and, moreover, often entails intensifying the "boundary" of the group such that the latter is conceptualized as a holy enclave in the midst of a corrupt or demonic world. The extent and intensity of such doctrinal commitments may at some later point be regretted by persons being proselytized. Such individuals ought to be "on guard" or in a *caveat emptor* mode, both with respect to cultic ideology and to their own inner tendencies which are responsive to it. However, the thrill or "high" that may sometimes be associated with becoming involved in a radical salvationist or a "world-saving" movement is inimical to caution. The sensation of *risk* may be part of the rewarding excitement!

It is certainly appropriate to warn the public of the possible consequences which emotionally intense movements may pose for participants. But civil and religious libertarians are concerned with several interrelated issues arising from direct or indirect (e.g., civil suits) state control impinging on sects when legal measures are grounded in a psychologistic mind control rationale. Behavior which is said to embody insidious mind control usually takes the form of persuasive *speech acts* such that state controls raise the issue of free speech (as well as "free exercise" of religion) under the First Amendment.[21] Court hearings involving mind control claims thus frequently involve extensive testimony about unconventional group *beliefs*, and it is all too likely that some judges and juries make intuitive inferences about mental enslavement on the basis of the perceived *non-believability* of aberrant notions which seemingly could only be accepted by persons whose minds are not whole or are in bondage. Thus most of an award against the Hare Krishnas for emotional injury was vacated in 1992 by the Massachusetts Supreme Court because of excessive prejudicial testimony about religious beliefs.

The litigation over processes of religious conversion has necessarily entailed "scientific" judgments about ultimate concerns, a subjective realm heretofore shielded from state regulation. Government intervention in the province of ultimacy, particularly when based on pseudoscientific judgments, is dangerous, as it threatens to create through state action the very thought control it is designed to prevent. To put the argument somewhat hyperbolically: the state could become our cult.

Beyond these issues are questions raised by the linked premises of paternalism and determinism. When the state undertakes to protect us from our own weakness and presumed helplessness before demagogues, it may make a self-fulfilling prophecy. We could be led to think of ourselves as the state would see us: frail reeds blown hither and thither by manipulative leaders, and therefore we may possibly make less effort to exercise responsibility. And if the state attributes exclusively to our leaders and their machinations all responsibility for our acts when we are in sects, does it not make it easier or more convenient for us to surrender responsibility for our decisions?

We have seen Jonestown, and a decade and a half later we have seen Waco. There have been other—smaller—lethal altercations within other movements and between such groups and authorities. There will probably be more such events. Apocalyptic ideologies, charismatic leadership, rigid group boundaries, and intense internal solidarity are among a number of factors which enhance the volatility of many unorthodox religious sects.[22] Is it possible for the state to respond in a manner which reduces the likelihood of violence and destruction while not infringing upon religious liberty? Arguably, anti-cult brainwashing theories encourage confrontational state actions which trigger the very violent and self-destructive activities they are ostensibly designed to prevent. In both the Waco and the Jonestown tragedies, intemperate cultic actions responded to federal intervention allegedly encouraged by anti-cult interpretations of religious realities. Perhaps the single most beneficial activity the state could perform would be to do as the late Supreme Court Justice Jackson suggested: relinquish any attempt to interfere with the "spiritual and mental poison" which some "false prophets" disseminate.[23]

Notes:

[1] On the conversion patterns and indoctrination procedures of the Unification Church see Eileen Barker, *The Making of a Moonie: Brainwashing or Choice?* Oxford: Blackwell, 1984.

[2] A number of recent articles have critiqued the allegedly pejorative concept of "cult" and related its emergent "hegemony" to the triumph of the "anti-cult movement" in the 1980s "politics of meaning." See James Richardson, "Definitions of Cult: From Sociological-Technical to Popular-Negative," *Review of Religious Research,* Vol 34(4):348-356, 1993; and Jane Dillon and James Richardson, "Social Construction of the 'Cult' Concept," Presented to the Association of the Sociology of Religion, Cincinnati, 1991. According to one scholar the application of the "cult" label to the Branch Davidians reflects the fact that "the showdown in Waco was reported [by the media] in a mindless vacuum of historical and religious ignorance," p. 486, Robert Fogerty, "Cults, Guns and the Kingdom," *The Nation,* April 12, 1993, pp. 485-87. In particular, media reportage on the events in Waco generally proceeded in ignorance of the violent American sectarian-millenarian tradition. On the Branch Davidians and the American tradition of religious apocalypticism, see also Paul Boyer, "A Brief History of the End of Time," *The New Republic,* May 17, 1993, pp. 30-33.

[3] Indeed many of the most violent American religious groups correspond to the sociological construct of "sect" defined as a schismatic offshoot of a church or sect. Thus the Branch Davidians emerged from the Davidian sect, an offshoot of the Seventh-Day Adventist Church. The latter, through its institutionalization and gradual accommodation to conventional values, and by diminishing the salience of prophetic-apocalyptic concerns, generated reactive schismatic sects. Similarly, the Mormon Church, by departing from its tradition of patriarchal polygamy, provided the impetus for the emergence of various "fringe-Mormon" patriarchal sects, a minority of which are violent.

[4] Marc Galanter, *Cults: Faith, Healing and Coercion,* New York: Oxford University, 1989.

[5] Moral entrepreneurs decrying mind control in cults often emphasize "hypnotic" trance states allegedly produced by cultic rituals such as meditation, repetitive

chanting or speaking in tongues as the linchpin of coercive mind control. See for example, Flo Conway and Jim Siegleman, *Snapping: America's Epidemic of Sudden Personality Change*, Philadelphia: Lippincott, 1978. In the view of the present authors this analysis is too facile. Given some degree of emotional intensity, group solidarity and experiential ritual behavior such as meditation, practically any group can be accused of employing psychological coercion by virtue of alleged hypnotic trance states, emotional manipulation and pressure for conformity. Physical constraint or threat, which might provide an objective standard or cutting point, tends to be rejected by theorists of cultic brainwashing since practically all of the disvalued groups do not employ systematic physical coercion.

[6]A rather moderate form of this argument has recently been applied to the followers of Jeffrey Lundgren, a disfellowshipped teacher/guide in the Reorganized Church of the Latter-Day Saints, who led a breakaway group and organized the murder of a family of potential defectors. See Sandra McPherson, "Death Penalty Mitigation and Cult Membership: The Kirtland Killings," *Behavioral Sciences and the Law*, Vol. 10(1):65-74.

[7]On the Patty Hearst trial and the brainwashing issue, see pp. 63-85, Alan Scheflin and Edward Opton, Jr., *The Mind Manipulators*, New York: Paddington, 1978.

[8]For an overview of legal issues and developments involving "cults," see David Bromley and Thomas Robbins, "The Role of Government in Regulating New and Nonconventional Religions," pp. 205-40 in James Wood and Derek Davis (eds.), *The Role of Government in Monitoring and Regulating Religion in Public Life*, Waco, TX: Dawson Institute of Church-State Studies.

[9]See Maureen Orth, "Blueblood Wars," *Vanity Fair*, April 1993, beginning p. 184.

[10]See Scheflin and Opton, *The Mind Manipulators*, op. cit. See also Thomas Robbins and Dick Anthony (eds.), "Brainwashing and Totalitarian Influence," forthcoming in *The Encyclopedia of Human Behavior*, V. S. Ramachandran (ed.), San Diego: Academic Press. See also Dick Anthony, "Religious Movements and 'Brainwashing' Litigation," pp. 295-343 in Thomas Robbins and Dick Anthony, *In Gods We Trust*, New Brunswick, NJ: Transaction.

[11]See Robert Lifton, "Cult Processes, Religious Totalism and Civil Liberties," pp. 59-70 in Thomas Robbins, William Shepherd and James McBride (eds.), *Cults, Culture and the Law*, Chico, CA: Scholars Press.

[12]See Dick Anthony and Thomas Robbins, "Law, Social Science and the 'Brainwashing' Exception to the First Amendment," *Behavioral Sciences and the Law*, Vol. 10(1):5-30.

[13]On the history of discourse over "brainwashing," see Scheflin and Opton, *The Mind Manipulators*, op. cit. pp. 22-105, and Anthony and Robbins, "Brainwashing and Totalitarian Influence," op. cit.

[14]See M.S. Moore, *Law and Psychiatry: Rethinking the Relationship*, Cambridge: Cambridge University Press. See also Anthony and Robbins, "Law, Social Science and the 'Brainwashing' Exception to the First Amendment, op. cit.

[15]See Anthony, "Religious Movements and 'Brainwashing' Litigation," op. cit, p. 295-344.

[16]See Anthony and Robbins, "Law, Social Science and the 'Brainwashing' Exception to the First Amendment," op. cit.

[17]The events leading up to the *Fishman* procedural ruling were in part the basis for a civil suit filed in 1992 by the "experts" whose testimony was excluded by Judge Jensen against the American Psychological Association, the American Sociological Association and a number of individual professionals including Dick Anthony, co-author of this paper. The suit, which accused defendants of conspiring to defame and injure the plaintiffs through making false representations to federal judges and other actions, was dismissed "with prejudice" in August 1993.

[18]See David Bernstein, "Junk Science in the Courtroom," *Wall Street Journal,* March 24, 1993:A15.

[19]As law professor Douglas Laycock comments with respect to civil actions against religious movements which entail claims of mind control, "From the beginning to end these cases consist of subjective and intangible elements . . . it is difficult to separate the actionable wrongdoing, where there is any, from protected free exercise. These cases provide maximum opportunity for juries to act on their prejudices and minimum opportunity for judges to control juries." Douglas Laycock, "The Remnants of Free Exercise," *Supreme Court Review 1990.* Reprinted for private circulation by the University of Chicago Press, 1991.

[20]See the following commentary on the Court's opinion in *Daubert,* which is generally viewed as actually enhancing the responsibility of judges to screen expert testimony proffered to juries: Jeffrey Mervis, "Supreme Court to Judges: Start Thinking Like Scientists," *Science,* Vol. 261, p. 22; Linda Greenhouse, "Justices Put Judges in Charge of Deciding Reliability of Science Testimony," *New York Times,* June 29, 1993:A10; David Bernstein, "Hauling Junk Science Out of the Courtroom," *Wall Street Journal,* July 13, 1993:A14.

[21]See note #18 above.

[22]See Thomas Robbins, "Sects and Violence: Factors Enhancing the Volatility of Marginal Religious Movements," forthcoming in Stuart Wright (ed.), *Armageddon In Waco: Critical Perspectives on the Branch Davidian Conflict.*

[23]The reference here is to Justice Jackson's famous dissent in *U.S. v. Ballard* (1944). For an extrapolation of Jackson's dictum and its implications for litigation involving new religious movements, see William Shepherd, *To Secure the Blessings of Liberty: American Constitutional Law and New Religious Movements,* New York and Chico, CA: Crossroads Publishing Co. and Scholars Press. See also William Shepherd, "The Prosecutor's Reach: Legal Issues Stemming from the New Religious Movements," *Journal of the American Academy of Religion,* Vol. 50(2):187-214.

Thomas Robbins, a sociologist of religion, is the author of *Cults, Converts and Charisma* (1988) and co-editor of *Cults, Culture and the Law* (1985) and *Church-State Relations* (1986). Dick Anthony, a psychologist, is the author of *Spiritual Choices* and co-editor (with Dr. Robbins) of *In Gods We Trust* (1989).

Chapter 20

The Cult Awareness Network:
Its Role in the Waco Tragedy

Andrew Milne

The tragic legacy of the campaign waged relentlessly by Cult Awareness Network (CAN) against new religious groups was the death of eighty-six Branch Davidians including twenty-four children, in a final inferno in Waco.

As Alexander Cockburn put it in the *Los Angeles Times*, "The role in Waco of the Cult Awareness Network, whose members are respectfully cited in the press as 'experts,' may well have been crucial." Consider these facts:

* None of the Davidians had been charged with any crime.

* It was not necessary to raid the compound to arrest the Davidians' leader, David Koresh. He ran a mile a day and went into town twice a week. He could easily have been served by the ATF during one of his regular trips. Outsiders, including neighbors, friends, family members of residents, also frequently visited the Mount Carmel compound.

* During a recorded phone conversation between Koresh and the ATF in the first few hours of the raid, Koresh said to federal officials, "It would have been better if you just called me up or just talked to me. Then you all could have come in and done your work."

* The powerful tear-gas which the FBI pumped for six hours into a compound containing children too small to wear gas masks has been banned for military use. "It can't be used militarily on Iraqi soldiers, but apparently it's OK against six-year-olds in this country . . . . Eventually, they [the children] would have been overcome with vomiting in a final hell," Benjamin C. Garrett, executive director of the Chemical and Biological Arms Control Institute in Alexandria, has stated.

* In the aftermath of the first deaths, former prosecutors who had previously dealt with the Davidians came out with strong criticism of the tactics used by the ATF. Vic Feazell, former district attorney for McLennan

137

County, explained how he had arrested Koresh in 1987 without bloodshed. "If they'd called and talked to them, the Davidians would've given them what they wanted," Feazell told Associated Press. "We had to arrest them to prosecute them . . . . we treated them like human beings, instead of storming the place. They were extremely polite people," he said.

CAN's Role in the Tragedy

CAN's involvement in events in Waco began before the initial raid on the compound by the Bureau of Alcohol, Tobacco, and Firearms (ATF) took place on February 28, 1993. That raid, carried out by more than one hundred federal agents who tried to storm the compound and arrest Koresh, led to a shooting match which left four agents dead and sixteen wounded. Two members of the Branch Davidians were also reported to have died in the gunfire.

After the tragedy, it was learned that CAN deprogrammer Rick Ross, who was arrested following a failed deprogramming in January 1991, had advised the ATF prior to the raid. During an interview with the CBS program *Up to the Minute,* Ross, a convicted jewel thief with a history of psychiatric problems, stated that he had warned the ATF that there were large caches of arms inside the compound. After the conflagration, Ross claimed on *NBC News* that he had been in touch with the FBI "over the long haul ever since March 3."

Ross's "advice" to the ATF and FBI helped create an adversarial position between, on the one hand, the ATF and the FBI, and the Davidians on the other. In an interview with the *Waco Tribune-Herald*, he described the Davidians as "a very dangerous group" and issued dire warnings of their potential violence.

Dr. James Lewis of the Association of World Academics for Religious Education (AWARE) stated that "whatever Ross may have communicated to the ATF, it is certain he promoted the worst stereotypes of alternative religions . . . , scholars have time and time again rejected this stereotype as simply unfounded, provable by simple observation."

CAN's contribution to the Waco disaster goes deeper. David Block, a former Branch Davidian, was deprogrammed in the summer of 1992 by three deprogrammers including Rick Ross and Priscilla Coates. The deprogramming took place at Coates's house in Glendale, California.

Block was later interviewed by the ATF. The information he supplied concerning firearms allegedly stockpiled by the Branch Davidians was included in the search warrant the ATF drew up to authorize the February 28 raid that precipitated the tragedy. Block's information contributed to the decision by the ATF to storm the compound instead of negotiating with the Davidians. Block's description of the Davidians is bound to have been influenced by his deprogramming.

CAN Inflames the Waco Standoff

After the raid on the compound, CAN spokespersons had been all over the media, offering "advice" which portrayed the Davidians as sub-human zombies with whom it is impossible to negotiate. CAN's president, Patricia Ryan, told the *Houston Chronicle* that officials should use whatever means necessary to arrest Koresh, "including lethal force." That is exactly what the government did on April 19. In an interview on *A Current Affair,* CAN spokesperson Jan Keith from Houston stated, "They [the Davidians] are never going to come out. They [the FBI] are going to have to go in and get them. I don't expect a good ending to this."

Instead of providing constructive advice which might have brought about a peaceful end to the standoff and prevented the deaths of over people, CAN continually promoted stereotypes of new religions to the media and officials—stereotypes which have been rejected by qualified scholars as unscientific and inaccurate. Unconcerned with the final consequences of these actions, CAN sought to exploit the tense situation in Waco to promote its own fascist-style agenda of hatred and intolerance.

CAN's picture of the Davidians as an assortment of brainwashed robots is probably the reason the government, instead of calling upon respected and qualified religious scholars to mediate with Koresh, decided to invade the compound with armored vehicles and teargas. As an example of the unsubstantiated allegations about the Davidians which CAN dished out liberally to the media as well as to government, Priscilla Coates of CAN told the *Washington Post* on April 25, "I know how these groups work and children are always abused." Cynthia Kisser and other CAN spokespersons also made allegations of child abuse.

Patricia Ryan, CAN's president, alleged abuse in a joint statement she made with the president of the American Family Foundation, Herbert Rosedale, to the U.S. House of Representatives' Subcommittee on Health, Committee on Ways and Means. After insisting how potentially dangerous the Davidians were, Ryan and Rosedale continued, "The second fact highlighted by the Waco situation is the risk cults pose to the health, and sometimes even the lives, of children." In true CAN style, Ryan and Rosedale failed to provide any evidence to back up this statement and skidded off instead into generalized allegations against "cults."

However, the Texas Department of Protective and Regulatory Services conducted a nine-week investigation into allegations of child abuse at the Davidian compound and found that there was no evidence to bear them out. Even the FBI director, William Sessions, admitted that he had no evidence that child abuse was occurring. Furthermore, according to Texas officials, none of the twenty-one children released from the compound during the siege showed signs of physical or psychological abuse, and they were all in good health. Yet the federal authorities cited alleged child abuse as the major reason for the heavy-handed methods that were used by the FBI to end the standoff, showing that despite the lack of evidence of abuse, CAN's propaganda had impinged on them.

CAN Has Incited Action against Other Groups

Waco is not the first time that children have been victimized by the Cult Awareness Network. In 1984, Priscilla Coates and CAN deprogrammer Galen Kelley (who was convicted in May 1993 of kidnapping a woman whom he had violently seized for the purpose of deprogramming) so alarmed the authorities with fantasized allegations of child abuse by members of a religious commune in Island Pond in Vermont that the movement was illegally raided and its children removed into custody. The incident became notorious after it was learned that the only abuse that occurred had been the raid itself. A judge ruled that the raid had been "grossly unlawful" and ordered the children released.

Exactly how to incite tax and law enforcement authorities against new religious groups is even explained step by step in a manual co-written by Larry Zilliox, a former board member of CAN's New York/New Jersey chapter. The book, subtitled "An Investigator's Manual," meticulously details how to collect public records information on religious groups, how to conduct surveillance on their members, how to lie if caught in a compromised situation during the investigation, and many other investigative techniques. The manual contains such headings as "Intensive Investigation and Infiltration Techniques," "Debriefing Former Members," "IRS Rewards" and "Books about Investigative Techniques." Zilliox and his co-author, Larry Kahaner, a private investigator with a history of inveterate animus towards new religions, give examples of how to stir up official action against targeted groups without being identified:

> Place all your information in a well-organized, anonymous letter with as many facts and figures as you can gather. Most agencies will treat your complaint with skepticism, especially because it's unsigned, so make sure you put as much meat into it as possible . . . , you may also benefit if there's a government investigation as a result of your letter. Some or all of the material generated by government investigators may be made public and you'll have more information—information you couldn't have gotten on your own—to add to your files.

The "anti-cult groups" that Zilliox cites to be used as resources by the investigator include Cult Awareness Network, American Family Foundation, and the Jewish Federation "cult commissions" in LA, New York and Miami.

CAN Seeks to Alter Survivors' Testimony

CAN spokespersons are now threatening to "deprogram" the survivors of Waco to ensure that their testimony about events during the final day confirms CAN's propaganda about a mass suicide having taken place. In the *New York Daily News* of April 24, Brett Bates, a deprogrammer from CAN's Texas chapter, stated that "before they [the survivors] become productive witnesses in the prosecution, they have to realize they were the victims of mind control." Bates, who stated that the Davidian survivors were "a unique challenge" has already started to meet with their families to arrange deprogrammings.

However, it is clear from the statements of the survivors that no mass suicide took place, and that the Davidians tried, but could not escape. The *Washington Post* of April 24 described attempts by the terrified Davidians to flee the fire. "The survivors offered a picture of a chaotic morning within Ranch Apocalypse as armored vehicles rammed holes in the flimsy frame buildings and cult members in gas masks read Bibles and prayed. . . . [T]he survivors said they believe that the fire started when armored vehicles overturned kerosene lanterns being used inside after authorities disconnected the electricity in mid-March." The article describes how "as the armored vehicles slammed into the walls, the cult members were driven farther into the 50 room building." One, Renos Avraam, moved from the rear near the gymnasium into a second-floor hallway and was able to dive out a window when the flames became unbearably hot. Another, Derek Lovelock, was huddled with a crowd in the chapel and escaped through a hole made by the battering tanks. His right hand was afire.

> Others were not so fortunate. "I don't know how many wanted to go up in flames, but it is my understanding the choice was taken away," said Don Ervin of Waco, who represents Lovelock, a British construction worker who had joined the cult. "The people were isolated and trapped." While most of the men were on the first floor of the 50 room house, the women and children stayed on the second floor. Ervin said he believed that, after a staircase collapsed, they had no avenue of escape.

House Judiciary Hearings Throw More Light on CAN's Role in Waco
The House Judiciary Committee hearings into the Waco tragedy revealed that CAN has been in regular contact with at least one congressman, and that through him, CAN supplied information about the Branch Davidians to the attorney general.

On March 30, 1993, when the Waco standoff was at its height, Patricia Ryan of CAN, Herbert Rosedale and psychologist Margaret Singer of American Family Foundation submitted statements on "cults" to a congressional committee considering health benefits. Singer's "research" has been rejected by the American Psychological Association as lacking scientific merit, and several courts have refused to admit her testimony on this basis. Rosedale and Ryan cited the writings of psychiatrist Louis Jolyon West— known for his promotion of mind-altering drug use and his proposals to use ethnic and racial minorities as experimental subjects for psychiatric testing. The submissions sought to obtain government funding for deprogramming. CAN is now following up by exploiting the deaths of the Davidians to instigate federal government action against new religions. During the House Judiciary hearings, an exchange took place between Congressman William Hughes of New Jersey and Attorney General Janet Reno. Hughes, who stated that he had been in touch with CAN for a number of months, began by asking Reno whether she had spoken to "the folks from the American Family [Foundation] . . . or the Cult Awareness Net-work possibly during this time." Reno denied having done so, but reminded Hughes that she had met with him and that she has been "following up on some of your suggestions and doing everything I can to make sure that we determine all available experts that can advise us in terms of how we address these problems in the future; what do we do now to address the cults that exist, what actions should be taken if any." She also confirmed that she had a copy of an article entitled "How Many Jonestowns Will It Take?"

Reno stated that she had taken advice, apparently from the FBI, as to whether it was possible "to get them [the Davidians] out and isolate them" outside the compound and that her advisors had told her it was not.

Later during the hearing, Hughes urged Jeff Jamar, the FBI special agent who led the government's strategy, to start compiling information on "cults." Jamar stated in response to Hughes's questioning that prior to the events at Waco, the FBI had been in possession of "a white paper on cults" that was "very, very useful to us."

These exchanges indicate that Congressman Hughes, the FBI, and, through them, the attorney general were being fed CAN's hate propaganda concerning new religions. Based on this data, Reno decided to storm the compound instead of to negotiate—with tragic and fatal results.

This terrible incident at Waco occurred on the fiftieth anniversary of the Nazi assault on the Jewish ghetto in Warsaw. But it did not happen in Germany, it took place in America. As Dr. George Robertson, executive vice president of Friends of Freedom has written, "The tactics and hysteria stirred up by the Cult Awareness Network deprogrammers is one of the worst affronts against religious freedom this country has ever experienced yet. What is frightening is that the Cult Awareness Network and the deprogrammers are leveling similar charges against local churches all over the country and exploiting their own blunder in Waco, Texas, in a concerted effort to destroy religious freedom in America."

In the aftermath of Waco, the *Los Angeles Times* of May 8 reported that a wide range of civil rights and religious groups have urged the government to refrain from using its investigation into the tragedy to define a valid religion. The statement concluded that "to deny religious liberty to any is to diminish religious liberty for all."

Chapter 21

The Media and New Religious Movements

James A. Beckford

Introduction

In order to avoid misunderstanding, let me begin by making it clear that I am not going to retract any of the critical remarks that I have made in the past about the portrayal of new religious movements (NRMs) in the mass media of communication. I stand by the claims that I, along with Jim Richardson and others, have made about the tendency for journalists to sensationalize NRMs (Beckford, 1985; Beckford & Cole, 1988; van Driel & Richardson, 1988a, 1988b, 1989; van Driel & van Belzen, 1990). Journalists usually do this by accentuating those aspects of the movements which appear to be threatening, strange, exploitative, oppressive and provocative. The overall effect is two-edged. On the one hand, it reinforces ideas about the normality of non-cultic religion. On the other, it creates an apparently objective category of cults as, by definition, destructive and dangerous.

I see no reason to modify the views that I first formulated in the late 1970s about the typical ways of depicting NRMs in the mass media. But I want to add some different considerations here. In particular, I want to discuss some aspects of the relationship between journalistic and academic interests in NRMs. My remarks are an attempt to place mass media portrayals of the movements in a broader context in the hope that a clearer understanding will emerge of the difficulties facing journalists and academics. These two broad and heterogeneous categories of people have different and equally legitimate reasons for wanting to know more about NRMs. But it may be naive and unhelpful to expect that they should ultimately agree with one another.

The Political Importance of Mass Media

The French statesman and scholar Alexis de Tocqueville was among the first to recognize in the mid-nineteenth century that newspapers, magazines and other printed media of communication would become more and more important to industrial societies. They would be important as replacements for "parish pump politics" in an age of accelerating rates of social and geographical mobility. They would also act as a check on the power of politicians. They would therefore be essential to the stability and dynamism of democracy. But Tocqueville was equally far-sighted in his fears that the print-media might become an instrument of manipulation and tyranny. In fact, he had few illusions about the fragility of democracy or about the temptations for democratic majorities to act and think in thoroughly oppressive and stifling ways. His only hope for the health of democracy rested on the criss-crossing, countervailing play of different interest groups and voluntary associations serviced by self-critical journalists and owners of the news media. No single group, majority or publication could be trusted to protect democracy from their separate selfish interests in controlling it.

Tocqueville's fears about the fragility of democracy have been echoed over the past 150 years by commentators from virtually every political persuasion. There is widespread agreement that free and lively media of mass communication are vital to the health of all societies. We are therefore in the debt of journalists. But, just as importantly, we must not become dependent on them. Non-journalists need to keep a critical distance from journalists' work and to maintain a constant dialogue with them. Let me try to substantiate these general arguments by reference to the different interests that journalists and academic researchers typically have in NRMs. I shall analyze three dimensions on which the interests of journalists and researchers are markedly different.

Journalists and Academic Researchers

1. Time

For a variety of good reasons, very few journalists can afford to work on items about NRMs for longer than each "cult controversy" lasts. This is because the owners and managers of the mass media lose their audience if the focus is not kept on "newsworthy" stories. NRMs are only newsworthy when a problem occurs. Scandals, atrocities, spectacular failures, "tug-of-love" stories, defections, exposés, outrageous conduct—these are the main criteria of NRMs' newsworthiness. When the controversy has passed, the journalists usually have to move on to other stories. Exceptions may occur, of course, when a journalist takes time out, for example, to compile a book-length publication. But even then, the structure of journalists' books tends to reflect the same criteria of newsworthiness. And, of course, the unspectacular, non-sensational NRMs are permanently invisible in journalists' accounts.

By comparison, academic researchers who are professionally concerned with NRMs tend to be just as interested in them when no controversies are apparent as when there is clear evidence of problems. This greater continuity of interest is dictated by the nature of scholars' interests and methods of research. They tend to ask questions about, for example, patterns of recruitment, retention and defection which can only be answered methodically on the basis of time-series data. Ideally, scholars also try to compare NRMs, to compare their operations in different countries or to compare their operations in different periods of time. It is almost as if researchers considered the occasional cult controversy as a rude interruption of the routine life of NRMs—quite the opposite of most journalists. As a result, dull or boring NRMs could be just as exciting to academic researchers as the most eye-catching cult. The public may interpret academic interests in NRMs as a form of appeasement or as ivory tower indifference. Neither interpretation is fair.

2. Objectivity

One person's objectivity is another person's bias. This is not a sign of cynical world-weariness on my part. It is a recognition that criteria of objectivity are variable and socially constructed. Everyone wants to be seen to be objective—but only in their own way.

How do journalists create objectivity? Their favorite strategy is to combine a dash of *vox populi* with a squirt of balance. The vox pop aspect usually consists of comments elicited from passers-by or by-standers. If these comments can be attributed to identifiable individuals, it heightens the appearance of verisimilitude and realism. Balance requires something more artful. It usually requires finding space for opposing views, in the belief that readers, listeners and viewers will mistake this adversarial structure for a representative sample of opinions. The journalist seems to have made obeisance to objectivity if a story or program is not one-sided but two-sided. Arguments with more than two sides are usually considered too complicated for "good" journalism. The inclusion of a non-committal contribution by an academic frequently serves as another journalistic device for constructing a kind of objectivity. It can be very uncomfortable being the filling in the sandwich!

There is no universally agreed version of objectivity among academics. And there are conflicts and tensions between academics about the objectivity of their work. But certain strategies are conventional. They include filtering out personal values and emotive language; basing findings on representative samples; comparing NRM members with matched samples of non-members; conducting research over relatively long periods of time; taking account of all available publications on a topic; and, in the sharpest contrast to journalists, participating in both mutual criticism and self-criticism. This list is far from exhaustive but it gives a clear enough indication of how academic researchers construct their versions of objectivity. It is unlikely that the items, individually or collectively, will be considered adequate grounds for objectivity in the eyes of non-academic critics.

3. Practical and Theoretical Interests

As I said earlier, NRMs are interesting to journalists by reason of their newsworthiness as deviant, threatening or simply weird. "Cult" is therefore a self-contained and self-standing category which is of interest to the mass media for its own sake. Journalists need no other reason for writing about any particular NRM except that it is counted as a cult. This categorization is sufficient to justify a story, especially if the story illustrates many of the other components which conventionally make up the "cult" category. This puts pressure on journalists to find more and more evidence which conforms with the categorical image of cults and therefore confirms the idea that an NRM is newsworthy to the extent that it does match the category. It is no part of conventional journalistic practice to look for stories about NRMs which do *not* conform with the category of cult. Nor do journalists methodically chart the activities of NRMs which never display supposedly cultic tendencies. Journalists are in the business of, among other things, "moral gatekeeping." Gatekeepers do not need to concern themselves with people whose right to pass through their gates is not in moral question.

Self-critical academic researchers question why and how particular moral boundaries are established and protected. The fact that some NRMs are newsworthy because they act illegally or immorally is not in itself sufficient reason to study them. It is much more likely that NRMs will be of interest to researchers because they represent part of a broader, theoretically interesting topic. NRMs may challenge, for example, prevailing sociological ideas about secularization, the dilemmas of the liberal state, the limits of tolerance in democratic societies, the processes of religious conversion, the routinization of charisma, and so on. In short, NRMs are interesting just as much for what they reveal about *other* aspects of society and culture as they are for what they reveal about themselves. The interpretations that social scientists place on NRMs' activities are then subjected to constant criticism and testing.

Conclusion

The mass media *can* function as one of the vital foundations of healthy democracies. But it would be a mistake to forget that they can also serve the interests of dominant groups by stifling new ideas and change. This is why portrayals of NRMs in the mass media tend to favor conservative, majoritarian distrust of novelty, dissidence and rebellion. Nevertheless, journalists have on occasion played a significant role in exposing problems and scandals in NRMs and in putting pressure on errant movements to change their ways.

On the other hand, for the reasons that I have already discussed, the prevailing interest among journalists (or, at least, the owners and managers of the mass media) is not well adapted to the task of understanding NRMs as historically changing, but not always sensational, phenomena which reflect features of the societies and cultures in which they operate. In my opinion, the progressive growth of dispassionate, but compassionate, understanding of NRMs as social and cultural phenomena which are related in complicated ways to other phenomena is also a contribution towards a better society.

It might be tempting to conclude that journalists and academic researchers should work together in the best of all possible worlds. But the imbalance of power between them is too great for this to succeed. No, my proposal is that democratic, open societies require critical and self-critical scholarship as a counterbalance to the commercial and political forces which drive even the best journalists to limit the scope of their work on NRMs. We should not pin our hopes on the search for common ground between journalists and academic researchers. Instead, we should concentrate on improving our objective understanding of NRMs. The challenge is to counterpose information based on careful, critical scholarship to the rash generalizations and stereotypical images which all too often pass for "in depth" journalism.

References

Beckford, J.A. *Cult Controversies, The Societal Response to New Religious Movements.* London: Tavistock, 1985.

Beckford, J.A. and M. Cole. "British and American responses to new religious movements," *Bulletin of the John Rylands University Library of Manchester* 70:3. 1988:209-24.

van Driel, B and J. van Beizen. "The downfall of Rajneeshpuram in the print media: a cross-national study." *Journal for the Scientific Study of Religion* 29:1. 1990:76-90.

van Driel, B. and J.T. Richardson. "Print media coverage of new religious movements: a longitudinal study." *Journal of Communications* 38:3. 1988a:37-61.
van Driel, B. and J.T. Richardson. "The categorization of new religious movements in American print media." *Sociological Analysis* 49:2. 1988b:171-83.
van Driel, B. and J.T. Richardson. "Journalist attitudes toward new religious movements." Paper presented at the CISR conference, Helsinki, 1989.

Paper presented at the INFORM conference, London, March 28, 1993

James A. Beckford is Professor of Sociology at the University of Warwick in England. His main publications include *The Trumpet of Prophecy* (1975), *Religious Organization* (1985), *Cult Controversies* (1985), and *Religion and Advanced Industrial Society* (1989). He is the editor of *New Religious Movements and Rapid Social Change* (1986) and co-editor with Thomas Luckman of *The Changing Face of Religion* (1989). He was Editor of *Current Sociology*, 1980-1987, and President of the Association for the Sociology of Religion, 1988-1989.

Chapter 22

Television and Metaphysics at Waco

Constance A. Jones and George Baker

The purpose of this discussion is to open three arguments. First, television news coverage creates media events by the use of polarized opponents, scripted reporting and stereotypical images. A second argument concerns the degree to which the Waco disaster was a metaphysical placebo in the lives of television viewers. Finally, the crisis at the Branch Davidian Church of February-April 1993 constituted, for both participants and television viewers, a meta-event, that is, an event the facts of which have a political meaning totally unsupported by data accessible to either investigative journalists or social scientists.

Waco: Programming a TV Docudrama?

Television demands drama, forward-moving action, narrative, and speedy moral judgments. In the case of Waco, television associated a new religious movement unknown to the general public with the Peoples Temple and the horror of the 1978 apocalypse at Jonestown. Language, visual images, and escalating reports of unconfirmed allegations created an artificially heated environment which precluded any reasoned analysis of events. The television environment polarized the actors in the drama: the participants were the "authorities" and the "cultists," and the ensuing polarization increased the probability that Waco would culminate in a tragedy.

The deaths at Waco were caused in part by the creation of a "media event" through the media's use of inflammatory language and images. The probability of a violent outcome was increased by pandering to stereotypical assumptions about non-traditional religious behavior. Television framed the conflict in terms of good versus evil, suggesting the worst sort of Manichaean dualism. Initially and consistently afterwards identified as a "cult," the Branch Davidians were from the outset classified as "weird" and a challenge to conventional morality. Use of the word "cult" itself is quite enough to evoke in the collective sensibilities of the American public the most depraved of images—sexual promiscuity, child abuse, brainwashing, mind control, and involuntary captivity. (How the word "cult" became so consistently and pervasively imbued with this pernicious complex of associations is a larger question of media influence.)

Set in opposition to "cultists," the FBI and ATF were portrayed as protectors of national values and morality. Once the dualism was established, the federal authorities, the "exemplars of absolute good," were entitled to violate conventional human rights with impunity; unlike the Rodney King incident, no charges of civil rights violations were brought against federal agents. As the dualism became incorporated into the story line, visual images, innuendo, and witnesses were produced in rapid succession to confirm the dastardly nature of the "cult" and the multiplicity of evils being carried on behind the compound walls.[1] (Evidence that might break down such polarization was largely omitted: the walls were crossed daily by members of the group; numerous visitors [including government investigators] had witnessed life inside the Davidians' compound; and allegations of human rights violations had been declared spurious by local officials.)

As the fifty-one-day siege wore on, whatever violent images the camera had on file, such as the assault, or even the last images of Jonestown, were repeatedly aired. Because of the element of suspense induced by narrative and inflamed by visual cues, viewers were prepared, and came to anticipate, that the siege would culminate in a dramatic climax.

Events at Waco demonstrated the existence of a ready-made script defining how a cult operates and how intractable a cult can be to reasonable intervention by public authorities. Waco serves as yet another confirmation of the validity of the script—"another Jonestown," in which sexual slavery, child abuse, stockpiling of arms, and mind control were perpetrated upon a cast of naive actors by a Svengali who called for "suicide" rather than capitulation to the outside world. Thus, instead of learning of the varieties of religious experience and group commitment, the American public gleans yet another example of the horrors of cult life and its inevitable tragedy for all.

Sociologist Todd Gitlin finds Alexis de Tocqueville's writing of the 1830s strangely prescient in this regard, as Tocqueville observes that American culture in that era was already given to "comfortable, sensational, mass-produced amusements, 'vehement and bold,' 'untutored and rude,' aiming 'to stir passions more than to charm the taste.'"[2] Gitlin goes on to define television's spectacles as "having roots in centuries-old myths, just as they recycle and transform them." That the dualism of Waco went unchallenged, except for a postmortem analysis conducted ingenuously with belatedly summoned scholars, testifies to the training toward conventionality which television imposes.

The ante at Waco was upped because of the intervention of television reporting. Lives were endangered because the story line was created and embedded in a pernicious dualism which legitimated the "authorities" and discouraged unconventional perspectives and opinions. The shared mentality—the corporate mentality—was served as the cultural mainstream was reinforced, not challenged.

Waco's Branch Davidians, then, were victims of a media-induced disaster, executed before the eyes of the nation on television. The polarization that led to the catastrophe at Waco was inherent in neither the religious group itself—nor even the FBI.

Waco as a Metaphysical Placebo

Every serious person's experience includes an occasional feeling, as recognizable as it is indescribable, of unconnectedness. In words, such a feeling might be something like, "I feel on the periphery of my own life. I feel marginalized, a fifth wheel in the collection of persons, schedules and agendas of the people who supposedly form my most intimate circle. There is nothing, no resting point inside my own head or heart in relation to which these conflicting schedules, images and priorities can be viewed, understood." From the perspective of the teachings of both traditional as well as new religions, the state just described is an ideal one in which a search for the truth of one's life can begin. The loss of moorings from stereotyped social, gender and professional roles can provide a new access to energy in life that, previously, had been absorbed in role-playing.

In such a state—and in reaction to the growing alienation of contemporary life—a person may turn to religion or other redemptive movements. Notably successful movements such as Human Potentials, New Religions, Ecology and Evangelicalism emphasize a sense of the immediacy of one's life and of one's connection with others in the movement. In this context there is the strong impression of an engagement with one's life at a level of intensity previously unknown. For many participants in such movements, alienation (or at least the most visible signs of it) has been overcome.

Television coverage of the type reported on Jonestown in 1978,[3] the so-called Gulf War of January-February 1991, the Rodney King beating and aftermath in Los Angeles in 1992 and the military confrontation in the compound of the Branch Davidian Church in March-April 1993 provides viewers with a pseudo-engagement with their world. This is important because the real market for much news coverage is not motivated by hunger for sex and violence, per se; rather, fundamentally, the market is driven by an underlying metaphysical need for connectedness with others and a sense of the lawfulness and orderliness of life.

The television viewer's metaphysical needs are addressed by providing a negative foil that allows the viewer to regard his lifestyle, values and associations as preferable to those of the persons filmed on television. Here, the sense of immediacy, of intimate connectedness with other, is provided by television's ability to establish Manichaean-like subsets of "us" and "them."

The addictive character of (typically negative) television news reporting, then, arises from a profound disquietude in contemporary life. It is as if the emotional and spiritual stability of a great number of people required the periodic sacrifice, Aztec style, of the lives of a small number of people on the sacrificial stone of the television camera.

Waco as Meta-event

We introduce the concepts of meta-events, meta-facts, and meta-conditions as tools for the analysis of reporting within the electronic and print media. Meta-events are news stories that concern those public actions of government agencies, the authority and purpose of which are beyond the reach of investigative journalism.[4] Meta-events are made up of meta-facts, descriptive images and narrative reporting that implicitly contain pointed messages for other groups. In the reporting of both meta-events and meta-facts, there is a coded message for other individuals or groups in society that might share similar beliefs, habits or affiliations. It follows that meta-conditions constitute the medium in which meta-events and meta-facts operate. A meta-condition is the underlying absence of fit between what is reported and what is happening; it is the cognitive inconsistency which goes unrecognized and exempted from a reality check.

The confrontation at the Davidian compound qualifies as a meta-event in the ostensible "raid" for search and seizure of arms and abused children. The event contained meta-facts in the transparent message that the raid has (or was intended to have) for other alternative religious organizations. The meta-condition of an apparently unverifiable motive of the initial ATF raid-inspection on February 28 completes the scenario.

The federal authorities treated the crisis with the Branch Davidians as a political, military confrontation in which raw power and technology would decide the outcome. The fact that the Davidians were a group with apocalyptic and survivalist beliefs was not incorporated into the social calculus of the FBI and ATF officials. The fundamental historical and metaphysical conditions at Waco, then, went unrecognized by the public authorities. In the standoff between federal authorities and Davidian church members, federal officials were in denial about the real risk to their lives and those of church members that the firearms inspection and the ensuing crisis represented. As so many observers have emphasized, there was no practical need for such an inspection. The Davidians, apparently, had broken no federal or state law, and, in any case, the physical apprehension of its leader, David Koresh, would have been a trivial, administrative matter that local police could have handled.

Often news events are reported exactly counter to their historical fact in order to convey specific political messages to one or more audiences. In many cases such events appear empirically verifiable, but, on closer inspection, are not; and the message is considered delivered in the publication of the original version of the alleged event, not by its subsequent verification. The "buck-stops-here" speech of Attorney General Janet Reno after the holocaust at Waco on April 19 demonstrates how counterfactual precedents get established as fact: she gave a courageous, if wholly implausible, explanation of the "decision" at the Justice Department to use greater levels of armed force against the Davidians. The political meaning of her speech had little to do specifically with the Davidians, however; the meaning, apparently, was intended for other non-traditional religious and cultural groups, the existence or activities of which could come to be opposed by program administrators of lobbyists acting within the Department of Justice.[5]

The occurrence of both meta-events and meta-conditions raises serious issues for academic observers for whom, at least officially, meta-facts do not exist: U.S. social scientists (as well as prosecution and defense counsels in the U.S. judicial system) report on facts; nothing in their training prepares them to process meta-facts. This same shortcoming in the professional preparation of U.S. social scientists does not exist in journalists, publishers and social scientists in other countries (such as Mexico) who, readily and easily, are able to incorporate meta-facts into their understanding of facts and trends in Mexican society.

Social scientists from the United States and other countries, therefore, may view the media from two quite different viewpoints. The U.S. academic reads the press under the belief that the events reported actually took place, and that, at least in principle, they are empirically verifiable. The Mexican academic (to continue with the example), in contrast, holds to no such suppositions. In his view, the Mexican press in its political reporting is seen as a class of political poetry, the raw material for a national ballad, a *corrido,* a novel, but not as a sure guide to historical events.

Television's well-known tendencies toward hyperbole and standard script-reporting were displayed in the Waco confrontation between federal authorities and a local church.   The Waco confrontation became an artificially heated and sensationalized account portrayed through selected images and escalating allegations.

Our second contention is that the Waco confrontation gave television viewers two months of what we have called metaphysical placebo: viewers were given data and impressions that served to validate their values, lifestyles and personal commitments. The story of the Waco Davidians fed our appetite for images of what could go wrong in someone's life. Our argument, however, is that the story also provided the viewer with a false promise of a new connection to the world, an evocative immediacy owing to the real-time reporting of the events.   In this way, the viewer then experienced the illusion of being brought to life by the drama at Waco. Such an interpretation, in turn, suggests the lack of a real metaphysical vitality in American society.

Our final, counterintuitive argument is that there is a class of media reporting for which the concept of historical event is insufficient. We refer to such reporting as meta-events. The key element in meta-events is the application of arbitrary governmental power in defining the terms and implications of a story. Invariably, such a use of power has a collateral purpose of signaling policy goals to other groups and constituencies. In the case of Waco, the Clinton administration signaled that abuses of power by federal agencies like the ATF and FBI against nontraditional religious groups will not be challenged.   It is predictable that the authoritarian potential in some non-traditional religious groups would be activated by an initial authoritarian stance on the part of federal agencies. The bombing of the World Trade Center in New York by members of a Muslim sect may have been abetted by the message of a violent retribution given by attorney general Reno and her subordinates. Was this a self-fulfilling prophesy? Television, in turn, collaborated with the government's efforts to undermine the claims to moral and religious integrity of the Branch Davidians, formerly of Waco, Texas.

Waco could be recognized early on as a probable "media event" because of its potential for great grief, sex, violence, and death, a potential exacerbated in an American context by the religious nature of the group. Although this country's history is replete with religious experimentation at almost all levels, the country's sensibilities remain curiously unsympathetic to religious innovation. The history of religious experimentation in America amply demonstrates patterns of public distrust and open oppression. Is it the case that, since the advent of television, the American predisposition to be suspicious of religious innovation has become more widespread and forceful? Is it also the case that the effect of a constant barrage of visual images surrounding a "media event" is to force viewers to rush to an instant judgment about the merits of each side in opposition?

Notes

[1]Constance A. Jones, "Exemplary Dualism and Authoritarianism at Jonestown," in Rebecca Moore and Fielding McGehee, eds., *New Religious Movements, Mass Suicide, and Peoples Temple: Scholarly Perspectives on a Tragedy* (New York: Edwin Mellen, 1989).

[2]Todd Gitlin, *Watching Television* (New York: Pantheon, 1986), pp. 4-5.

[3]A discussion of television coverage of Jonestown is in George Baker, "The Ethics and Psychology of Media Consumption," in Eileen Barker, ed., *New Religious Movements: A Perspective for Understanding Society* (New York: Edwin Mellen, 1982).

[4]The paradigm case (cf. Weber's ideal type) of meta-event was the reported arrest on January 10, 1989, of a Mexican oil union leader Joaquín Hernández Galicia ("La Quina"). There are a few eerie parallels to Waco. The national and international press covered this story intensely. Mexican government press releases recounted how four police officials had come to La Quina's house in the northern town of Cd. Madero (near Tampico) for the purpose of making an on-site inspection of the premises to determine if La Quina illegally possessed firearms. According to the press release, La Quina's bodyguards opened fire on the police, killing one. La Quina and two dozen others were then arrested and flown to a Mexico City penitentiary where they were kept in solitary confinement. In the course of the following eighteen months the historical details of what actually happened came to light: there had been no police officers present; none were killed; the entire operation was conducted by commando army units. La Quina was a political prisoner jailed because of his opposition to the privatization policies of the new presidential administration headed by the young, recently inaugurated Carlos Salias de Gortari and because of his allegedly having supported the campaign of an opposition candidate. All Mexican union leaders, government officials and university graduates in general understood the unwritten political messages in this event. No one in Mexico believed the literal account given by the government-controlled press. George Baker, "The Mexican Border Print-Media: Facts and Meta-Facts," paper presented at the Annual Meeting of the Association of Borderlands Scholars, Corpus Christi, April 22, 1993; George Baker, "Take My Word for It," *El Financiero International* (Mexico City), August 30, 1993, p. 7.

[5]San Francisco psychologist Jane Hawes suggested to the authors that the subsequent bombing of the World Trade Center in New York by members of a militant Muslim sect may be connected with the message of violent retribution given by Attorney General Reno and her subordinates.

Constance A. Jones, Professor of Sociology at Mills College in Oakland, California, does research on new religious movements and women's issues.

George Baker, formerly associate director of the Program for the Study of New Religious Movements at the Graduate Theological Union, co-editor of *Understanding the New Religions* (1978), and currently director of a consulting firm in Oakland, publishes on topics relating to the media and other issues of public policity. Since 1989, he has give special attention to U.S.-Mexican relations.

Chapter 23

Waco and the *War of the Worlds:*
Media Fantasy and Modern Reality

I. Lamar Maffett

In 1938, a live radio program, adapted from H. G. Wells's *War of the Worlds,* made journalistic history. It was the story of how Martians were invading Earth. The young Orson Welles narrated the script "as if a normal evening of broadcasting was being interrupted by bulletins about the invasion," according to Don R. Pember *(Mass Media in America*, Macmillan, 1991, p. 126). The program, aired by CBS, became a famous radio broadcast. Pember continues:

> The people at CBS thought it was believable enough from the beginning. They made Welles make 38 script changes—renaming the National Guard the militia, the U.S. Weather Bureau the Government Weather Bureau, and so forth. But that apparently didn't help listeners distinguish fiction from reality.

The public, many of whom tuned in late to the program, believed they were hearing a blow-by-blow account of how the world was being destroyed by aliens. The next day, after a night of hysteria and suicides, the *New York Daily News* carried this heading:

FAKE RADIO WAR STIRS TERROR THROUGHOUT U.S.

Fraud in the media did not begin with this CBS broadcast or electronic journalism. The news media has never had a great age by which to measure itself. In spite of occasional signs of brilliance, usually by individuals, it has

157

left a tarnished legacy, characterized by sensationalism, distortion, and bias. It learned, from DeFoe's *A Journal of the Plague Year* and *Robinson Crusoe,* that it could create news where none existed before, such as CBS's choreographing of student riots in the 1960s.

Some media have also become "experts" in religion by assigning a reporter to "cover the religion beat" for the public. Qualified reporters may have a genuine appreciation and understanding of religion. Many do not. As a recent example of the latter, The *Atlanta Journal/Atlanta Constitution* carried several front-page, "soft" news stories on "Women of the Veil," a series purporting to expose anti-feminism in modern Islam. They continued printing the series in spite of outrage expressed from the Islamic community that they were confusing the culture of individual countries and personal behavior with what the Quran actually teaches, and were totally ignoring the brutal history of woman abuse in the Middle East before the coming of Muhammad. Muhammad, at the risk of his life, opposed the abuse of women in his time, when women were subject to the whims and pleasure of males. Newly born baby girls were commonly buried alive in the desert and left to die. Muhammad also suggested the use of the veil, already in use by other cultures such as the Hindu, to protect women from the leering eyes of males. One article like those in the "Women of the Veil" series can produce great public misunderstanding, reinforcing centuries-old stereotypes and prejudices.

Earlier this century, the University of Missouri School of Journalism introduced "objective news reporting," ignoring the warnings from psychology and the new sciences, particularly Heisenberg's Uncertainty Principle from 1920, that "objective reporting," or objective anything, even science, is impossible. During the 1970s, something called "precision journalism" made a brief and limited appearance in news reporting; it attempted to saturate a story with all of the garbled, nonsensical data behind the story, forcing the reader to draw his or her own conclusions. From the underground press, advocacy journalism, gonzo journalism, and the increase in yellow tabloid journalism came the "investigative journalism" of the 1980s and 1990s.

Guardians of honesty in journalism, the journalism reviews, appeared in the 60s and 70s, but have virtually disappeared today, becoming only a footnote in the history of the media, while the yellow tabloids continue to dominate media format and content.

It was from this feckless history that a fascinated public viewed the Waco tragedy, as the media was fed "data" from the government, data that was beefed up by the media for public consumption. A "good" story, editors know, can be milked further by the use of sidebars and special reports. As the Waco standoff moved toward a conclusion, the media files discovered the answer for extending the tragedy: the cults.

Why extend it? The answer is not pretty. Money, promotion, prestige, and journalism awards were at stake. Front-page news can be chosen from a formula, a sliding scale of public interest. War is usually more important than Wall Street news. High on the list are celebrities, scandal and sex-related stories, preferably all three in one story, which accounts for the ongoing attention paid to the British royal family. Combine any or all of the above, such as sex and scandal, with religion, as in Jim Bakker, and the editors shout, "Hold the presses!"

The Branch Davidian group seemed to fit several of these news categories, including a perceived war with the U.S. government. It was not until weeks after the fire that the media reported how David Koresh had criticized the "federal authorities for using force and indicated he wouldn't have resisted if ATF agents had given him a chance, according to tape recordings obtained by the *Houston Chronicle*" (The *Atlanta Journal/Atlanta Constitution*, May 25, 1993). And it was not until mid-June 1993 that the public learned how the FBI had given edited tapes to a congressional subcommittee of Koresh's 911 call for help, tapes that left out his repeated appeals to the police that the church was being fired upon and would be forced to fire back if help was not quickly forthcoming. Before these disclosures, fundamental questions bothered many citizens. The *Atlanta Journal/Atlanta Constitution* (May 11, 1993) carried this question/answer:

Q: Have authorities found evidence of any of the *illegal* [italics added] weapons they were looking for at the Branch Davidian compound? *Tommy Haddaway, Marietta*
A: Neither the FBI, the Bureau of Alcohol, Tobacco and Firearms nor the Texas Rangers would give us that information.

The media, always under pressure from their competition, had already planned documentaries and sidebars on how the Branch Davidians were just the tip of an iceberg, but they needed a live target. And they found one: the Church Universal and Triumphant. With military precision, newspapers, magazines and radio-television special reports were warning the public that the Church had "dozens of underground bunkers" and more, deadlier firepower than the Branch Davidians. The frenetic media bandwagon was off and rolling.

Several newspapers, lacking budget or desire to investigate for themselves, carried word for word from the wire services an article created by the *Boston Globe,* entitled "U.S. Cults: Dozens of More Potential Time Bombs." It begins:

Boston—If you think Waco, Texas, was bad, consider who could be next. Consider Elizabeth Clare Prophet's Church Universal and Triumphant, which has constructed dozens of underground shelters near Yellowstone National Park and stocked them with sleeping bags and batteries, first-aid

kits, flashlights and enough food to feed hundreds of members for months—
along with what critics insist [italics added] is a cache of weapons.

A long, rambling article with no real documentation, the Boston story quotes
only the "cult watchers," die-hard enemies of the Church.   The old
journalism cliche, "We don't make the news; we just report it," is not always
true.   This article clearly was intended to persuade, not inform.   The article
continues:

> Mr. Enroth said the Prophet's [Elizabeth Clare Prophet's] Church Universal
> is a possible hot point. "They're very much into an armed status and have
> a tightly controlled camp."
>
> Kathy Grizzard Schnook, who lives near the church and is about to
> publish a book on it, is even more alarmed. "It's much more dangerous than
> Waco because the weapons are 100 times what they [the Davidians] had
> down there. If these people go underground, you're not going to get them
> out. They have survival supplies for seven years . . . and an armored
> personnel carrier inside their main shelter."

Clark Morphew, staff columnist for the *Saint Paul Pioneer Press*, and
Gustav Niebuhr, staff writer for the *Washington Post*, wrote reports in stark
contrast to those in other media.   Niebuhr states that the media had focused
on the purchase of guns by two individual church members and the
construction of bomb shelters on the Church property.   Niebuhr continues:

> Filtered through such reports, the church's public image is often spooky. "It
> was only after spending time with them that I was able to let go of those
> [negative] impressions," said James R. Lewis, a senior research associate at
> the Institute for the Study of American Religion in Santa Barbara, Calif. .
> . . "I was actually favorably impressed . . . . I liked the Church Universal
> Triumphant people," Lewis said.   He called the situation "extremely
> healthy—there's no danger of them becoming another Waco."

Morphew writes in his column (February 28, 1993):

> New religions are always persecuted by the ignorant and the fearful. But
> eventually, they are seen as legitimate pieces in the American religious
> puzzle.
>
> I predict that is exactly what will happen to the new religions of this
> age. They will be persecuted. But determined leadership will carry the day.
> Elizabeth Clare Prophet is a part of our religious history, and someday
> Church Universal and Triumphant will be as honored as Mormonism is
> today.

How many of the allegations about the Church carried in the negative media
are true?   Exactly none.

First, contrary to what the Church neighbor Schmook reported in the
media, U.S. citizens cannot buy a tank.   If a museum buys one, its barrels

are cut off and plugged so they cannot be fired. The "communications tower" shown on the CBS *48 Hours* program is located on private land twenty miles from Church headquarters. Finally, Mrs. Prophet stated that the only guns on the property are privately owned by church members and are used for such things for hunting. Although invited to do so, CBS's *48 Hours* never filmed anything on Church property. The negative effects upon the public were enhanced by having the camera peer over a fence at the "next Waco."

Many television news and talk shows, national and local, simultaneously compared the Waco group to the Church Universal and Triumphant. Noteworthy for their blatant sensationalism were *Inside Edition*, with Nancy Glass; *Dateline NBC*, with Jane Pauley and Stone Phillips; *48 Hours*, with Dan Rather; *The Jane Whitney Show*; and KDFW, Dallas. Only Jane Whitney attempted to present both sides in an emotionally charged program.

Several of these programs featured interviews with former Church members Talita and Kenneth Paolini, who said they met and married while on the staff of the Church and, after leaving the Church, had become paid deprogrammers; they said that they were speaking out publicly against the Church and its leader, Mrs. Prophet. One of their acts after leaving the Church was to kidnap for "deprogramming" (that is, brutal brainwashing while held against one's will) a thirty-nine-year-old mother, a Church member who lives in Idaho. She was taken by force while her small children watched. The following allegations, coming primarily from the Paolinis and a few other dedicated critics, appeared time after time on television programs: I have added my response:

> *Allegation:* The Church holds its members against their will by brainwashing.
> *Response:* Since most of the Church's membership does not live on the Montana property but in over forty countries around the world and since its membership includes people from the highest professional levels—doctors, nurses, lawyers, psychiatrists, college professors, teachers, ministers and scientists—it would be impossible to keep these highly trained and/or intelligent people brainwashed day after day. There must be other incentives to keep this loosely organized congregation so unified and faithful.
>
> The Church's hundreds of publications (books, tapes, advertising brochures, letters to Church members) produced in the highest journalistic standards absolutely do not support the brainwashing charge. By airing charges by the Paolinis and two disgruntled neighbors of the Church, the media were hoping that the public would smell smoke and assume a fire was burning. In contradiction to the charge of controlled thinking, the Church's central message is *spiritual freedom and Self-sufficiency*, an ancient and honored theme also found in the writings of Emerson, Thoreau and Whitman. The Self is the atman, God, the *Yod He Vau He* ("I AM THAT I AM") within each person. In other words, one should worship only God, not a human being. Mrs. Prophet has repeatedly warned Church members

not to worship her, which she says would be idolatry, and she is on record opposing any form of hypnotism, self- or otherwise.

Allegation: The Church mixes its doctrine with the education of its children. *Response:* The Church strongly maintains that children in American public schools are not being given an adequate education in the 3 Rs, geography, history, math and science comparable to that of other cultures, such as the Asian. The Church supports a strong basic education for children in order to produce well-informed, responsible citizens; and for this purpose it conducts regular seminars and practicums on education for the public. The seminars feature recognized national and international speakers and educational theory, such as the Montessori and Glenn Doman methods and Spalding phonics. It has its own higher religious educational institution, Summit University.

As for including "church doctrine" in the education of its members' children, the Church believes that religious dogma is man-made. A modern mystery school, the Montana Church does not have a dogma, but rather teachings which students and church members may prove in the laboratory of their daily lives. However, if adding church doctrine to education were forbidden by law, it would be the death of Catholicism, Eastern Orthodoxy, Mormonism, much of Protestantism, Islam, Buddhism and Bahaism—in short, most religions today.

Members of the Church Universal and Triumphant are encouraged to read the great books, poets, and writers, such as Homer and Shakespeare, and listen to the great musical compositions of Mozart, Beethoven, and the Strausses. From their carefully developed research, the Church offers specific psychological and spiritual reasons for not watching much television programming, such as soap operas, and general entertainment today. Golden ages of the past thrived as long as they reinforced their lofty cultures with idealized art and enlightened leadership. The ancient Greek chorus in drama, for example, was on stage to make certain through its chanting that the citizens watching the play understood the moral points and theme.

Allegation: The Church controls the food, lifestyle, marriage, and sex life of its members.
Response: The Church describes itself as a modern mystery school. The Paolinis, as most people today, do not understand the requirements for a historical mystery school, such as the several Greek mysteries, Roman, Chaldean and Egyptian mystery schools. Casual Church members who must be spoon-fed by "Mother" can become a serious problem for a mystery school. This highly disciplined order of gentle (but determined) people absolutely requires a spiritual harmony for accomplishing its purposes: the elevation of its members and mankind through an exemplary scientific, mystical unity. Church members who feel out of place in this setting are invited to find another path of their preference.

The Church Universal and Triumphant, however, responding to the needs of this age, permits anyone to join and progress at his or her own level, including the choice of his or her own foods. The Church does recommend, on the basis of historical research and personal experience, the most effective diet and living habits for achieving its exalted aims as a mystery school.

Allegation: They chant.

Response: So do Buddhists, Hindus, Muslims, Catholics, Protestants (such as congregational responses), sports fans, rights marchers, political conventions, children at play and most everyone else.

Allegation: The Church has underground bomb shelters and defense systems.

Response: A ministerial student friend of mine told me that he paid his college tuition and supported a large family in the 1950s by building atomic bomb shelters for citizens. Many contractors made a good living after WWII by building the shelters, and history shows conclusively that by 1962 it was a very wise investment since the Soviet Union and the United States were on the brink of nuclear war. The international proliferation of nuclear weapons today reveals that the shelters are like a good life insurance policy. The American federal government certainly knows this and has built massive, well-stocked underground nuclear bunkers outside Washington, D.C. Funded by taxpayers' money, the shelters are quickly accessible by helicopter for political and military leaders in case of nuclear attack.

The media, while attacking private citizens for having their own shelters, have also ignored the federal government's desire for several decades to move its national headquarters to the Midwest as added protection against surprise nuclear attack. Some state governments, such as that of Alabama, also have built well-stocked shelters in the past decade for their governors and staff. Nor has it been well-reported that for decades the former Soviet Union, China, Switzerland and Canada (*Maclean's,* September 13, 1993), among other countries, built enormous well-stocked underground nuclear shelters for their leaders and citizens.

The media's attack on the cults and the Church Universal and Triumphant has been deeply flawed by several common types of false logic: among them, ignoring the question, *non sequitur,* and *argumentum ad hominem.* "Doomsday Prophet" they have labeled Mrs. Prophet, totally ignoring her point that, with proper preparations, we *can survive* nuclear fallout and that a nuclear war does not mean the end of the world (as the term "doomsday" suggests). The Church does not teach that the world is about to end in a flaming Armageddon.

An honest investigation of the Church Universal and Triumphant on its beautiful Montana property evokes an image of the stereotypical American pioneer, who was God fearing, hard working, squeaky clean, morally pure, helpful and vision-led. The Church, like early American settlers, uses organic farming methods, without dangerous pesticides or herbicides. They have a deep love and reverence for the land, their nation and the earth. Bison, elk, deer and other native game graze on their wilderness property, which is adjacent to Yellowstone National Park. The Church conducted a

1993 summer conference, Healing the Earth, inviting authorities in ecology from major universities, private groups such as the Sierra Club and a national environmental columnist to help conduct the conference.

A lead letter-to-the-editor of The *Atlanta Journal/Atlanta Constitution* states:

> Waco Recalls Witch-burning of 300 Years Ago
> The Editors: As we try to change the subject and slither away from Waco, it is important to remember that Waco was no more than government-sponsored witch-burning of men, women, and children driven by the cries of the media: "Cult, cult, cult." This is probably not much unlike the cries heard in Salem, Mass., some 300 years ago . . . .

The media's war on the cults has all of the signs of a war on religion itself. Every thirteenth of the month in a farm field outside Conyers, Georgia, a homemaker, Mrs. Nancy Fowler, delivers a message that she says comes from the Virgin Mary, and many agree with her. Mary's appearance is a worldwide phenomenon today. On June 13, 1993, over eighty thousand pilgrims from around the world came to hear Mary's latest call through Mrs. Fowler to America and the world. A follow-up article in The *Atlanta Journal/Atlanta Constitution* (June 14, 1993) about Mrs. Fowler, however, focused on the complaints of three former followers who became disenchanted with her personality. Sound familiar? The article concludes:

> Across White Road, unhappy neighbors alternately beat on metal pipes, blasted rock music on automobile radios and fired weapons.

The *Pioneer Press'* Clark Morphew may well be right Persecution assured the success of America's distinctive religion, Mormonism, and of most other faiths in history, and persecution may well help establish the Church Universal and Triumphant as a major religious force in the next century. In the crucible of white-hot hatred, religious bigotry and ignorance, the dross of fantasy is burned away and one discovers what is worth living or even dying for.

Professor I. Lamar Maffett teaches world religions at DeKalb College, central and north Campuses in Clarkston and Dunwoody, Georgia. He has served as a newspaper, magazine and book editor, and taught journalism at DeKalb.

Chapter 24

A More Righteous Seed:
A Comparison of Polygamy among the Branch Davidians and the Fundamentalist Mormons

Martha Sonntag Bradley

At 9:00 a.m., Sunday, July 16, 1953 the voice of Arizona Governor Howard Pyle traveled over the airways of KUTR radio to announce a raid on the polygamist community of Short Creek, Arizona. He said:

> Before dawn today the State of Arizona began and now has substantially concluded a momentous police action against insurrection within her own borders. Arizona has mobilized and used its total police power to protect the lives and future of 263 children. They are the product and the victims of the foulest conspiracy you could possibly imagine. More than 129 peace officers moved into Short Creek, in Mohave County, at 4 o'clock this morning. They have arrested almost the entire population of a community dedicated to the production of white slaves who are without hope of escaping this degrading slavery from the moment of their birth.[1]

The raid culminated two years of careful planning and investigation about the polygamous and communal lifestyle of the Fundamentalist people living in northern Arizona.[2] Pyle felt the raid was justified because of the way women and children were treated in the group. "Highly competent investigators have been unable to find a single instance in the last decade," he would say, "of girls reaching the age of fifteen without having been forced into a shameful mockery of marriage."[3]

It is haunting how familiar Governor Howard's Pyle's words are, forty years after the raid on Short Creek. They might have been spoken by Janet Reno as she stood before television cameras to explain away the raid at Waco. There are striking parallels between the lifestyle of the Branch Davidians and the Fundamentalist Mormon people of Short Creek, Arizona.[4] Polygamy and communalism play prominent roles in both groups, defining the boundaries between insiders and outsiders, testing the faithfulness and loyalty of members, and forming connections between individuals that are fortified by belief. But perhaps even more important for the purpose of this discussion are similarities in the methods and the scope of the government's reaction to the groups.

Governor Pyle's findings and the FBI's rather abortive investigation of the Branch Davidians' compound in Waco suggested the presence of firearms, substandard living standards, and scarce supplies. Both identified the polygamist lifestyle of certain members of the groups, the effect of polygamy on the women involved, and what they perceived to be an abusive, immoral environment for the children. In both cases, the government's extraordinary reaction was based on a surface examination of the way things looked; the police agents saw the simple frame houses and plain clothed children of Short Creek as proof of neglect. They saw pregnant teenagers and families with five or six wives as harems, and therefore evidence of lustful controlling patriarchs. They failed to push any further than the veneer to measure the degree of religious commitment that drove this people, that filled them with a feeling of goodness that far compensated for the poverty of their lifestyle and imbued with religious significance every sacrifice they made for their faith. They made decisions in 1953 to arrest and remove virtually an entire community; and forty years later, in 1993 the decisions that led to the death of eighty-six individuals were based on intolerance, on fear, on perception not fact, with a lack of substantive information that might have led to greater understanding rather than the tragedies that did result.

Polygamy among the Branch Davidians differed in important ways from the Fundamentalist practice. Polygamy in Waco centered around the personality and position of David Koresh. According to reports coming out of the group, Koresh was the only man allowed to have additional wives. This was because he saw himself as the literal seed of David, a king chosen by God to wed righteous women who would renounce their families and join his new order. His charismatic leadership demanded the complete and unquestioning loyalty of his followers. Accepting his instruction to become a polygamous wife was one of many changes the group's women made to adjust their lives to Koresh's vision of the path to God. By introducing plural marriage to the most trusted inner circle of Davidians, David Koresh created a new community order, a secretive and exclusive system of loyalties and familial ties based on his authority.

This surrender to the authority of David Koresh is the key to understanding the origins of his teachings on polygamy and the creation of this new marital order. When Koresh reinvented a world through revelation, he created a condition of anomie, throwing all norms into flux, casting out and recasting all assumptions about morality, theology, law, and community. For these women and, perhaps more important, the husbands who willingly gave them to Koresh, he was the central unifying character in a new, often confusing state of reality. Koresh became the gatekeeper, and as such he specified the conditions upon which the faithful could pass on to salvation. They became dependent on him for their redemption and thus were peculiarly vulnerable to each new idea he presented. Regardless, polygamy was only a measure of their commitment, of their devotion to an ideal, and perhaps to the person of their leader. It was not evidence of a potential for violence, for abuse, for perversions that threatened the lives of the children. It is certainly not a compelling enough justification to defend the action at Mt. Carmel.

Furthermore, despite differences between the Mormon Fundamentalist type of polygamy and the Branch Davidian version, in each case a preoccupation with procreation and the importance of creating a more righteous seed led members of both groups to enter into a marriage form that offered more challenges than rewards. Clearly, for both, polygamy created complicated relationships at the same time that it established associations that were intended to last into the millennium. Polygamous unions were based on religious commitment, on a willingness to relinquish one's own interests on behalf of the group, and an ability to forsake happiness, perhaps even contentment on this earth for rewards in the next. Polygamy became a rite of passage for the women of these groups—a process through which one separated from the world outside, relinquishing the parameters of laws, customs, conventions, and ceremonies, and took on a new order, a new way of being.

Finally, it is ironic that these people put so much faith in the constitutional form of government. They trusted the government to protect them, to guarantee that they could live out their lives in peace. Despite the fact that such groups have been so badly treated by the government, they continue to believe that America is a place that respects the rights of individuals to pursue their own interests.

Clearly, we didn't learn the lesson of Short Creek. Within two years all the polygamists returned to their homes and took up their broken lives again. Within twenty years the community's population had increased tenfold. Forty years later, the men, women and children of Waco weren't so fortunate. Many of those who were out of the compound at the time of the conflagration are confused about what course their lives should now take. But those of us who watched this tragedy unfold like a dark unbelievable science fiction must express our outrage and call for a re-examination of the horrors we have ourselves created, and learn from our mistakes.

Notes

[1] "Statement of Governor Pyle," July 26, 1953, KUTR Radio, Phoenix, Arizona. Copy in the Howard Pyle collection, Luhr Reading Room, Hayden Library, Arizona State University.

[2] Since the early twentieth century Mormon polygamists have been excommunicated for failing to obey direction of the Mormon Church forbidding the practice. The Mormon Church ended the official practice of polygamy with the Manifesto of 1890, a document that took two decades before it was truly invoked by the church.

Martha Sonntag Bradley formerly taught at Brigham Young University. Her book on the Short Creek community has recently been published.

Chapter 25

Who Committed Child Abuse at Waco?

Lawrence Lilliston

In his classic work *The Myth of Mental Illness*, Thomas Szasz argued that words and phrases can be reified and acquire power to control behavior and to limit human freedom. In his analysis of the social uses of the term "mental illness," Szasz has demonstrated how labels can serve the purpose of control over behaviors and values that lie outside of social norms. The use of such labels by persons in power, such as psychiatrists, political figures, law enforcement personnel, and media icons, can serve as a rationale for all sorts of social control including inappropriate control which limits individual or group freedom. Labels and terms may be used to indicate that a person or group lies so far outside the norms that it is acceptable, or even necessary, to take strong measures to control them. The imperative to control those labeled as mentally ill becomes even stronger if they are viewed as a threat to themselves or others. The label of mental illness, as employed by the media, law enforcement officials, and mental health experts, played a major role in the events in Waco. Whether he was given a clinical diagnosis, such as psychopathic or paranoid, by mental health professionals or whether he was crudely referred to as the "Wacko from Waco" by late-night talk show hosts, David Koresh was clearly seen by most Americans as being mentally ill. And a dangerous mentally ill person, at that. Because of accusations that he had a cache of guns and that the Branch Davidians were highly trained in the use of these guns, the group was seen by most Americans as a threat to their surrounding community. In addition, and crucially, Koresh was portrayed as dangerous to the children within the Branch Davidian compound. Stories of child abuse circulated widely in the media. These stories included allegations of physical abuse, such as unusually severe beatings of infants, and sexual abuse, including charges that Koresh routinely had sex with children and had impregnated several young teenagers. These charges resonated quite well with the general public since the topic has been widely discussed and written about in recent years. Because of a greater awareness and sensitivity to the issue, an ever increasing number of real cases of child abuse, particularly sexual abuse, have been reported and successfully prosecuted. Most experts agree that these cases of real, substantiated child abuse constitute the considerable majority of cases reported. However, there has also been an increase in accusations of child abuse that appear to have little substantiation. Such accusations have become quite common in child custody cases related to divorce. Charges of abuse have also become almost *de rigueur* for critics of new religious movements. Because of their representation in the media as cults, NRMs are particularly vulnerable to these characterizations since they lie far outside acceptable norms for religious practice. Indeed in the public's consciousness, people who would join such groups must either be mentally ill to begin with or are deviously manipulated into joining and then made mentally ill through the cult's practices. And according to this view, as a result of their mental illness, they are likely to be child abusers and society is justified in controlling their behavior (e.g., attacking and destroying them). Thus, we see a newer updated version of the use of the metaphor of "mental illness" as a mechanism for social control as it was written about so perceptively by Szasz over thirty years ago: the involuntary mental hospitalization Szasz attacked then has been replaced by attempts to force people to involuntarily give up their right to religious freedom.

Reports of child abuse played a particularly significant role in the events at Waco since this alleged abuse was the initial reason given by the FBI and Attorney General Janet Reno for the initiative that led to the conflagration. Reno had, in a sense, risen to her position partly on the child abuse issue. Her prosecution in child abuse cases in Florida, including an unsuccessful but highly newsworthy prosecution of an accused seventeen-year-old worker in a day care center, clearly furthered her political career. According to Reno, children at the Branch Davidian compound were routinely being abused and the abuse was growing worse with each passing day. Thus, immediate intervention was called for. In brief, then, David Koresh was characterized by the media and by federal authorities as a mentally ill leader of a group of mentally ill followers. In this view, one symptom of his mental illness was his ritualistic abuse, including sexual abuse, of children with the apparent sanction of the children's presumably mentally ill parents. Public opinion polls indicate that the overwhelming majority of Americans believe that the government acted appropriately. These polls also indicate that most Americans believe that child abuse was occurring in Waco.

Child abuse was occurring in Waco. But by whom?

First, we should look at the case *for* child abuse by David Koresh and other members of the Branch Davidians. The evidence in support of this case comes solely from three sources: a member who had left the church, a parent of a member who had visited the compound and had unsuccessfully attempted to persuade his son to leave, and a psychiatrist who examined several of the children who had left prior to the holocaust. All other charges of child abuse came from individuals who had no knowledge—either as first-hand observers or as scholars—of the church, its history, structure, or beliefs and practices. In short, these were either individuals who make a substantial income by attacking NRMs or mental health professionals who were willing to violate professional ethical standards by making long-distance clinical interpretations and diagnoses about people they had never seen, in exchange for their one minute of fame on national television.

In the first instance of evidence meriting serious consideration, a disgruntled member made charges against Koresh that included holding members hostage against their will, coercing the behavior of adults and children through violence and threats of violence, having sex with and impregnating minors, and preparing members for a Holy War with the outside world that would result in the Apocalypse. In response to the charges of child abuse, caseworkers from protective services in Texas conducted a complete investigation, including home visits to the compound and interviews with children and adults. According to an interview on National Public Radio with the caseworker supervisor, there was absolutely no evidence of abuse. Children were characterized as happy and well-adjusted, and their needs were well taken care of. There was no evidence that any minor had been sexually abused, and there were no cases of pregnant minors. The church was given a clean bill of health and the case was closed. The supervisor also stated that since their investigation, no new charges or evidence had emerged.

Another source of evidence for abuse is the report of the father of a member. The father visited the compound in an attempt to persuade his son to leave. Although he described being well treated during his stay, he reported on national television that he had seen Koresh spank an infant for several minutes as a lesson in discipline to the other members. Since the father did not report the incident to authorities at the time and has only talked about it subsequent to the destruction of the ranch, neither confirmation nor disconfirmation of the allegation is likely.

The third relevant source of evidence for child abuse was the chief of psychiatry at a medical school in Texas who examined several children who had voluntarily left the compound prior to the FBI's final initiative. This psychiatrist's conclusions were widely reported in the media, including a lengthy article in the *New York Times*. He concluded that the children had been abused, and cited as evidence marks on their bodies. These physical marks, described as round red marks on the skin of several children, comprised the only specific evidence reported. The psychiatrist otherwise described the children as being friendly, happy, and likable, and as having good interpersonal skills and being open to others. They were also described as generally being bright and above average on cognitive and educational tasks. This picture is clearly not consistent with expectations for children who have been abused. The only other support offered by the psychiatrist is his "interpretation" that when these children said, as they did, that they "loved David," they were really confused and meant that they "feared David."

The evidence *for* abuse from these three sources must be compared with evidence *against* abuse. In addition to the obvious point that none of this evidence for abuse is very persuasive, there are the counterarguments that protective services concluded there was no abuse, that the father's report of infant spanking was reported only on television after the fact, and that the psychiatrist described children who sound as if they have been treated well rather than abused. Moreover, we do have the observations of others who visited the compound both before and during the siege. These visitors include attorneys and one person—an itinerant evangelist who had no connection with Koresh or the Branch Davidians—who walked through FBI surveillance during the siege and spent eight days inside. All visitors reported that they saw no evidence whatsoever of abuse of children and that, in fact, the children were loved and well treated. It is probably for these reasons that the FBI and Attorney General Reno so quickly dropped the child abuse explanation as reporters began to raise questions about specific evidence for abuse.

But there was child abuse in Waco. Consider the following: knowing that there were many children inside, federal agents conducted a raid on the compound, firing a fusillade of bullets through windows and walls, killing one child and surely terrifying the others. Knowing that there were many children inside, federal agents cut off electricity and other utilities necessary to the maintenance of health and safety standards for these children, and then, incredibly, criticized the adults because children had to perform elimination functions in buckets. Knowing that there were many children inside, federal agents bombarded the building with spotlights twenty-four hours a day in an admitted attempt to disrupt sleep and rest. Knowing that there were many children inside, federal agents incessantly assaulted the building with loud music and bizarre sounds, such as rabbits being killed. Knowing that there were many children inside, federal agents used tanks as battering rams, crashing into the building and punching holes in the walls even though they were aware that the building was a potential tinder box and that the people inside were using lanterns which could easily be knocked over. Knowing that there were many children inside, federal agents pumped in tear gas—tear gas of such strength and capacity for producing pain that it has been banned by international law—and they did this, knowing that there were no gas masks inside small enough to protect children. Certainly these children's last living moments must have been filled with unbelievable horror and agony. Who, considering these facts, could dispute the charge of child abuse in Waco? If firing bullets at them, disregarding and disturbing their health and tranquility, destroying their home while placing them in clear danger, and intentionally inflicting intense pain on them is not abusive to children, what is?

So, why did federal agents abuse these children? The answer is clear. Koresh made them do it! Through some fantastically contorted mental exertions, the federal government, the media, and Americans in general have blamed Koresh and the other Branch Davidian adults for the suffering of these children. The reasoning goes something like this: Koresh cannot be dealt with rationally because he is mentally ill (a real live Wacko from Waco) and, as part of his sickness, he is abusing the children. And because he is abusing children, we have an obligation to stop him, and if necessary we are allowed to take strong measures. Of course, there could be problems. Some people may get hurt. We may lose a few kids. But what the hell—at least they won't grow up crazy!

Lawrence Lilliston, Ph.D., is Chair of the Department of Psychology at Oakland University in Rochester, Michigan, and a clinical-child psychologist in private practice. He has published research on the psychosocial development of children in new religious movements and in the areas of religion, values, and coping.

Chapter 26

Suffer the Little Children

George Robertson

As far as anyone can tell, there were about forty children in the Branch Davidian compound during the Sunday morning church services when the BATF agents began their raid.

There was at least one infant killed by the government agents during the gunfight—Koresh's sixteen-month-old baby—and reports of another infant killed.

During the first few weeks, twenty of the children left the compound. Most of these were accompanied by relatives and other members who had decided to leave. Leaving or not apparently was a personal choice and no one has reported that they were coerced into staying or leaving.

Each person was free to choose as they felt God led. In the case of children who had not reached the age of accountability under the Mosaic Law, the parents decided.

As with many fundamental Christian religious beliefs, the children who had not reached the age of accountability (usually at puberty) when they stand or fall spiritually for their decisions—remained under the protective covering of their parents or custodial guardians. It is generally held that God will protect young children from harm; and if physical death may take them, they will immediately be safe in the arms of Jesus Christ.

All of the children who left the Davidian compound were immediately taken into custody by social service workers of the Department of Children's

Protective Services of the State of Texas. Their parents and other adults who chose to leave were immediately arrested and whisked off to jail by the government.

This action on behalf of the government was not in accordance with the understanding of those inside the compound. The news of the treatment of those who were arrested made a tremendous impact on the remaining members. It proved that the government agents, who by this time were held in very low esteem by those inside, could definitely not be trusted to keep their word. Some members had even been shot indiscriminately by the government agents.

It was apparent to those still inside that anyone leaving would probably face greater danger, losing whatever protection the compound and their leaders could afford them. The decisions to leave dropped dramatically.

In most cases when people face a dangerous choice, the fear of the unknown is always much greater than that of the known, even if the known is distasteful, unpleasant, or even dangerous in itself. Nearly ninety people chose to stay and wait it out, and, with them, at least a dozen small children whose parents would not be separated from them.

Some of the children, like Misty Howell, seventeen, and Rachel Sylvia, thirteen, probably did make their own choice to stay. It may even be that they could and would participate in the protection of the others in the compound. Other children like the Howells and Martinez, who were barely teenagers but old enough to decide, would choose to stay with their parents and smaller brothers and sisters.

During the siege, the children continued in their studies, maintained their chores as best they could, and participated in the religious services. The constant rumbling of the tanks and military vehicles, and the helicopters circling overhead, became a type of routine during the day-by-day ordeal. The children were often seen at the windows and doorways of the compound for brief moments, but as the military vehicles would pass by or danger seemed to loom, they would quickly retreat to an inner room.

Most of the time, for them, was spent in the children's sleeping quarters on the second floor of the main building. It was here that they later found themselves trapped when the tanks knocked out the stairwell leading to their quarters during the final assault. In all likelihood, those who were trapped would have been the younger ones like Cyrus and Star Howell, ages six and eight, and Joe Martinez, eight, or Melissa Morrison, six. The older children were most likely working at their chores or standing guard with the men, and the infant children were with their mothers or one of the women who stayed behind.

Child Abuse Accusations
It was the issue of the children that was being hyped continuously from the very beginning of the Davidian problems. From the first complaints of the Australian renegade Marc Breault to the final assault approved by Attorney General Janet Reno, the battle cry was "to save the children."

Horror stories abounded of sex with teenagers, beatings of little babies, and abusive activities towards the children in the act of disciplinary punishments. As the investigations unfold, it is becoming increasingly obvious that very little of the allegations had any substance; this was, in fact, only a ploy to capitalize on America's latest "action trigger": Child Abuse!

Although there was virtually no substantiation of the claims against the Davidians, and even though the BATF specifically—and the attorney general's office generally—has no authority in matters of child abuse, these unfounded allegations were reported to be the primary motive for the raid, the siege, and the final assault.

Since in this area of concern there was absolutely no authority on the part of any of the officials conducting the attack on the Davidians, the whole matter of child abuse should not even be a consideration in the issues surrounding the tragic events at Waco. In a proper court of law, it would not be. But in the interest of justice and truth, we will reiterate the allegations, the sources, the circumstances, and the facts or questions which surround each instance.

The allegations of child abuse first surfaced in 1991, when Marc Breault, a former leader in Waco and a defector who plotted to take over Koresh's Australian church group, contacted the non-custodial father of one young teenager, Kiri Jewell, who was living in Waco with her custodial mother. Breault easily convinced him to file custody charges in Mr. Jewell's home state, Michigan.

The Jewells had been divorced for nearly ten years. He and his new wife maintained visiting rights and had spent the holidays with Kiri at their home in Michigan practically every year for the ten years since the divorce. It was during the last of these holiday visits that David Jewell arranged for Kiri's deprogramming and then filed for emergency custody. This was later discovered to be a very well orchestrated and planned action involving several former members and legal maneuvers executed with precision by Cult Awareness Network experts.

After nearly four months of deprogramming and rehabilitation sessions while being kept a prisoner in Michigan, Kiri was taken by her father to a judge in St. Joseph, Michigan. Former members flown in from Australia related detailed horror stories of child abuse, sexual improprieties, and other allegations—but all without evidence—and the court allowed Kiri to choose with whom she wanted to stay. She chose her father and stepmother. Kiri then became the latest "testimony" of child abuse by going on the national television and news media circuit to talk about her spanking (admittedly only once in ten years) and stories related to her by the other former members during the deprogramming sessions.

Shortly after the Michigan custodial battle in early 1992, Breault and his new ally and convert, David Jewell, contacted the Department of Children's Protective Services in Texas about the allegations and related stories about alleged abuses taking place in the Davidian compound at Mt. Carmel.

The department dispatched social service workers, interviewed the children and members, inspected the living arrangements and the conditions and gave the Davidians a clean bill of health—no evidence whatsoever of any kind of child abuse.

The second instance of allegations came from a twenty-one year old living in the group's La Verne, California, group home. Robyn Bunds was an admitted rebel in the strict Davidian lifestyle and worked as a local receptionist near the group's home. She had grown up in the group and maintains that a baby she had at eighteen was fathered by David Koresh. Other reports indicated that the baby was the result of a brief marriage to a Davidian from England.

Robyn had had a number of disagreements with Koresh. She had made contact with the Cult Awareness Network and the Australians and apparently was being voluntarily deprogrammed. One evening during the tense relationship, she arrived at the home from work and discovered that her clothes and belongings had been removed from the house along with her young son. She went to the La Verne Police and reported her son had been kidnapped by Koresh. The police investigated the family dispute, but refused to let Koresh speak with Robyn because she was in the process of being "deprogrammed." Koresh was instructed to return the child to Robyn.

Other than these two sources, no other reports of child abuse have surfaced against the Branch Davidians. All of the allegations come from disgruntled former members who have been subjected to the deprogramming techniques of the Cult Awareness Network. The tactics and methods are not new. They have been used frequently and with alarming success against a host of religious groups.

There had been reports abounding throughout the siege of the Branch Davidians' home in Waco about "lots of babies" having been fathered by Koresh. The list of children in the group obviously belies those reports, with every child listed accounted for with a proper mother and father. The only substantiation is the offhanded remarks of Koresh himself who frequently referred to all the children as "his babies," and to the women of the group as "his brides in Christ"—a manner of conversation not unlike many fatherly figures of small religious groups.

What Is Federal Child Abuse?

According to the recently enacted federal child abuse statutes and those that have been adopted by most states in America, the subject of child abuse is a vague and nebulous condition. It is interpreted with varying degrees of consistency from state to state and, indeed, differently within jurisdictions.

Child abuse falls into three basic categories:

Physical abuse indicated by bruises, scalds or burns on children's bodies, welts, or marks on the skin which may be caused by gouging, puncturing, or piercing.

Sexual abuse which may be indicated by specific symptoms related by the child to professional workers, physical evidence of penetrations, or repeated problems of genital area infections.

Neglect in the proper and appropriate care of the child, including proper food, water, clean clothing, appropriate medical attention, adequate supervision, and proper education.

None of these conditions existed or were found by the investigators during repeated visits to the Branch Davidian compound.

Upon the release of twenty children during the first two weeks of the siege, after they had been living in a virtual war zone for days, the Texas Department of Children's Protective Services conducted full-scale investigations of the released children and found that none of them, regardless of age, exhibited any evidence of child abuse; and in fact, they were found to be "surprisingly healthy, happy, well adjusted, well educated, and only wanted to return as soon as they could to their friends and relatives in the compound."

None of this was sufficient to satisfy General Reno. The fifty-four-year old professional attorney from Miami, Florida, who has never had children of her own nor even ever married, still maintained that she knew what was best for the care of children.

Reno's experience with children as a federal prosecutor in Miami was in prosecuting people for cases of satanic and ritual child Abuse. By a not so strange coincidence, the ritual-child-abuse issue which swept the country during the late eighties and early nineties was largely the work of media hype promoted by the national Cult Awareness Network and supported by many fundamentalist Christians.

The whole scheme was later exposed by a Law Enforcement consultant after a number of hoaxes were uncovered. The consultant, Robert Hicks, wrote a book, *Pursuit of Satan,* and a special report for FBI offices which was later correlated and substantiated by sociologists David Bromley and Jeffrey Hadden. Many of the stories promoted by the satanism sellers were proven to be false or grossly distorted. Some of these were Christian best-sellers which had to be refuted in later writings, and some of the leaders submitted to church disciplinary actions.

Although the substantiation for widespread ritual child abuse seems no longer valid, General Reno's concern for the safety and welfare of America's children in this regard has not diminished. During a hearing before the House Judiciary Committee in May, 1993, she sincerely agonized over her decision which led to the deaths of the Branch Davidian children. She reported that her only motivation for stepping up the aggression against the Davidian church was her misguided concern based on unfounded and inaccurate reports of "continued abuse."

She had been "conned" again by the professional anti-religion con artists!

From *Watching Religious Freedom Die* (19993) by Dr. George Robertson.

Dr. George Robertson teaches at Maryland Bible College, and serves as media spokesperson for Friends of Freedom, a religious-liberty information center and advocate group.

Chapter 27

Lessons from Waco:
When Will We Ever Learn?

James T. Richardson

The Greek tragedy that played out in Waco is finally over, save the recriminations and repercussions. The episode started badly and ended worse. At least eighty people are dead—a half dozen at the beginning and over seventy at the end. Two dozen of those were children, and two of the women were pregnant.

The unbelievable beginning of the tragedy hit the world's television screens like a made-for-TV movie titled "Rambo 6." It was "Shootout at the OK Corral" times 100. Viewers were titillated with scenes of people being shot live on camera. We had not seen such good theater since live shots from Vietnam.

The tragic Keystone Cops beginning also contributed one of the most unforgettable excuse lines of the decade. An ATF spokesperson said, "We had an excellent plan and we practiced it for months. Everything would have been fine, except their guns were bigger than our guns."

Hundreds of media people arrived at Waco, making management of the media, which shares in the culpability for this tragedy, a bigger problem than getting Koresh and his followers out. The media "feeding frenzy" that developed in Waco for the first two weeks was an embarrassment to the media and to American society. The *demonization* of Koresh and his followers was a joint undertaking of the media and law enforcement officials, an effort that led to predictable results.

We lapped up every word as media reps interviewed each other, glossing over their ignorance of what was happening by using the obligatory word "cult" hundreds of times a day. Particularly creative media reps would expand their coverage and apply the hot word "cult" to other minority religions, just to stir up viewer interest, if not hysteria. The CBS *48 Hours* hit a new high (low?) with its "timely" program that contained more footage from Montana than from Waco.

Then sanity seemed to set in. We heard reports that law enforcement was prepared to "wait them out." Claims were made that this situation would be solved with no more loss of life. Negotiations opened, directly with Koresh and through the media briefings, which often took the form of "disinformation," served up because officials assumed Koresh was listening to every word.

And wait we did. For fifty days law enforcement waited, showing patience, and some three dozen people were extracted alive. However, there were growing reports of "how expensive this is," and there were claims that the situation was costing a half million dollars a day or more. Negotiations went on sporadically, with Koresh manipulating and teasing officials, who showed increasing anger and impatience at being treated so casually.

Then came day fifty-one. Officials approved a total switch of strategy, ramming the building with armored vehicles, knocking gaping holes in the flimsy wood construction of the building. Unbelievably, these officials were oblivious to threats from Koresh, delivered earlier, that any direct attack would lead to massive destruction.

Officials seemed incapable of understanding the strongly held beliefs of Koresh and followers. Agents claimed to be studying his theology during the siege, but they missed the crucial point of Koresh's interpretation of the Book of Revelation: the end of time is here; Armageddon has arrived, and all will die in the conflagration.

Law enforcement personnel became Koresh's foil in this tragedy, and they played their role perfectly. He teased them until they were goaded to action. Their action drew the world's attention back to Waco, and then the conflagration began. It was over in about thirty minutes, with the entire compound reduced to smoldering rubble before any fire truck arrived from Waco, twelve miles away.

What happened was very predictable, even understandable, for those who would take seriously the religious ideas and claims of Koresh. The surprise shown by officials was as disingenuous as their claims that no lethal force was used, and that "no one died at the hands of the FBI."

The Lessons of Waco
  Lesson #1: When confronting an armed apocalyptic group in a wooden structure, have some fire trucks handy. Keeping the fire trucks in Waco "to protect them from the weaponry" of Koresh sounds strange, especially when there were hundreds of media people within a mile of the compound.
  Lesson #2: Reconsider the frontier mentality about guns that pervades our country. When someone gets the strange idea that Armageddon is about to happen, and that they should defend their remnant during the apocalypse, it is easy to implement such ideas. Just drive to town in pickup trucks and load up the weapons. Order hand grenade cannisters through the mails, as well as kits to make weapons into automatic ones.
  Lesson #3: Take religious beliefs seriously. Defining as "a nut" anyone with a religious idea different from the mainstream is too simple, and can lead to tragedy. Koresh was probably not nuts in a technical sense, but he did have some strongly held beliefs, which he articulated rather well at times. Defining such people away into the category of crazy deludes policy-makers, makes tragic events more probable, and justifies bad policy decisions. Not to have believed Koresh was capable of what happened shows a remarkable ignorance about Koresh and millions of Americans and others who do hold minority religious views, sometimes very strongly.
  Lesson #4: Have law enforcement work on contingency plans which are not derived from Rambo movies. Two violent episodes separated by fifty days of calm do not a good plan make. We must learn patience and alternatives to the massive and expensive show of force that was made at Waco. And something a little less provocative than tanks ramming the building might have been a good idea, especially if a nonviolent solution was, in fact, being sought.
  Lesson #5: This is the tough one. We need to lower the level of hysteria about new and minority religions in this country, and increase the amount of understanding of religion among citizens and policy-makers. The ignorance shown by media and law enforcement about the Davidians was appalling, and contributed directly to the tragedy. Some major statements made since by national leaders perpetuates this ignorance and contributes to continued demonization of Koresh and his followers and, by implication, other minority religions. Our tradition of freedom of religion in this country has suffered some severe blows in recent years, as governmental action and court decisions have rewritten traditional understandings of freedom of religion. The Waco episode may cause a new round of "getting tough" with religious groups that are not in the mainstream. We forget that 99 percent of minority religious groups (often called "cults" by the media) are benign and peaceful, and most just want to be left alone. When laws are broken, then action must be taken. But, when religious groups abide by the law, they have the right not to be harassed. The Waco tragedy should not lead

to more harassment of the 99 percent. Regrettably, however, Waco may be just the excuse some need (want?) to exercise more control over minority religious groups.

Lesson #6: Remember the children. At least twenty-four innocents died in the conflagration. Their status was closest to that of hostages, which raises a hard question about why federal authorities were using tanks to ram a building containing twenty-four hostages? The demonization of Koresh and his followers, including even the children, was so successful that many Americans think this tactic was acceptable. But, maybe the memory of children dying gruesomely by fire or gunshot will remind us all of the importance of the other "lessons of Waco" listed above.

James T. Richardson is Professor of Sociology and Judicial Studies at the University of Nevada, Reno. He has been researching new religions for over twenty years, and has published five books and nearly seventy-five articles in journals and books.

Chapter 28

Why *Did* Waco Happen?

Larry D. Shinn

There are many voices clamoring to be heard after the tragic immolation of the followers of David Koresh in Waco, Texas. Some have focused on the insanity of David Koresh, some on the helplessness of the children who died, others on the persistent blunders of the ATF and FBI, and still others on the justification of their anti-cult views. Few persons, however, have commented upon the twin factors of our culture that conspired to create the Waco tragedy: the increasing secularism and the increasing violence of American culture and institutions. These two factors had as much to do with the deaths at "Ranch Apocalypse" as did the seven seals of Revelation.

We learned in an April 21 national poll by *USA Today*/CNN/Gallup that 57 percent of the American public thought the agents had waited too long to attack the Branch Davidian compound, 73 percent thought the use of the tear gas was responsible, and 93 percent blamed Koresh for the death of his followers and their children. An undercurrent running through the survey's questions and answers was the assumption that cults are dangerous and must be dealt with firmly and decisively. With this logic, the cult leader bears full responsibility for any consequences. But, as we assess the Waco disaster, the picture is not so simple.

Consider how the events unfolded in Waco. Rumors of child abuse and gun violations had already heightened fear among law enforcement officials. Rick Ross, a well-known deprogrammer associated with the Cult Awareness Network (CAN), claims to have deprogrammed a Branch Davidian member from Waco (and later to have served as an advisor to the ATF office). The word "cult" itself intensified negative images of the Branch Davidians. A UPS shipper found empty grenade shells in a broken parcel addressed to Koresh's farm and this was the last straw that prompted the Alcohol, Tobacco, and Firearms agency to secure search and arrest warrants. The strategy used to deliver these warrants was one of surprise, a high level of armed force, and the time-honored technique of bursting through the door to overwhelm the gangsters inside—including children, of course. Because the Branch Davidians had been alerted ahead of time, they met the ATF agents with a fusillade of gunfire. Four ATF agents and several Branch Davidians were killed. At this point, the window of the world opened on Waco and the rest of the tragic story is now history. What does this series of events tell us about religion and violence in America?

The first thing the Waco story tells us is that the ATF and FBI were woefully ignorant of the power of religious symbols and, thus, overestimated their own ability to design a successful plan of attack prior to February 28. This may seem surprising given the fact that the whole world has focused on the power of religious world views in the form of Islamic fundamentalism in its different guises in Iran, Iraq, and Egypt over the past decade. The connection between religion and violence came recently to America's doorstep in the World Trade Center bombing. What is less obvious to most observers is that powerful religious images and world views direct the behavior of millions of Americans every day. This fact was unheeded by the ATF prior to its February 28 action. If the ATF and, later, the FBI had tried to understand their opponents in Waco *in religious terms,* they would never have proceeded as they did. Religious symbols are powerful because they can create a conceptually plausible world view and appeal to primary emotions such as love, hate, and fear. Only political movements gain the same level of commitment and devotion and often evoke powerful symbols to attract their adherents.

Unlike what CAN would have us believe, the ATF and FBI were not dealing with a "destructive cult" of generic description. David Koresh did not brainwash his followers into compliant robots. Rather, most of the Branch Davidians had come to their beliefs through the powerful imagery of the biblical book of Revelation. They came to believe that there were loose in the world powers of evil that denied God and His judgment. Many of the global events of recent years confirmed their belief that the last days were upon us. Furthermore, as God's chosen disciples, they would be attacked by the godless and needed to arm themselves for their own defense.

The initial raid and subsequent behavior by the ATF only confirmed Koresh's message to his followers. These followers had varying degrees of commitment to Koresh's cause and multiple reasons to stay at Ranch Apocalypse. While Koresh, himself, had become delusional and psychologically unstable, numerous scholarly studies have shown that followers can become invested in the "sanity" of the charismatic message and person (e.g., Hitler), and deny all evidence to the contrary. This, too, the ATF should have known. To attack the Koresh compound—with this perspective in mind—would have been deemed foolish. So why did the ATF use the strategy it did?

The first reason has to do with the fundamentally violent nature of our culture. It is not just that we lead the world in the rate of murder of our population; it is that violence, both overt and covert, lies at the basis of our very institutions. Whether in the home or in our legal and law enforcement practices, Americans often choose violence as a preferred means of self-expression. Gandhi led a movement for self-rule in India that took as its motto, "The means are the ends in the making." How else could the ATF "invaders" have expected an armed millennial religious movement to respond when they attacked with brute force? Violent means certainly lead to violent ends. Then, to compound an already botched initiative, the ATF and FBI proceeded to barrage the Koresh compound with light and sound and then expected those held captive inside to react "rationally." How could the highly informed Waco law officers neglect to consider the reciprocal response to the violent techniques *they* were using? Violence as a means of conflict resolution in America is seldom challenged and, in this case, led to predictable violent ends.

The second reason for the miscalculation by the ATF and FBI is the pervasive secularization of American culture. Yes, America is still one of the most heavily church-going nations on the globe. Yes, our presidents still refer to our Judeo-Christian heritage in major speeches. But do we really understand or appreciate the kind of deep religiosity that produces a Mother Teresa—or a David Koresh? Such deep devotion can be used for good and noble causes; it can also deteriorate into personal pathologies and evil outcomes, as history has taught us. Yet, do we understand in what ways troubled people in a culture that is secular and morally adrift seek simplistic answers and fundamentalistic retreats to an idealized past? Can we not see the substitutional values and images the ATF held when their fallen colleagues became the motivation to end the siege and bring to justice those who killed him? That the law enforcers were willing to sacrifice even the children for the righteousness of their cause when they decided to bring an end to the standoff reveals the same level of devotion to symbols and values that those inside the Koresh compound held. One agent said that the ATF agency was "not simply going to stand by, suck our thumbs and wait."

Another admitted that the ATF officers were eager to put Koresh on trial for the murder of four of their own. On one level, what occurred in Waco was a conflict between two passionately held violent world views, one based in biblical prophesy, the other in a tradition of violence often expressed in the values of the American West. Neither understood the basic symbols and values of the other, and the death of seventy-one men, women, and children was the result.

Could there have been another conclusion to this story? Perhaps the difference between the violent repression of the Attica prison siege versus the nonviolent tactics in the recent Lucasville prison riots holds one possible answer. Violent means used against an enemy who was only partially understood produced the fiery holocaust in Waco. Dispassionate assessment of the Branch Davidians as a religious and paramilitary community *before* the February 28 assault would almost certainly have led the ATF to a different initial strategy. The failure to understand the power of religious symbols, and the tendency in America to use physical force to resolve disputes, are at least two reasons why ATF agents can only blame these deaths on "brainwashing" and attribute the cause of the violence to Koresh. The Waco tragedy was ultimately rooted as much in the secularization of America and its penchant for violence as in the Davidians' particular theology or David Koresh's mental illness.

Larry D. Shinn is Professor of Religion and Vice President for Academic Affairs at Bucknell University. He is the author of *The Dark Lord: Cult Images and the Hare Krishnas in America* (1987).

Chapter 29

Reflections on the Waco Disaster:
Trying to Make Sense of Insane Events

Charles L. Harper

The main facts about the outrageous debacle at Waco are beyond dispute: the initial assault, killings and woundings, a multimillion dollar fifty-one day siege, the final invasion of a religious community's compound by a virtual armada of federal agents with specially equipped tanks, poison gas, and the resulting fiery holocaust that destroyed the community and most of the men, women, and children living there. The search warrant that was its legal basis is undoubtedly to become the most expensive one in the nation's history—in both financial and human terms. But other important facts about the incident are still murky and clouded in dispute and controversy: Was the group storing illegal weapons and training its members to use them? Or was one of its members, Paul Fatta, a gun dealer and simply storing his guns there, as some testified? Were children being abused, sexually or in other ways? Why then did local officials after investigating similar charges against the community a year before dismiss them? Both of these allegations, made initially to government officials by a competing Australian religious group, were the basis of the BATF search warrant, but neither has been firmly established, either by official investigation or testimony of surviving members of the Branch Davidians. Finally, how did the fires that destroyed the community get set? Were they part of a planned "mass suicide"? Or were they set unintentionally during the assault by knocking over kerosene lamps in the rickety old wood frame building full of straw and flammable materials, fanned by a thirty mile an hour Texas prairie wind?

Important as these and other unanswered questions surrounding the incident are, I am certainly not qualified to address any of them. So I will put them aside. But still, as a student of alternative or marginal religious movements I have struggled, and still do, to get some comprehension of events that are bizarre, to say the least. How *can* one understand the assault and destruction of a religious community, intentionally or not, by the federal government, particularly at a time in which the legal guarantees of freedom of religious practice and due process of law are more firmly established than ever before in the history of the nation?

I have heard different people—some scholars, some not—claim that (1) the Branch Davidian cult was beyond reason or civility because they were under the nefarious spell of a charismatic but malevolent psychopath, (2) they deserved what they got because they resisted legitimate authority, and conversely that (3) the government agents were a bunch of gunslinging yahoos using Gestapo-like tactics, or (4) were simply stupid and blundered everything. Yet for my taste, saying that the Waco outcomes were dictated by some combination of insanity, vengeance, maliciousness and stupidity explains "everything and nothing." To be sensible, there must be more to it than this.

I have come to believe that there are some ideas useful for understanding the devastation at Waco to be found in the accumulated works of scholars of alternative religions, and in more general social science ideas. Some of these are indeed so elementary that they can be found in any recent introductory sociology text. On reflection, I have found them useful as perspectives, even when the particulars of the case are very much in doubt. I have found them useful in conversations with local newscasters seeking orientation (though I admit that they don't translate into very good "sound bites"). Here's a not-too-well-organized "laundry list" of a few of them. There are undoubtedly others.

1. *Reality is not "out there" alike for all persons or groups; it is a social construction. Different constructions of reality underlie and facilitate social conflict between persons, groups and organizations.* For the most part we are so naturally enmeshed in shared constructions of reality that we assume them to be "really" real, rather than constructions, interpretations, and definitions of what is real (Berger and Luckmann, 1967). But groups of people who are "different" for some reason or another have reality constructions that are obviously different—both to themselves and outside

observers. And the development and maintenance of a "different reality" is easier in small, isolated, tightly bonded communities. Indeed, different reality constructions and belief systems are important for maintaining the cohesion and rationale in such communities.

How is this a useful notion for understanding the Waco affair? It is a way of answering what is nearly *always* the first questions people ask about alternative religions ("cults"): How could anyone in their right mind choose to be in such a cult? How could anyone believe those things? Aren't they just crazy, deluded, naive?

Well, not necessarily. But they seem "crazy" because they live in a different reality, with a constructed set of meanings and logic of its own. From their history as an Adventist splinter group, the Branch Davidian worldview was drenched in apocalyptic and millennialist themes—and religious prophesies of the "end time" and "signs" of its immanence. They probably also believed that they were God's chosen to perceive, survive, or at least live out, in a special way, the coming struggle between the forces of good and evil, while surrounded by a corrupt and ungodly social world. Minimal cooperation with that world is necessary, but it is delegitimated and assigned to the realm of corrupt "powers and principalities" which God will eventually destroy. In this context the arrival of armed forces storming their compound undoubtedly had a theological significance that was not widely appreciated. The belief system, emphasizing apocalyptic and millennialist themes, separates them from secular reality constructions and from most Christians. But it is shared, in one form or another, with perhaps 15 percent of the Christians in America today.

A broader construction of reality about alternative and marginal religions emerged from the "cult scares" of the past two decades. Alternative religions have come to be almost universally perceived to be "cults"—crazy systems led by powerful, charismatic, and demonic or at least psychopathic leaders in which innocent followers are deceived, brainwashed, exploited, and lose critical faculties as humans. The Unification Church, as it was perceived by the anti-cult movement and the media in the 1970s, became the prototype of the contemporary malevolent "cult." While scholars of alternative religions know that the real picture is quite a bit more complex and diverse than this, it has become a powerful and entrenched popular "reality." My experience is that to suggest problems with this view usually elicits disbelief. Indeed the Waco affair demonstrates how compelling this conception of alternative religions has become. Combined with allegations of illegal weapons and child abuse, a nutty cult was vulnerable to treatment by federal authorities (with much popular support) in ways that more "respectable" organizations would not be. Can you imagine government agents storming the chancery of a Roman Catholic Diocese in such a manner, even if there were official complaints about weapons or child abuse? I can't.

2. *American culture possesses some embedded themes which provided broad contexts that shaped the drama at Waco.* America has often been noted as a violent society among comparable industrial nations. Americans tolerate high levels of violence, in reality and in media portrayals, and, although we may dislike it, are accustomed to violence as a problem-solving strategy. Related to this, foreigners marvel at how Americans have enshrined the "right" to freely own and circulate firearms. Any serious attempt to abridge or regulate this "right" or address the problems that attend it (such as the possession of lethal weapons in school environments) has been met by howls of protest from gun enthusiasts and a well-endowed arms industry combined into a powerful political force.

Another powerful cultural theme in America is the importance of "getting things done." Americans value "can do" individuals and organizations that can "cut to the core" of complex problems and solve them simply and quickly. The way of dealing with the Waco situation hatched by the BAFT and FBI resembles a plot ripped from an old John Wayne western movie, in which the "good guy" (sheriff) defeats the "bad guys" (criminals and scoundrels) by extralegal violent means (a Texas-style shootout?). But it is "pro-social violence," presumedly in the interest of the community, rather than the "anti-social violence" of criminals. An important difference, of course, is that the final act of the Waco drama didn't have the happy resolution of the old western films (newer films don't either).

Eileen Barker underlined these American cultural themes in an interview for *National Public Radio News* last spring by pointing to differences between British and American ways of handling such problems. In Britain the private circulation of firearms is so much lower and more tightly regulated that it would be unlikely that a determined individual or organization could amass a stockpile of weapons (minimizing the likelihood of lethally violent outcomes). And in Britain, when authorities don't know what to do, they do nothing for as long as possible. In America authorities feel that doing something is better than doing nothing. Violence, guns, and action are profound themes embedded in American culture.

3. *While officially neutral about religious doctrine, the state in America has historically been involved in the most severe conflicts involving alternative and minority religions.* Since the beginning of the American republic, alternative and minority religions have often provoked controversy and conflict. Sometimes the state has protected religious minorities; but in the most intense conflicts, the state has been a part of the process of opposing and stigmatizing alternative and minority religions. In the nineteenth century, officials were often helpless to intervene or looked the other way as mobs and vigilantes harassed Shakers, Roman Catholics, and Mormons. In the late nineteenth century the federal government itself opposed the Mormon Church as its threats to American political sovereignty became clear. The Mormon Church was officially disbanded by an act of Congress, and federal troops en route to Utah were called off only when Mormon officials conceded to the rule of the federal government and courts. In the twentieth century for the most part the mobs are gone, and conflicts between the state and alternative religions take the form of (sometimes punitive) investigations by regulatory agencies protecting their own interests and "turf," such as the rights to control taxation, licensing, and legal compliance in general. There are many contemporary examples of this: the conviction of Reverend Moon for tax fraud (despite legal protests from most mainstream religious bodies), the FBI and FDA investigations and "raids" on the Church of Scientology in the 1960s, and the attempt to convict the Alamo Foundation under the Faith Labor Standards Act (Beckford, 1985:282-86; Robbins, 1984:48-49; Harper and LeBeau, 1993:187). The events at Waco are another case in point, even though the destruction of the Branch Davidians is more extreme than any of these examples.

4. *Bureaucratic organizations can, through their own internal processes, develop a powerful momentum toward narrowly defined goals that can be difficult to stop or reverse—even when pursuing such goals may be not effective in addressing the broader concerns of the organization. In addition, bureaucratic organizations can develop important but unstated goals related to their own needs for jurisdiction, budgets, political security and favorable publicity.* The BATF has an obvious legal interest in regulating the flow of firearms, and was compelled to investigate allegations made through official channels. But one would think that a search warrant would be executed in private, with a minimum of public commotion. Why were the media invited by BATF to witness the assault on the Waco compound by a hundred armed BATF agents? Was there another agenda here, of favorable publicity for the BATF "doing their job"? When BATF agents were killed, then there was a whole different set of issues: killing federal agents and resisting arrest. The most common source of conflict between religious groups (or any group, for that matter) and government is the denial of the rights to government agents and courts to rule, investigate and regulate—In other words, to challenge the very sovereignty of the government itself. And once the conflict at Waco was set in motion, *that* became the key issue.

5. *Situations of confrontation between authorities and isolated religious communities with apocalyptic and millennialist beliefs are particularly volatile.* There is evidence from far-reaching but rare historical cases. They may resist civil authority and identify it with the forces of evil corruption in the world. They may interpret the arrival of the authorities as signaling the beginning of the apocalyptic struggle. Most instances of "mass suicide" have taken place under such circumstances. Examples include the Jews at Masada, the Orthodox "Old Believers" resisting religious reforms of the tsarist system, and the Peoples' Temple at Jonestown (see Robbins, 1986, for an insightful analysis of this). Such confrontations in contemporary America resulting in actual shootouts—none on the scale of Waco—have come from groups that have often fused apocalyptic Christian beliefs with racist, anti-Semitic, neo-Nazi and paramilitary survivalist orientations (They have occurred in Idaho, Montana, Nebraska, Missouri, and Arkansas).

Apparently the government was advised about the possibility of violence and mass suicide, as well it should have been. After listening to all such advice, the attorney general and the president apparently urged a "cautious, go slow" approach to minimize the possibility of such a conflagration, but the plan—whatever it was—didn't work. Whether the fires were set intentionally by members of the Branch Davidians, by the invaders, or incidentally in the general conflagration may never be known with any certainty. Given the outcome it doesn't make a whole lot of difference.

These are five broad ideas and themes from the religious scholars and the social sciences. They have helped me to make some kind of sense out of the events at Waco. They make the outcomes more understandable—but not less tragic.

But let me now reverse the tables. Suppose an unlikely event: that the BATF, FBI, or the Justice Department had asked for input from the scholarly community about what to do at Waco. For openers, there must be better ways to execute search warrants than that chosen by the BATF. But suppose, further, that we were consulted after the initial assault, resistance, and killings. What would we have advised?

Perhaps a different strategy. Post the smallest effective (and minimally costly) armed guard to patrol the perimeter, preventing exit or entrance without apprehension. Wait for the press to get bored and go away, and then simply wait while attempting to negotiate a resolution—or for the situation to resolve itself through boredom and exhaustion. Attempt to de-escalate rather than to amplify the conflict. Cut off food, water, and medical care? Well, perhaps, but that's a hard one, particularly if there is unqualified concern for the lives of the children and other "innocents" on the inside, as officials claimed. At worst, that might result in a prolonged "stake out" of a religious community by federal agents—an unofficial "prison" of sorts. How much challenge to its sovereignty, even by marginal and insignificant groups, can a government tolerate? The answer has to be quite a lot, but not in the glare of publicity.

You can see why scholars are not consulted very often in such circumstances. A low-cost, patient, "wait them out," negotiate (and perhaps even—perish the thought—plea bargain) scenario would not be acceptable for a number of reasons. It is not the American activist "can do" tradition. It is not the stuff of which political careers are made. CNN would find it boring. It satisfies none of the BATF's or the FBI's need for favorable and public visibility. You can hear the hoots of derision at the prolonged challenge to government authority and the government "lack of guts" to do anything decisive. Was not part of Jimmy Carter's political demise due to his inability to free hostages from Iran? How much more embarrassing when an unresolvable situation is in Texas?

All this is true. But the public interest might have been better served by a low-profile, patient strategy than what was done, which cost hundreds of millions of taxpayers' dollars, killed virtually everyone, and besmirched the reputation and confidence in federal agencies anyway.

Whatever evils alleged to be practiced by the Waco "cult" seem vastly outweighed by the monstrous outcomes of "decisive" official reaction. Is this the best we can do?

References

Beckford, James A. (1985). *Cult Controversies: Societal Response to New Religious Movements.* (London: Tavistock).

Berger, Peter, and Thomas Luckmann. (1967). *The Social Construction of Reality.* (New York: Doubleday).

Harper, Charles L. and Bryan LeBeau. (1993). "The Social Adaptation of Marginal Religious Movements in America," *Sociology of Religion.* 54,2:171-92.

Robbins, Thomas. (1984). "Marginal Movements," *Society.* 4,47:47-53.

_____. (1986). "Religious Mass Suicide Before Jonestown: The Russian Old Believers," *Sociological Analysis.* 47,1:1-20.

Charles L. Harper is Associate Professor of Sociology at Creighton University and has scholarly interests in the sociology of religion, social movements, and social change. He is a board member of Creighton's Center for the Study of Religion and Society, and a member of the academic advisory board of the Association of World Academics for Religious Education.

Chapter 30

Deconstructing Waco

Michael York

With a growing awareness of the need for a society in which everyone can participate on an equal footing, the Waco debacle involving David Koresh and the Branch Davidians fully illustrates the problems which result in a civilization that seeks to eliminate differences and assimilate everyone to a single model of conformity. As a counterdevelopment to this long-standing Western trend, the French theorist Jacques Derrida has pursued what is coming to be known as "the deconstructive project." In essence, this is an attempt to rename all aspects of society in a spirit of openness. The aim of deconstructionism is to "let the other speak." The Branch Davidians are a classic case in which the other could not speak and, if it could, could not have been heard.

Today's deconstructive enterprise seeks merely to open structures—including dominant patterns of thought—which have hitherto remained closed and, in so doing, to allow passageway to the voice of those who live on the margins of society and culture. Deconstructionism recognizes that on the social fringe, the so-called "other" is to be found—whether these others are Jews, women, people of color, the poor, the physically or mentally handicapped, or adherents of alternate religious movements. The unifying principle connecting all outcasts is simply their difference vis-à-vis the social mainstream. But because of the West's relentless drive toward assimilating one and all to an acceptable sameness, marginalized subjects have tended to become written out of history. They are traditionally ignored by the society to which they belong. Consequently, it is within the historical margins of this disenfranchising situation that deconstruction seeks to find the inconsistencies and contradictions which appear as cracks in our official Western logic—the authoritative reasoning which endorses belief in an absolute similarity. Deconstructionism argues that by finding these gaps and opening them wider, the "space" is thereby created in which the other, the marginalized, the neglected and the misunderstood can begin to speak. Bill Martin sees this as an important step in the unlocking of our jaded society's frozen structures. He argues that if we can learn to see and appreciate the neglected historical experience and viewpoints which marginal subjects possess, we might be able to launch a renewed cultural period of interaction and growth.

From an additional point of view, the same processes which diminish and eliminate human possibility ultimately have the effect of marginalizing nearly everyone. The marginal become the unnamed and ignored or, as in the case of the Branch Davidians, the misnamed and misunderstood. Our cultural society has its dominant logic of identity with its enforcing police, army and other instruments of subjugation by which people are designated and coerced as particular kinds of subjects conforming to set classifications. Language is the chief tool by which we are labeled. According to Claude Levi-Strauss, as a means of communication, writing's primary function is to make it easier to enslave other human beings. To counter this process, one might resort to what deconstructionism calls intertextual analysis. This is a penetrating examination and deciphering of language in the attempt to break down the various fixed labels which restrict human identity, movement and expression.

The Italian theorist Theodor Adorno has pointed out that a language of sameness precludes the possibility that the other can speak in its terms. Nevertheless, Derrida's deconstruction recognizes that any established language of uniformity has cracks or inconsistencies in it. No language is monolithic and solid. Instead, it is by working in, through and around these gaps that language is able to replenish itself. The invariable inconsistencies that all languages possess, and the means which are found to circumvent them, provide a natural process through which languages can change and grow. Consequently, it is these breaks or fractures which the deconstructive strategy seeks to expose and make even bigger. A basic understanding of this philosophical approach is that truth is situational, relational and ever receding. In the historical processes of continual reinterpretation and subsequent perpetual syntheses of newer meanings, any unity of truth is, according to Nietzsche, completely indefinable. Instead, intertextual analysis chooses to concentrate upon falsity, error and self-contradiction within any given context and expose these on an ever open path to liberated understanding.

The unnaming which occurred with the Branch Davidians in Waco, Texas, is to be found in their being labeled with the "cult" stereotype. This stereotype automatically includes assertions of irresistible and overinflated leadership, mind control, brainwashing, powerlessness of devotees, lack of free choice, child abuse, weirdness, unacceptable sexual arrangements, fallacious thought, lying and even satanic evil. Through this categorization, the other—here David Koresh and his followers—could not be heard. They had no voice or no voice which could at least be understood. But by the mainstream culture's lumping any deviant or marginal expression under an erroneous and emotionally-charged designation, an accurate and legitimate understanding of the situation is routinely precluded.

Concerning the Mt. Carmel center, we are able to see the Cult Awareness Network and the Bureau of Alcohol, Tobacco, and Firearms themselves playing informative and enforcing roles which were bound by the "rules" of a predominant social model of conformity. In other words, CAN and ATF are instruments which are simultaneously both exacerbating of and victimized by a closed system of thought and language which cannot recognize—let alone tolerate—difference. They are themselves products of a political and socio-cultural action which brackets off spheres of meaning and truth-production as a means of marginalizing growing threats of disruption. But in its effort to expose these isolating "brackets," the intertextual and deconstructive movement itself delivers disruptive disturbances. These last, it stresses, are part of the very cutting-edge to future social growth. Without an open and unhindered exchange of new and different perspectives, we—and our social, political and religious institutions—become our own prisoners and casualties.

In the lamentable Waco saga, the media remains the key institution through its power to confer names—including that of the "cult" stereotype with its attendant and fixed associations of brainwashing and child abuse. With the discovery of marginalized history, however, one can come to see these identical accusations being laid on the doorsteps of all fringe groups from the past: witches, gypsies, the Knights Templar, the Jews and even the early Christians. Moreover, as another victim to its own power of naming in the Waco fiasco, the media perpetuated misinformation through its selective presentation of so-called "cult experts"—predominately drawn from the anti-cult school of thought. As Martin explains, the scriptural doctrine of *clarity* is not only impossible but also an undesirable quality. Nevertheless, it is under this secular banner that the unknowingly secular movement known as Christian fundamentalism flourishes. It is to the sociologist that the media must first turn, for he or she follows a discipline which in many essentials seeks, like deconstructionism, a multiple perspective and the call of the other. The grounding of sociology to the voice of the other is expressed by Bryan Wilson when he makes clear that sociologists in their study must begin with the self-interpretation of religious individuals and groups as their point of departure.

The legacy of Waco is the clearer realization that the deconstructive strategy is one which seeks to displace names, proper names and the single perspective of the proper and property. A community, including that of the Branch Davidians, is one which depends not on ownership but on the shared memory and language of a common narrative (intertexuality). Communities allow people to create shared meanings, values and ways of life. There are no guarantees, however—and cannot be, in any fully open and participatory society—that what is shared is good or bad. There is no *a priori* formula that can dictate "proper" behavior for any particular situation. Assessments and decisions must depend instead only on the responsibility for our on-going social enterprise, but this responsibility itself depends on our being liberated from erroneous concepts and presuppositions.

To displace a name and then rename without closed-off conclusions is an empowering act. The quality of caring which a truly human society requires does not arise from "knowing the truth" but from hearing the call to respect the other. Diversity precedes the postsecular community to be. This is not pluralism and eclecticism, which at best call only for tolerance but not obligation. As the Russian Mikhail Bakhtin assesses, toleration of difference is not enough; we must learn instead to celebrate it. Such counter-institutions as sociology, new social movements and communities of resistance must confront those more traditional institutions (the media, executive arms of government, the anti-cult movement among them) which have been integral to the imposition of conditions in which the other is unable to speak. Martin's formulation of "intertextual materialism," which is developed from the deconstructive project of Derrida, has two principles: (1) always to support the oppressed, downtrodden and marginalized. (2) to be open to learn from many sources. When such a strategy becomes established as the norm, the future inevitability of the Mt. Carmel-type scenarios may no longer have to be.

References

Behler, Ernst (1991). *Confrontations: Derrida, Heidegger, Nietzsche.* Translated by Steven Taubeneck. Stanford: Stanford University Press.

Derrida, Jacques (1976). *Of Grammatology.* Translated by Gayatri Chakravorty Spivak. Baltimore: Johns Hopkins University Press.

Martin, Bill (1992). *Matrix and Line: Derrida and the Possibilities of Postmodern Social Theory.* Albany: State University of New York Press.

Stam, Robert (1988). "Mikhail Bakhtin and the Left Cultural Critique." In *Postmodernism and Its Discontents, Theories and Practices.* Edited by E. Ann Kaplan. London & New York: Verso.

Wilson, Bryan (1982), *Religion in Sociological Perspective,* Oxford: Oxford Univ. Pr.

Michael York is with the Academy for Cultural and Educational Studies in London.

Chapter 31

Did the G-men Sleep through SOC 100?

William H. Swatos, Jr.

Every semester I teach two sections of "Soc 100." Where I teach currently, it is known as "Principles of Sociology." Over the past twenty-five years that I have been doing this more semesters than not, the course has more often been called "Introduction to Sociology," or, among peers, "Intro." The course frequently has a reputation for being less than demanding. Although it is generally required of law enforcement types, my impression is that they seldom are enamored of it. Perhaps that was the case for those involved at Waco.

In my present situation, I have the option of choosing the text that I will use, and my decision has been for Bassis, Gelles, and Levine, *Sociology: An Introduction* (4th ed., 1991, McGraw-Hill). From talking to colleagues, I gather that it's a middling sort of book—not a giveaway, but not overly challenging to the mythical average student. On page 187 of this book appears "Figure 7.2"—a graphic depiction of Neil Smelser's theory of collective behavior. The text provides a two-page illustrative analysis of the mass suicide at Jonestown, Guyana, to show how theory works. The authors also provide a critique of some of the theory's functionalist implications.

In teaching Soc 100, one of the problems is that theories and their illustrations often lack currency. After all, the Smelser theory is over thirty years old, and most of my students were in kindergarten when Jonestown broke. Waco was thus a real gift to this beleaguered sociology teacher. Since I also teach my students that the essence of sociology is not "helping people" but seeing social life as a puzzle, we could get over our initial horror and begin to dissect the remains. The case was a perfect fit.

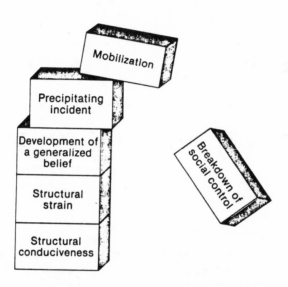

Reproduced from Michael S. Bassis, Richard J. Gelles, and Ann Levine, *Sociology: An Introduction* (4th ed., 1991, McGraw-Hill), with the permission of McGraw-Hill, Inc.

If you look at the graphic, what you see is that serious problems occur (i.e., the blocks begin to tumble) only after a precipitating incident—in this case, the ATF fiasco. Then mobilization takes place; over fifty-one days, David Koresh had plenty of time for this. Bassis et al. (p. 186) write:

> At this point . . . the ball has been set in motion. How far and how fast it rolls depends on whether or not social control is exercised. If someone is able to correct misinformation, to convince people that the threat is imaginary or the enemy has been vanquished, to provide leadership and a model for different behavior, or to intervene forcibly, the outbreak may be checked. If there is a breakdown of social control, however, collective behavior is all but inevitable.

A battering ram or two through the Branch Davidian compound wall was the guarantee of collective behavior inside. The claim of the G-men that Koresh had "promised" that his folk would not commit suicide (or murder) is an absurd defense: Koresh broke one promise after another throughout the siege.

A little less than a decade ago, while I was covering Durkheim's theory of suicide in Soc 100, a student who was not in my class was kind enough to below his brains out in his dorm room. Interest and excitement in my class grew enormously. Intense discussions took place over whether we had a case of egoistic or anomic suicide. I could hardly get students to leave the room after class. The Branch Davidian debacle was further away; people didn't hang around after class. Yet the effect was otherwise strikingly similar: Soc 100 was right on target. The model predicted. Wow, the teacher knew something!

What strikes me as so difficult to account for in this is how so many relatively well-paid, well-educated men and women could have missed what was so plainly obvious that it could be laid out to introductory sociology students in a community college in a half-hour's discussion. What bothers me even more is that so many individuals with whom I have talked in the larger community in which I live do not even seem to think there was a problem with how the situation at Waco was handled. But, then again, neither, as best as I can tell, does the president of the United States. Perhaps four points off on a multiple-choice test for having missed Smelser's theory doesn't have sufficient impact. Should I add another item? Maybe two?

I also teach Introduction to Philosophy, where I usually avoid Hegel. Perhaps I should not do that, either, for it was he who said in introducing his *Philosophy of History,* "Peoples and governments never have learned anything from history, or acted on principles deduced from it." No sentence, it seems to me, can be better applied to Waco than this one.

William H. Swatos, Jr., is Editor of *Sociology of Religion: A Quarterly Review,* the official journal of the Association for the Sociology of Religion. His most recent books include *For Democracy: The Noble Character and Tragic Flaws of the Middle Class,* with Ronald M. Glassman and Peter Kivisto (1993); *Gender and Religion* (1993); and *A Future for Religion: New Paradigms in Social Analysis* (1993). An episcopal parish priest, he is an adjunct member of the arts and science faculties of Scott Community College in Bettendorf, Iowa, and Black Hawk College in Moline, Illinois.

Chapter 32

Reflections on the Tragedy at Waco

Thomas McGowan

New religious movements in America have long been the targets of bigoted and misguided attacks. Most of us know that Shakers, Mormons, Christian Scientists and others suffered, at least in their early days, because of beliefs that were labeled peculiar. Most of us are also aware that immigrant Catholics and Jews had a difficult time assimilating into a hostile American culture. And some of us are even alert to the more recent ill-informed media criticisms of groups such as the Unification Church and the Krishna Consciousness Movement. But few if any of us were ready for the horror at Waco. Why? Perhaps because we naively believed that religious bigotry and ignorance were things of the past. After all, hadn't we been sending out over the years numerous liberated students from our universities? And hadn't we been writing and teaching about religious toleration? And hadn't we as a people matured enough to the point of accepting diversity? Maybe there still existed the occasional bigot, but surely our government was enlightened enough not to confuse religious belief with open sedition. The conflagration at the Branch Davidians' compound brought us back to the cruel truth that to be religiously different is to live dangerously.

An incident that made clear to me the "popular" view of the Waco events occurred when a casual acquaintance, who had just learned that I was

a teacher in the field of religion, immediately brought up the topic and
expressed his satisfaction with the deadly outcome because the government
would save the expense of imprisoning "those fanatics." He was amazed that
anyone could follow David Koresh or believe him to be Christ, since "he
bleeds like me." I refrained from commenting to this professed Christian
that traditional belief affirms that Jesus did in fact bleed. But his forthright
comments did serve to remind me of the underlying secular view our society
shares. There is no room in this mindset for genuine conversion. Rather,
there is an unreflective acceptance of the claims that the new religions are
dangerous cults and that whoever converts to one of them is brainwashed.
But how then can Christians, for example, claim consistency if they
acknowledge Paul's experience on the road to Damascus to be authentic
conversion but deny the same possibility to a Branch Davidian? Is it simply
that time legitimizes this unsettling experience? Or how can citizens cherish
religious freedom for themselves but deny it to members of alternative
religions? The problem for many contemporary Americans in accepting the
authenticity of conversion is that their scientific mentality has weakened
their ability to believe or even, at times, to comprehend the reports of those
who claim to have experienced the transcendent. Religious conversion has
become something to be treated as the subject of science alone.
Unfortunately, this approach usually ends by attempting to explain away
conversion and arguing it is not conversion at all but mind control.

The government, of course, must evaluate the admitted mistakes that
instigated, prolonged and finalized the tragedy. Was it proper to assault the
compound in the first place because of reported illegal guns?   Did
subsequent negotiations include honest dialogue and open communication?
And why was the final attack conducted so violently if, as Attorney General
Janet Reno stated, the purpose was to save the children? These questions
require answers which should lead to policy and procedural changes so that
the same mistakes will never be repeated. But beyond looking for better
ways to confront people engaged in apparently unorthodox religious
behavior, would it not be preferable for our government officials to learn
tolerance of religious diversity?   Admittedly, intense personal religious
feeling is difficult to deal with in the public arena. Such a private and
transcendent experience as religious faith is not the usual beat for law
enforcement officers. And that is why the most nagging question for me is
why experienced experts in the theology and psychology of the new religions
were not consulted in any meaningful way. At least they might have
challenged the unexamined assumption that Koresh's followers were duped
and that the situation called for "hostage" negotiations.

Each person who died in Waco must have had his or her own story of
conversion. If there had been the opportunity to interview them, I'm sure
some would have told their stories in the metaphor of a journey, beginning

with a departure from a former social and religious perspective, moving through a limbo of doubt and searching, and ending with their commitment to Branch Davidian. The reasons they would have offered for their change of life would probably have ranged from finding truth in the teachings of David Koresh to the hope for improving the world or at least themselves through this new community. The value of such stories would have been to personalize the Davidians and to take seriously the motivations for their actions. Since people seemed to have undergone a mysterious and radical change of personality, it was easy to presume that something untoward and even diabolical had happened to them. But an attempt should have been made to look at the belief system of the Davidians, which was obviously so compelling to its members, and to recognize the power of this faith commitment. If they had been treated more as a people with a story to tell, not only would the tragedy have been avoided, but they might have enriched America, much as earlier, previously misunderstood "cults" have.

But where does one draw the line between the First Amendment's ban on any law "prohibiting the free exercise" of religion and the government's obligation to protect us from anti-social acts? After all, the Branch Davidians were accused of storing illegal guns and of child abuse. The Supreme Court offered some guidance in 1972 *(Yoder v. Wisconsin)* by suggesting that government should not restrict or burden religious practice unless it was necessary to serve a "compelling" state interest and was the least restrictive way of doing so. More recently, however, in another case *(Employment Division v. Smith),* the Court decided that the exercise of religion deserves no special protection, so long as the law or regulation impinging on it is "neutral" and "generally applicable." The Court has a long tradition, going back to the late nineteenth century, of separating belief from practice. In other words, a person may believe what he or she wants, but the actions that result from that belief—as, for example, polygamy for the Mormons—may be deemed anti-social and illegal. The problem with this line of reasoning is that it compartmentalizes religion—something the man or woman of faith finds dishonest to attempt.

The constitutional issue, therefore, concerns whether the lifestyle of the Branch Davidians deserved to be protected from official interference. Personally, I feel that the First Amendment's guarantee of religious freedom was seriously jeopardized by the heavy-handed attempts to forcefully enter the compound and by the denigrating reporting of the group's beliefs. Simply put, the Davidians should have been left alone since there is no compelling evidence that they were either a danger to society or to themselves. This is not to say, however, that such communities should never be scrutinized. But government officials are probably the least qualified to do this overseeing. Better to have scholars of the new religions available, both to warn of any religiosity that could lead to loss of human dignity or even life and also to calm any unwarranted fears held by the larger society.

I'm sure the debate over the tragedy at Waco will take many turns; but if it is to have any redeeming grace, surely it should be to finally convince us to tolerate those among us who believe strange doctrines and live in strange ways.

Thomas McGowan is Professor of Religious Studies and Past Director of American Studies at Manhattan College in Riverdale, New York.

Chapter 33

How Future Wacos Might Be Avoided:
Two Proposals

Phillip Lucas

The conflagration that killed over eighty women, children, and men at the Ranch Apocalypse on April 19, 1993, was a tragic episode in the ongoing story of American religion and the state. While other commentators question motives and tactics, analyze the flow of events, and allocate blame, I have felt challenged, by the magnitude of this tragedy, to suggest concrete ways to avoid its repetition. In this short essay I will propose two initiatives that I believe would significantly lessen the potential for future decimations of small religious communities by state-sanctioned power.

The *first proposal* addresses the problem law enforcement officials face whenever they must negotiate with a religious community whose members understand the world in a way that is largely incomprehensible to them. This situation resembles an encounter between persons who speak different languages. If any meaningful communication is to occur, an interpreter must be present who understands both languages. If officials and non-traditional religious communities are to communicate clearly, they need "worldview" interpreters. It is now painfully obvious that such interpreters were nowhere in evidence during the Waco standoff. As a result, each side in the negotiations acted in ways that, in retrospect, completely misunderstood the other side's intentions, concerns, values. (Other essays in this volume provide ample evidence of misunderstanding.)

It is the responsibility of law enforcement officials, in my judgment, to ensure that they have ready access to such "worldview" interpreters before entering into any negotiations with a religious community in which the threat of violence exists. To facilitate such access I propose the formation of an advisory board of scholars who have studied individual religious communities in contemporary America and who have, therefore, learned the "language" of their worldviews. These scholars would constitute an intelligence clearinghouse that could be consulted prior to (preferably) or during (if necessary) negotiations with religious groups suspected of illegal activities. Their expertise would be available on an *ad hoc* basis, and the only expense to law enforcement agencies (whose budgetary restraints are well known) would be an agreed upon per-consultation fee.

It would no doubt be advisable that such a consultative body meet periodically with law enforcement officials, so that each body was well-informed concerning the other's methods, procedures, goals, and professional discourse. Should it prove feasible, this advisory body might even participate in periodic trainings of law enforcement officials in the sociology of new religious movements and the psychology of sectarian and cultic commitment. Aside from these activities, however, the scholars willing to participate in such a board would only be called into service as events warranted.

The advisory board would remain completely independent of governmental and religious institutions and be understood as a collective of civic-minded scholars whose chief intention was to encourage mutual understanding between religious communities and law enforcement agencies. In addition, the board would eschew all political or religious agendas—such as the promotion of some religious beliefs over others, or the support of partisan political bodies—and would maintain respectful relations with both the law enforcement community and individual religious movements. Indeed, such a nonsectarian and nonpolitical stance would be crucial to its credibility as a neutral advisory board.

As the investigation of the Waco tragedy unfolds, it becomes more and more apparent that the Bureau of Alcohol, Tobacco and Firearms (ATF) and the Federal Bureau of Investigation (FBI) themselves constitute particular subcultures with characteristic codes, rituals, agendas, and discourses. In these agencies' hierarchy of values, nuanced understanding of the worldviews of others ranks rather low in priority. Given this, as well as the complexity of contemporary religious subcultures and the fierce loyalties that members of religious communities hold (loyalties that in some cases can lead to collective suicide or violent self-defense), the need for an advisory board such as I have proposed becomes all the more urgent.

I am aware that the FBI's negotiation team at Waco included so-called "cult experts." However, some of these "experts" were members of organizations that have strong doctrinal loyalties and a history of hostility toward nontraditional religious communities. Their interpretation of these communities, therefore, tends to portray them as manipulative, exploitative, and dangerous—a perspective that invites violent action against these demonized "enemies" of society. An advisory board composed of scholars who are recognized by their academic peers as objective and respectful of religious diversity would avoid such obvious pitfalls.

My *second proposal* encourages nontraditional religious communities to cooperate with both scholars and the media so that they are accurately represented before the general public. Taking concrete steps in this direction, while by no means necessitated by law, would be a prudent way for religious communities to avoid the demonization that occurred with the Branch Davidians—a demonization that was used to justify the draconian measures taken against them. This proposal asks religious groups to take responsibility for how they appear to the general public and to realize that, in spite of the First Amendment, religious freedom in America is often a tenuous privilege, revokable under various legal pretexts. In short, nontraditional religious communities should not take their freedoms for granted and should act to preempt their public demonization by hostile institutions and organizations.

For instance, religious groups could invite academic researchers to visit their communities, talk to their members, and read their literature. They could also keep the scholarly community abreast of new developments in their organizations through regular communication with individual researchers and/or advisory boards like that proposed above. Such initiatives could result in scholarly articles or monographs that would give a more accurate portrayal of a group's beliefs and practices. It would also allow researchers to give informed perspectives on a group when interviewed by law enforcement agencies and the media.

As a further measure, nontraditional religious communities could issue regular press releases so that opinion makers and reporters would at least have the group's own account of their teachings, activities, and pending legal battles. Most reporters are willing to present both sides of an issue or event if they have accurate information at hand. Had David Koresh been more attentive to such public relations efforts, the half-truths, accusations, and hearsay used to demonize the Branch Davidians could have been effectively neutralized.

Clearly, in the aftermath of Jonestown and Waco, public suspicions will persist with regard to nontraditional movements. Nevertheless, a concerted effort by these groups to counter the biased representations produced by the anti-cult movement would go a long way to assuaging public fear and hostility. Nontraditional religious communities must accept the hard truth that, in the American context, overt disdain for public opinion and for open dialogue with neighbors and civil institutions is a recipe for Waco-like disasters. In short, extreme efforts to maintain group boundaries are potentially counterproductive to movement survival.

In the final analysis, tragedies like Waco occur because people and institutions become isolated within their own worldviews and discourse communities. Given our society's mushrooming religious diversity and its accompanying expansion of state police power, both sides would do well to keep the lines of communication as open and clear as possible.

Phillip Lucas is Assistant Professor of Religion at Stetson University. His current book, *From New Age Millennium to Orthodox Restoration: The Religious Odyssey of a Post-modern Initiatory Movement,* is forthcoming from Indiana University in 1994.

Chapter 34

Sticks'n'Stones May Break Your Bones but Words *CAN* Really Hurt You

Evelyn Dorothy Oliver

> Genocide does not begin with ovens; it begins with words.
> — Simon Wiesenthal

On April 19, 1993, the Branch Davidians were not the only victims of Waco. Janet Reno and Bill Clinton were also victimized when the sparks of misinformation, having been thoroughly fanned by the media and viciously fueled by hate groups, reached a point of critical mass. These two marvelous people and other gifted officials exemplify how even the best of us *CAN* become pawns when deprived of accurate information. The smoke screen was too thick and the sound bites too loud to counter the inertia of slander with the knowledge and experience our country's finest academic investigators were attempting to offer—hence the frustration that is expressed in some of the essays in this anthology.

Woe to those caught in the grasp of marketed fear. Shock'n'Horror, Sex'n'Riots is all you hear and read. "People eat it up," is the excuse to proceed. But, "You are what you eat," as someone aptly said. Let us examine the daily diet of those fifty-one days. First we devoured rumor and slander, while compassion and truth got shoved to the side like a pile of peas on a kid's dinner plate. The "brain bits" of scholars and other voices of reason were drowned in an oozing gravy of greed.

When the children were roasted, even the purveyors of this embroiling drama finally became nauseous. "Check your sources," I do believe, should have a whole new meaning. As we join the wake to mourn Waco, I now see the media to be a victim too. As more information emerges, I suspect we will all come to realize that the ultimate victim of Waco is the American public, you and me.

The moment a finger is laid upon another human being, the dispute ceases to be a religious issue and immediately becomes a civil rights/human rights violation. Looking back from the 1960s to the future of the 1990s, we collectively imagined that prejudice and bigotry would become a thing of the past. As we examine the components of discrimination we learn that it's the sum of the parts that make a whole. It's not just their size, their color, or their language that needs to be "allowed" or "legislated"; it's the culture of the people that must be learned and understood. How on earth can we ever hope to eradicate bigotry and prejudice without first educating our world about religions? Religion is the soul of the culture of the people we fear, hurt, and harm. The world is suffering and sick at a soul level. It's going to take massive inoculations of compassion laced with an educated understanding to allow the diversity of spiritualities to heal ailing souls.

To contribute to this end, the Association of World Academics for Religious Education (AWARE) was formed. We are an organization formed to accomplish the agenda set forth in Dr. Lucas's preceding essay (Chapter 33), and much more. We will offer accurate up-to-date information, researched and compiled by the finest academic specialists in the world today. Our statement of purpose reads, in part:

> The primary goal of AWARE is to promote intellectual and religious freedom by educating the general public about existing religions and cultures, including, but not limited to, alternative religious groups and world religions that are not part of the tradition of mainstream American religion and culture. AWARE's orientation is scholarly and non-sectarian; the organization is not religious and does not have a religious ideology to propagate. AWARE's purpose is to correct the inaccurate and often misleading information that many people—including the media, law enforcement, and other social institutions—hold regarding unfamiliar religions and cultures. AWARE also educates the scholary community and the general public about the severe persecution that religious and cultural minorities experience in the United States as well as abroad, and to support the United States government in its efforts to heal the prejudice that exists in our country and in the world.

Evelyn Dorothy Oliver is Executive Director of the Association of World Academics for Religious Education (AWARE).

Chapter 35

Christian Holocaust

The Family of Floyd Houtman (Branch Davidian)

Thank you, Mr. President, Janet Reno too.
We mustn't forget the ATF, the FBI, all the men in blue.

How well did you sleep last night?
Did you toss and turn?
I myself didn't get much sleep.
Did you know I saw my father burn?

We don't know how you did it.
You really must be brave.
You sat through all their screaming,
without emotion as they entered their fiery grave.

Save the children.
Well, not this time.
For patience we have none.
Enough time has been wasted;
we were ordered, "Get this over, get this done."

Patience is a virtue.
Good things come to those who wait.
It took only 51 days for you to decide their fiery fate.
Deep down inside your heart, you know the truth;
you cannot hide.
Christians who believe in God don't contemplate suicide.

The day will come we'll all be judged
as we stand before the Lord.
Koresh may have thought himself as Christ,
But you thought yourself as God.

    The Family of Floyd Houtman
    We Love and Miss You, Dad.

This poem was supplied by Stan Silva, a surviving Branch Davidian who lost his wife and two children during the fire at Mt. Carmel.

Chapter 36

Open Season on Messiahs?

Dean M. Kelley

[This statement was issued *following* the ATF assault, but *prior to* the FBI assault.]

The papers are full of news and conjectures about the "Davidian Branch"—a small sect headed by one "David Koresh" and located in a compound near Waco, Texas, that is now surrounded by hundreds of law-enforcement officers, ambulances, reporters and armored "personnel carriers." After a tragic and unsuccessful assault on Sunday morning, February 28, 1993, in which several sect members and several assaulters were killed and others wounded, the forces of the law are now apparently trying to wait out their quarry without further violence.

The media are having a field day with on-the-spot reports in every newscast—even when there is nothing new to report, which is most of the time. So they have been digging up anyone with any connection to the sect—including neighbors, former members and relatives of present members—to flesh out their rather sparse accounts. They have also given a lot of free air-time to the harpies of the anti-cult movement, who have been hovering round the scene like vultures, uttering their usual shrill cries about "destructive cults" and "mind control." Surprisingly, there seems to be almost no intimation in the media—except for the comments of Col. Charlie Beckwith, who called it "a disgrace"—that the whole scenario is bizarre (except for the sect, which seems virtually humdrum in contrast to the fuss being made over it). [See Chapter 11 of this for for a later analysis by Beckwith.]

It is certainly not unprecedented for a charismatic religious leader to attract a following of devotees who accord him or her great authority over their lives and who try to insulate themselves from the unbelieving world. The leader may even claim to be some kind of a messiah and to promise eternal bliss to those who follow and eternal damnation to those who don't. Being a messiah is often dangerous business (and the stage is rather crowded now with claimants of such a role, from Rabbi Schneerson to Sun Myung Moon), but humankind seems to crave a superhuman savior to deliver them from the feuds and phobias that beset us, so you can't blame folks for trying to fill the role.

Those who aspire to messiahship have chosen a hard and thankless role to play. They often seem unprepossessing or even "kooky" to the rest of us, but there's no law against that. They often attract a lot of criticism from the neighbors and may become paranoid about their safety in a hostile world—with some reason. (One recalls the lynching of Joseph Smith, founder of Mormonism, by a mob of furious "gentiles" in Carthage, Illinois, in 1844, and the vendetta by the U.S. government—Congress, the cavalry and the courts—against the Mormon settlements in Utah during the ensuing decades, despite which the Church of Jesus Christ of Latter-Day Saints has become one of the pillars of the republic, as it probably would have without all that hysteria.) (I happen to believe that the real Messiah came some nineteen hundred years ago, but He didn't fare too well at the hands of His enemies either.)

The degree of investment of human energy in one of these small groups is far out of proportion to their numbers. Their devotion to their cause— fanaticism, the world often calls it—is greater than the rest of us give to the achievement of our fondest ambitions, and so the concentration of energy is very threatening to the neighbors. Add to this the various unconventional domestic arrangements in such groups (such as the "complex marriage" of the Oneida Community, in which everyone was married to everyone else), and the public—which seems able to tolerate many other kinds of bizarre sexual practice, so long as it is recreational rather than religious—begins to become upset.

A final ingredient is the "stockpiling" of weapons—a natural enough development in a society that views resort to armed warfare as the normal mode of resolving conflicts and indulges the acquisition of assault guns as merely an adjunct to good clean sport. This factor then becomes the occasion and the justification for the government to take a hand for the sake of "public safety." But since small "fanatic" religious groups are nodes of very high human energy, intruding upon them can be like sticking one's finger into a dynamo—as the late Representative Ryan discovered when he took a posse of dissident former members (and television crews) down to Guyana to "investigate" their charges against Jim Jones: a sure-fire recipe for tragic disaster.

Few commentators seem to have asked what was the heinous offense or imminent peril that prompted that Sunday morning attack on the sect's headquarters (and the months of surveillance and infiltration that preceded it). Were the Branchites planning to take over Baylor University and subject the faculty to forced conversion? Perhaps Koresh was the mastermind behind the bombing of the World Trade Center? If threats of this magnitude might have justified the massive attack on Sunday morning, we have been given no intimation of them. There has been talk of "illegal" weapons in the premises—though most of them were admittedly acquired legally and openly. (One wonders what an "illegal firearm" would be in Texas anyway, short of a bazooka firing nuclear warheads.) Perhaps the fear might be that a paranoid group might launch a "preemptive strike" against supposed enemies, and that is just what happened—except that the launchers were the governmental agencies, and the supposed "enemies" were the Branch Davidians, who unfairly (and "fanatically") resisted being overrun!

So we are confronted with the prospect of a vast military assault worthy of the Keystone Kops, directed against a relatively small and thus far unaggressive religious band whose chief offense appears to have been acting like a "cult," whatever that is (beyond a religious outfit that we don't understand and don't approve of). The anti-cult harpies have suggested an ingenious rationale for this intervention: it was designed to "rescue" the "hostages" held "captive" by Koresh through—you guessed it—"mind control"! This notion of "mind control" is the modern equivalent of the old bugaboo of demon-possession that underlay the tragic history of witch-hunts and justified the burning of hundreds of suspect women. As a federal court held in *U.S. v. Fishman* (1990), the theory of "mind control"—that the human will can be managed at a distance without force or threat of force—is not accepted in the relevant disciplines of psychology and sociology and is therefore not admissible as "expert testimony" in court (to explain behavior that is more readily explainable as simple persuasion). The resulting implication is that anyone following Koresh is doing so because he has persuaded them to do so, and there is no law against that.

What is the law, then, that was broken by the Branchers and justifies their being targeted—however patiently—by hundreds of government employees at a cost of hundreds of thousands of dollars a day of our tax money? Let us hope that this question finds an answer soon, or that the feds go back of square one and start over again without the heavy weapons and flak vests.

Dean M. Kelley is Counselor of Religious Liberty to the National Council of Churches. This statement is a personal opinion derived from thirty years of studying religious movements, and does not necessarily express the views of the National Council of Churches or its member communions.

Chapter 37

Waco Probe Should Not Be Used to Define Religion, Leaders Say
(Press Release, May 4, 1993)

Larry Chesser, Baptist Joint Committee on Public Affairs

WASHINGTON—The federal government should not use its investigation into the tragic loss of life at the Branch Davidian compound in Waco, Texas, as an occasion to define "valid religion," say many of the nation's religious and civil liberties groups.

In a statement issued May 4, organizations including the National Association of Evangelicals, the National Council of Churches and the Baptist Joint Committee urged government to "resist any temptation to retreat" from the Constitution's guarantee of religious liberty.

The statement said it is appropriate for government to investigate what happened in Waco to prevent similar occurrences in the future.

"Under the religious liberty provisions of the First Amendment, government has no business declaring what is orthodox or heretical, or what is a true or false religion," the statement asserts. "It should steer clear of inflammatory and misleading labels."

"History teaches that today's 'cults' may become tomorrow's mainstream religions."

The statement calls the nation's religious diversity a source of strength, not weakness.

"We must fend off the inclination to shrink from our commitment to religious pluralism or to seek security at the expense of liberty," the organizations said.

The statement recognizes that religious freedom is not absolute and cannot serve as an excuse for violent or criminal conduct that harms others or threatens public safety.

"Absent some compelling justification, however, government should not restrict religious exercise," the statement declares. "And force—if ever appropriate—must be employed as a last resort."

BJC Executive Director James M. Dunn said the agency participated in the statement in the hope that the Waco tragedy will not be the occasion of an overreaction by government against religious minorities.

"The difference between a 'religious fanatic' and a devout believer is never clear," Dunn said. "Even to categorize would be a calamity; to do more would be a catastrophe."

Other organizations signing the statement are the American Baptist Churches, U.S.A., American Civil Liberties Union, the American Conference on Religious Movements, Americans United for Separation of Church and State, the Association of Christian Schools International, Church of Scientology International, the Churches' Center for Theology and Public Policy, the Episcopal Church, First Liberty Institute, the General Conference of Seventh-Day Adventists, the Greater Grace World Outreach, the Presbyterian Church (U.S.A.), Washington Office, and the Union of American Hebrew Congregations.

Chapter 38

A New Religious Movement's Response to the Waco Tragedy:
(Press Release, March 14, 1993)

The Family

In light of the recent tragic developments in Waco, Texas, at the Branch Davidian compound, *The Family*—on behalf of our membership wishes to state the following:

1. We deplore the loss of life in Waco. Had the authorities and the members of the Branch Davidian group been more level-headed and exercised more restraint, we believe the tragedy could have been averted. It is our earnest prayer that the standoff will be resolved peaceably, with no further casualties. We extend our condolences to the families and loved ones of those who have died.

2. *The Family* does not have and has never had any formal or informal ties of any kind with the Branch Davidian group.

3. *The Family* has always abhorred the use of violence. We do not condone the use of firearms as a means of settling disputes. Rather than rely on force or weaponry, our founder, Father David, has always advised us to rely primarily on God, and secondarily on the police and civil authorities, for needed protection from hostile forces.

The conduct of our membership worldwide makes it clear that nonviolence is not only the belief of our fellowship, but also very much the practice.

4. The only situation in which we feel the use of reasonable force may

be justified is in the case of self-defense, the defense of property and loved ones. This is only if the threat is clearly an illegal one, and all other solutions have failed. We do not espouse any means of self-defense prohibited by law.

5. *The Family* has always advocated respect for and compliance with officers of the law engaged in the performance of their duties. We have never approved obstructing such officers. We adhere to the Scriptural admonition which states that they are "the ministers of God, who bear not the sword in vain" (Romans 13:4).

Over the years, due to the authorities' being grossly misinformed by our detractors, several of our communities in different countries have been the target of police raids. Even though our members knew that such intrusions were misguided, and that their communities were innocent of any wrongdoing, they always peacefully yielded to and complied with the law enforcement officials. (Each of these communities were subsequently exonerated of any criminal wrongdoing.) We feel that such conduct clearly proves our commitment to respect and obey the law enforcement agencies.

6. *The Family* has never sanctioned, much less promoted, suicide as an acceptable act in the eyes of God.

7. We express concern and alarm at the way the anti-cult movement (ACM) is currently exploiting the tragedy in Waco. By lumping all new religious movements (NRMs) together, despite the extreme diversity of beliefs and practices held by the various NRMs, the ACM is attempting to label and stigmatize *all* such groups as "destructive cults" capable of violent anti-social acts. We decry such broad generaliaations which we believe foster intolerance, bigotry and hatred.

We therefore appeal to the media to exercise objectivity in their reporting related to the events in Waco. And we ask the public to remain fair and unprejudiced in evaluating religious groups whose beliefs may differ from those of the mainstream faiths.

We beseech all believers to continue to pray that the situation in Waco will be resolved peacefully and speedily.

The Family is a Bible-based fellowship of independent Christian missionary communities. We are united in our firm belief that Jesus Christ alone is the Messiah, the only begotten Son of God. Presently active in approximately fifty countries, we trace our origins to 1968, when our founder, Father David, began a Gospel ministry to American counter-culture youth. Young people began to work with Father David, and the movement became known as *The Children of God*. This organization was formally dissolved in 1978 by Father David, who then invited those who wished to remain in fellowship with him to form a new group, *The Family of Love*, with a new organizational structure. In recent years, we have become known simply as *The Family*.

Chapter 39

Church Universal and Triumphant not like Branch Davidians
(News Release, March 11, 1993)

Church Universal and Triumphant

Church Universal and Triumphant is not like the Branch Davidians in Waco, Texas.

"There are some superficial similarities," said Murray Steinman, the church's spokesman. "But there are also profound differences—starting with the fact that we are not armed, isolated or expecting the end of the world. Those who make assertions to the contrary simply do not know what they are talking about," he added.

Steinman was reacting to news reports, including stories in this week's editions of *Newsweek* and *U.S. News & World Report*, that carried inaccurate reports about the church. The two publications only called him an hour before deadline and their stories did not fairly represent the church's point of view. "I'm going to talk to both publications to see what we can do to open up better lines of communication," he said.

Steinman referred to the standoff with the Branch Davidians as "a double tragedy." "The first tragedy," he said, "is events that have and continue to take place in Waco. The second tragedy is the hysteria and the unwarranted cloud of suspicion that has descended on us and other religious groups across the country."

Steinman corrected some of the common errors reported about the church:

1. *Church Universal and Triumphant is not a cult.* The term "cult" as it is generally used is a pejorative. While the media now avoids using negative racial stereotypes, they have not done so with negative religious stereotypes.

Church Universal and Triumphant is rooted in the Judeo-Christian tradition and embraces some Eastern beliefs as well. Members study the mystical paths of the world's religions.

2. *Elizabeth Clare Prophet, the church's leader, has never predicted the end of the world.* Prophet never made such a prediction. She is on record taking a position to the contrary. She doesn't believe the world is going to end even in a worst-case scenario.

Prophet has encouraged people to build fallout shelters for more than two decades. The church built a fallout shelter for its staff in 1990. Other church members have built shelters in Montana, throughout the United States and in some foreign countries. Prophet sees the shelters as an "insurance policy" against any form of a nuclear disaster—from a Chernobyl-like reactor accident to a terrorist attack to an authorized or accidental use of a nuclear weapon.

The church does not have a paramilitary, survivalist or garrison mentality. Members are guardedly optimistic about the future.

3. *Church Universal and Triumphant members are not isolated.* The church's headquarters are located on the Royal Teton Ranch in southwest Montana. The facilities are spread out over 40 miles into a number of different locations, including a publishing and data-processing center in Livingston, Montana. The church has 600 full-time staff members. The headquarters serves the needs of its centers in approximately 120 cities across the United States and additional centers in 40 nations throughout the world.

The staff at the church are not isolated. The church staff frequently conduct public seminars at the headquarters and throughout the U.S.A. The vast majority of church members live in their own homes in the United States. "We are fully integrated into local, state and national communities—even the international community," said Steinman.

4. *The church does not stockpile weapons.* In 1989, Edward Francis and Vernon Hamilton, two church members, attempted to purchase 15 rifles that were legal to buy, but in an illegal fashion (using an assumed name). The

church did not finance or sanction their activities—nor would it have done so. The weapons were seized by federal authorities in Washington State and were never transported to the ranch. The Bureau of Alcohol, Tobacco, and Firearms and the Justice Department concluded the church was not involved in the activities of Francis and Hamilton.

Francis' and Hamilton's convictions led to speculation that the church has stockpiled weapons. But that is not the case. Like millions of Americans, some church members in Montana own firearms, mostly for hunting. But the church does not stockpile or even own any weapons, other than a couple of rifles used by shepherds on the ranch to defend sheep from coyotes.

5. *The church does not use mind control.* One frequently cited theme is that so-called cults use deception and mind control. Most of the sources that have been used to advance this idea come from the Cult Awareness Network (CAN) or people associated with CAN.

Their material is not reliable and has not found acceptance in the scientific community. In fact, it is considered fringe.

Dr. Margaret Singer, a frequently quoted source, is CAN's leading theoretician. The American Psychological Association (APA) has rejected her ideas on brainwashing because they lack "scientific rigor." Federal courts have repeatedly rejected her testimony as a witness on coercive persuasion (the technical term for "brainwashing") on the grounds that her ideas, as Judge D. Lowell Jensen wrote, "are not generally accepted within the scientific community."

The APA does not accept the thesis that mind control, or brainwashing, is possible without physical restraint. What they mean by "physical restraint" are conditions approaching a Korean prisoner-of-war camp.

Deprogrammers formerly associated with CAN allege that the organization helps coordinate and financially benefits from deprogrammings that involve illegal kidnapping. An FBI affidavit states that a group who conspired to kidnap Lewis Du Pont Smith, heir to the Du Pont fortune, was "associated with the Cult Awareness Network."

Steinman also commented on the current activities of the church and its future. "We are interested in our religious life, our schools, publishing and building our community," he said. As for the future, he pointed to a recent column by Clark Morphew, religion writer for the *St. Paul Pioneer Press*, which said:

New religions are always persecuted by the ignorant and the fearful. But eventually, they are seen as legitimate pieces in the American religious puzzle.

I predict that is exactly what will happen to the new religions of this new age. They will be persecuted, but determined leadership will carry the day. Elizabeth Clare Prophet is a part of our religious history, and someday the Church Universal and Triumphant will be as honored as Mormonism is today.

Chapter 40

FBI Uses "Cults" as Bait

Phyllis Goldberg

> A portrait of the final day inside the Branch Davidian cult, a day that would
> end with raging fire, horrified screams and the deaths of 86 people, has
> begun to emerge . . . The F.B.I. has acknowledged that it foresaw a high
> probability of casualties. "We knew the chances were great that the adults
> would not come out unharmed," Mr. Ricks [one of the agents in charge at
> Waco] told *The Dallas Morning News*. "So we felt that if we got any of them
> out safely, that would be a great bonus."
> —— *New York Times*, April 26, 1993

About 120 people belonged to the sixtey-year-old religious group known as
the Branch Davidians, whose roots were in the Seventh-Day Adventist
Church. Most of them lived together in a communal three-story home they
called Mt. Carmel in Waco, a small city halfway between Austin and Dallas
in eastern Texas that was nicknamed the Baptists' Rome because it has so
many wealthy Baptist churches. The leader of these fundamentalist
Christians (they were among those who interpret the Bible literally) was a
thirty-three-year-old man named David Koresh.

On a Sunday morning in February 1993, more than one hundred agents
from the Treasury Department's Bureau of Alcohol, Tobacco, and Firearms

descended on Mt. Carmel to serve search and arrest warrants on the Branch
Davidians, who allegedly were in possession of illegal weapons.
(Government documents released later, indicating that the bureau began its
investigation in June 1992, contain a hodgepodge of other allegations; they
include the charge that the two dozen children at Mt. Carmel were being
sexually abused.) Although the ATF subsequently acknowledged that it
knew Koresh had been forewarned of the raid, and that therefore it had
forfeited the crucial element of surprise, it went ahead with the planned
"ambush" anyway. A shootout ensued during which four agents and several
Mt. Carmel residents died. The Federal Bureau of Investigation took over
after that, placing the Branch Davidians under siege until the conflagration
April 19 when as many as eighty-six people—including at least seventeen
children—were burned alive.

Most of the facts of April 19 have been well publicized. They are
horrifyingly simple. At dawn an armored tank tears a hole eight feet high
and ten feet wide in the wall of the main building near the front door. Tear
gas is pumped in. Four more tank assaults between dawn and noon. More
tear gas. Flames are visible a few minutes after twelve. For five minutes
the fire, whipped by thirty-mile-an-hour winds, devours everything in sight.
At twelve minutes after noon an FBI agent calls the Waco Fire Department:
"If you could, roll some apparatus to the checkpoints out here, please?"
How many trucks were needed? "Sir, I'd say it's a pretty good fire. The
entire compound is going up right now." Ten minutes later two fire trucks
arrive but are not allowed to pass the FBI checkpoints for another fifteen
minutes.

Why did agents of the federal government (who as yet have presented
no evidence whatsoever that the Branch Davidians were guilty of anything
other than collecting weapons, a popular pastime in Texas) descend on Mt.
Carmel?

Since the inferno, the public has been subjected to conflicting
explanations by government officials, as well as a variety of "scientific"
analyses by psychiatrists, professors of religion, representatives of the Cult
Awareness Network (which on April 9 counseled the FBI to use lethal force
against Koresh if necessary) and other "experts" on cults.

"Really, [April 19] was not meant to be D-Day," says Attorney General
Janet Reno. "[Rather, it was to] induce serious negotiations or the
evacuation of the compound . . . We had information that babies were
being beaten . . . These are concerns that we had." But she explains later
that she had agreed to authorize the action because no replacements could
be found for the "exhausted" agents who had been on duty at Mt. Carmel
for fifty-one days, and that nothing else—including negotiations (as well as
cutting off the telephone and electricity, surrounding the Branch Davidians'

residence with concertina wire, bombarding them at night with the sounds of dentists' drills, locomotives and rabbits being slaughtered)—had worked.

At a Senate hearing on April 22, Republican and Democratic senators added their voices to that of Bill Clinton, applauding Reno's "handling" of an assault that ended with the agonizing death of dozens of people.

Now come what will be weeks, perhaps months, of a grisly forensic investigation. Now come the endless media accounts of the surviving children being told about their parents' deaths. Now come the internal and public reviews of "handling" and "mishandling," which may lay blame and even lead to some bureaucratic reshuffling—up to and including the dismissal of embattled FBI Director William Sessions. But whatever lumps Treasury, Justice and even the president might take for their part in the Waco debacle, they have succeeded in at least one aspect of their mission; there is an insidious new public enemy on the American political/legal/ideological landscape: the cult. And there are some who believe that this was the ultimate objective of the entire Waco operation.

"Don't be fooled by the *appearance* of incompetence and blundering on the part of Washington and its agents in Waco—although there was plenty of incompetence and blundering," says Dr. Fred Newman, Stanford University-trained philosopher, student of mass psychology, political activist and a leader of the New Alliance Party (NAP)—which has, like the Branch Davidians, been labeled a cult by the FBI. "I believe that the operation, from start to deadly finish, was the product of a far more rational, self-conscious process than the powers-that-be choose to let on."

The FBI was trying out a new *modus operandi* in Waco, to suit the new conditions created by the end of the Cold War. For the past two decades, and particularly since the collapse of European communism, we no longer live in a bipolar—left versus right—world held together by a center which derived its political legitimacy and stability from the appearance of a broad majoritarian consensus. Attempts to reconstruct that center by coming up with reconciliationist solutions to the profound structural problems in the American economy have not worked; the center has given way to pluralistic extremism, in government as well as outside it.

Fred Newman, with a sense of the satirical, calls himself an "extremist"—and is proud of it. As he told a New York City-wide meeting of the New Alliance Party a few months ago, "I believe that every person in America has the *right* to quality health care. If what that will take, which I believe it will, is an 'extreme' measure like the redistribution of this country's wealth from the insurance companies and the pharmaceutical industry and the AMA to ordinary working-class and middle-class people—then I'm for it!"

Because there is a social and economic basis for extremism in America
(Bill Clinton, after all, is merely a post-modern Huey Long), the extremists
in power must find new ways to control, and ultimately destroy, extremists
of all kinds who threaten them. Over these past fifteen years, many of the
covert investigative operations conducted under the counterintelligence
programs (COINTELPRO) of the FBI—exposed in the seventies and
eighties to unwanted (and highly negative) publicity—have been taken over
by private entrepreneurs (including the Anti-defamation League of the B'nai
B'rith, "opposition research" teams associated with the two major political
parties, and the Cambridge, Massachusetts-based Political Research
Associates). The bureau, meanwhile, is exploring and testing new,
"apolitical" categories suitable for direct action by the FBI itself in this
depoliticized era.

Categories such as "cults," which can be used to label "extremists," are
potentially useful to the FBI.

When the liberals were in power in America (1932-1968) they regarded
communists as their arch-enemies. They were aware that since *they* were in
power, there was a social basis for other kinds of left-of-centrists to come to
power. The liberals and their cohorts in the FBI found a category for those
other leftists, who threatened their hold on America—"armed and dangerous
communists or revolutionaries." This label was effectively used by the
liberals and the U.S. intelligence to bury their leftist enemies. "Cults" are
the "communists" of the post-modern, post-political world.

What did the Branch Davidians do to deserve their fiery deaths?
Nothing. Few in numbers, poor, politically powerless and not connected to
mainstream religion, the Branch Davidians were profoundly *inconsequential*
to the people in Washington who authorized the attack on them. Bill
Clinton, Janet Reno, the armed body of men who take orders from them
and assorted unofficial advisors like the Cult Awareness Network in effect
conducted a "social experiment"—carried out with such inhuman precision—
in Waco.

The FBI wasn't attempting to *defuse* the situation that the Bureau of
Alcohol, Tobacco, and Firearms provoked in February. No. The agency
was trying something out, on people they had reason to think no one would
give a damn about—just some "cult." It had less to do with the Branch
Davidians and more to do with establishing what kinds of direct action the
U.S. government and its agencies could get away with once a group had
been identified as "extremist" or a "cult."

"Most civil libertarians in post-modern, post-political America think civil
liberties don't apply to members of 'cults,'" Newman charges. "This sets the
stage for new definitions of what may be considered 'reasonable' action by
the government. In Waco it was 'reasonable' for the federal government to

protect children who may have been being abused, by waging psychological warfare against their parents for weeks on end, and—when that didn't do the trick—precipitating a nightmarish calamity in which they burned to death . . . all because the adults were members of a 'cult.'

"There's been a self-conscious effort on the part of the country's elite—it was openly talked about in the writings of the Trilateral Commission twenty years ago—to create a narrow plurality rule as opposed to majority rule," Newman explains. "More and more this country is being run by fewer and fewer people, politically and economically. A 'cult' is just a made-up name for an extremist grouping that's *not* in power. Everyone else is a 'legitimate' opponent, a political enemy—not a special category to be demonized, dehumanized, and ultimately destroyed."

"There are no experts on cults, because there's no such thing as a cult," Fred Newman argues bluntly. "It's a classical post-modern 'counter-gang' strategy. You create a 'gang'—a 'cult'—and then you develop standard operation procedures, based on that created definition, to destroy it. It's like schizophrenia, another phony social control category, which was invented to justify depriving poor people labeled as 'schizophrenics' of their civil rights while creating a lucrative industry to manage them."

On April 22 WNET-TV, a local PBS affiliate, aired a segment of its roundtable show *Informed Sources*. The guest of the four host reporters was William Goldberg of the phonier-than-thou Cult Awareness Network; aided by heavy prompting from National Public Radio's Maria Hinojosa (who claims to know that the New Alliance Party is involved in "weapons training") and Eric Breindel, the editorial page editor of the *New York Post*, Goldberg said, "The people I've worked with who have left the New Alliance Party—and they have *left* it—have described it in terms that make me feel it is a political cult. It's their experience that it's a political cult." The show was aired again five days later.

"Although statements made about public figures and organizations have a lot of latitude under the First Amendment, in my opinion this program went beyond the bounds of that protection," NAP attorney Arthur Block told the *National Alliance*. "WNET has sufficient knowledge of NAP to have known that those statements were false—or to have displayed a reckless disregard for whether they were true or false. The word 'reckless' couldn't apply more strongly. In the wake of the FBI assault on the Branch Davidians, this defamation was tantamount to an invitation to kill members of the New Alliance Party before they made other people 'casualties' of their alleged cultism."

Cults have been constructed as an official category by the FBI in our post-modern world. The building material? The dead bodies of men, women and children in Waco, Texas.

Reprinted with permission from The *National Alliance*, May 6, 1993, Vol. 14, No. 17.

Phyllis Goldberg is a Senior Editor of the *National Alliance*, a weekly newspaper that covers the democracy movment in the United States and internationally. She holds a doctorate in sociology from New York University.

Chapter 41

Waco: Bill Clinton's Bay of Pigs

Eldridge Cleaver

Like most observers, I watched with a horror that evolved from panic and sorrow for my fellow human beings coupled with indignation towards the government, to complete outrage, as the sickening events unfolded during the fifty-one-day siege of the Branch Davidian Church's compound outside Waco, Texas. In the name of rescuing the children from David Koresh, the government massacred them, along with everyone else in sight, inflicting upon them the most cruel, horrible, savage death imaginable. Nothing done by Hitler's murderous hordes was worse. The terror, pain, and desolation felt by those children at the moment of truth must cause every American heart to weep, even that of the perfidious fiends who decreed and/or perpetrated this most wicked of deeds.

Through long, personal, bitter experience with the government's agencies and methods of repression, I recognized early on that the government was systematically poisoning and prejudicing public opinion with a blitz of inflammatory disinformation to stir up hatred against David Koresh and to foment a thirst for his blood. According to the government news, children inside the compound were being abused by Koresh and other "cult" members. People were being held hostage, unable to leave, even though they clearly wanted to surrender themselves into the loving embrace of the Gestapo authorities who already had assaulted them. The government said that Koresh had many wives and/or had had sex with scores of zombified women of the "cult," who had been brainwashed and reduced to sex slaves by Koresh's mumbo jumbo.

Sifting through the tons of verbiage dished out by the government and spewed forth by the genuflecting mass media, I am yet unable to discern any justification for the government's initial, tactically stupid raid on the compound. There's only the arrogant, abusive, fascist exercise of state power. In all fairness to the then sophomoric President Bill Clinton and Attorney General Janet Reno, I do not believe that they knew what was happening until the egg started splattering them in their faces and they were forced to take a closer look. What they saw was the emperor standing there under the klieg lights, naked, while the TV cameras churned out a report card on their first hundred days in office.

The sin of Clinton and Reno is not that they conceived and perpetrated this dastardly carnage, but that their response to it was that of weak rulers who are captives of the power they are supposed to wield, as opposed to the masters of power, who would have pulled the plugs, kicked ass from Washington to Waco, and rolled bureaucratic heads for days. Clinton and Reno closed ranks with their culpable underlings, as is the wont of tyrants, even though these particular underlings were hangers-on from the Reagan/Bush regime. They sided with the powerful perpetrators against their weak and powerless victims.

The clamoring chorus of civil libertarians, whose shrieks and screams would have been audible clear up on Mars had this event happened under Reagan/Bush, have been strangely quiet. This can only be explained by their pro-Clinton bias and their fawning over Janet Reno, The First Female Attorney General, *et cetera*. The civil libertarian establishment does not want to rock their own boat. What they have forgotten, or perhaps have never understood, is what Mr. Love said: "Silence is the language of complicity."

No doubt the actual perpetrators will be canned later on by Clinton and Reno, at the snail pace of the juggernaut of government doing a self-critique, but the people and the cause of Truth, Justice, and Freedom of Religion will have been ill-served by the very people who are sworn to protect them.

What the power structure did to the Branch Davidian folk in Waco has been done over and over again in our history, from the burning at the stake of witches at Salem, to the incinerating of the Symbionese Liberation Army in Los Angeles, and the torching of the MOVE militants in Philadelphia. Trial by fire is a standard military tactic for dealing with people under siege who refuse to buckle under to the "authorities"—never mind how illegal, provocative, and unacceptable the behavior of those authorities. In 1968, the Oakland police set fire to the house in which Little Bobby Hutton and I made our stand, murdering Little Bobby *after* we surrendered, and then lying, saying that he tried to run.

According to the historical tradition of illegal action by the government, political dissent and new religious movements are treason and heresy, punishable by fiery death. For whom did the bell toll in Waco? Not just for the Branch Davidian Church, but for each and every one us, for the U.S. Constitution, and for the Spirit of God in every one of His/Her/Its children.

Chapter 42

Letter from James Dunn and Dean M. Kelley to President Clinton

March 11, 1993

The President
The White House
Washington, D.C.

Dear Mr. President:

Please demilitarize the confrontation in Waco, Texas. It does not call for hundreds of heavily armed federal employees and Abrams tanks waiting for a showdown.

We are concerned that more people will be killed before the protracted encounter in Waco is over. Is there not some way to stand down from this stand-off without throwing more lives after those already lost? We are reluctant to judge from a distance the tactics of law-enforcement personnel who have been asked to risk their lives in the line of duty, since we are informed only by sensationalized media coverage, but we wish to urge a different way of thinking about this problem.

The law enforcement agencies are not being helped to understand this situation by the many anti-cultists on the scene uttering their shrill cries about "destructive cults" and "hostages" being held in "captivity" by a "cult leader" using "mind control." Neither they nor the officers seem to have any real understanding of what is involved in a high-energy religious movement, where the members are drawn into a tight circle of devotion and commitment to a charismatic leader whose spiritual insight and guidance they value more than life itself. The leader may seem eccentric or egotistical to outsiders, but there is no law against that.

Threats of vengeance and the mustering of troops and tanks are but proof to the "faithful" that the powers of the world are arrayed against them, evidence of their importance in the cosmic struggle—confirmation of their worst fears and validation of their fondest prophecies. Their level of commitment to their faith is higher than most other people give to anything and is therefore very threatening to others. To invade a center of energy of that kind is like sticking a finger in a dynamo. Whether it explodes or implodes, the result will be tragic for all. The ordinary strategic calculus of physical combat is as useless here as it was in understanding how the followers of the Ayatolla Khomeini could overthrow the Shah of Iran.

According to the press, some anti-cultists are claiming that they have been working for months on the Davidian "problem" with the federal agency that mounted the attack, which suggests that they helped to shape the conceptualization that led to the scenario of disaster. Central to their definition of the situation is the notion of "mind control"—that there is a technique for controlling the human will at a distance without use of force or threat of force, and that "cult" leaders have this power (though no one else seems to) and can use it to gain and keep and manipulate followers. This hypothesis is not generally accepted in the relevant disciplines of psychology and sociology [see the rejection of "expert" testimony to this effect for this reason by the federal district court of the Northern District of California when it was offered by the defense as justification for criminal conduct, *U.S. v. Fishman*, 745 F. Supp. 713, 719 (1990)], and it ill prepares those whose lives are at stake to understand what they are up against.

We are deeply distressed to suspect that an approach that should—at most—have been a last resort was used as the first resort. What opportunity were the members of the religious group given to surrender peaceably or to accede to arrest—if that was required—without violence? (A former prosecutor is quoted as saying that they did not resist an earlier investigation and arrest—*New York Times*, March 9, 1993.) This situation is not a problem that can be handled either with force or with arguments over biblical interpretation. It is better let alone as much as possible until it either runs down or stabilizes as a more conventional religion (as did the Mormon movement and the Christian faith itself, both of which began with a small group of faithful followers whose leader was killed by the authorities—in Joseph Smith's case by a band of militia after his arrest and jailing in Carthage, Illinois).

It would be even more tragic if the government has invested so much money and credibility in this no-win situation that it cannot be satisfied with less than a total eradication of the offending sect (without ever explaining what offense justified the assault in the first place). And if there must be a "victory" to save face for the government, can it not be brought about in a humane way? Surely there are technological means of immobilizing resisters without slaughtering them—and others—in the process. In any event, the public that is paying for all of this deserves a fair and objective post mortem on how this debacle ever developed.

Yours sincerely,
Dean M. Kelley   James Dunn
Counselor on Religious Liberty   Baptist Joint Committee
National Council of Churches

Chapter 43

Letter from Dean M. Kelley to Donald Edwards

Congressman Donald Edwards, Chair
House Subcommitee on Civil and Constitutional Rights
Washington, D.C.

Dear Don:

It is good to hear that you are holding hearings on the tragic holocaust at Waco, Texas. There is much that needs to be explained about what happened there, and I am sure that you will provide a thoughtful and non-sensationalized forum to explore the matter.

Much of the criticism of the federal agencies involved has focused on whether they used the best tactics for carrying out their mission of subduing and apprehending the "cult" leader, but I think a prior and more profound question is *whether they were carrying out a proper mission in the first place.*

The warrants that the Bureau of Alcohol, Tobacco and Firearms were trying to serve are reported to have involved alleged firearms offenses. In order to serve those warrants, the ATF mounted a huge assault on a group of relatively inoffensive religious devotees who may not have possessed the *mens rea* or criminal intent essential to the definition of a crime.

In any event, why was a tactic that would have been questionable even as a *last* resort employed as the *first* resort? What immense and urgent threat did the Branch Davidians pose to society that had to be countered by a Keystone Kops version of Desert Storm? Even if it had been "successfully" carried off as planned, would it have been justified? Were the victims given an opportunity to comply with the law peaceably before the tanks were called in?

241

A deputy sheriff has been quoted as saying that he could have called Howell/Koresh on the phone and asked him to drop by the office, and H/K would have gotten in his pickup and come into town, where he could have been told to get rid of whatever armaments were illegal. If he failed to comply, then there would have been time for sterner measures, of which one can think of many before reaching the Sunday morning "surprise" onslaught by more than a hundred heavily armed federal agents in flak vests and ski masks. (Some of the agents have subsequently complained that they were not armed heavily *enough* for the occasion, which typifies the macho thinking that seems to have defined the situation from the start.)

Was the object to remove the supposed threat of illegal weapons from the Texas countryside, or was it to "*get* Koresh"? Unfortunately, the result was neither until the tragic denouement of April 19. What scenario were the federal agents acting out, and who scripted it? Perhaps the ATF thought this was another paramilitary survivalist enclave like the Posse Comitatus or The Order and failed to realize that this was a different kind of situation. These were not determined, extremist militant rebels against society but religious devotees caught up in an apocalyptic vision, trying to live out the Will of God as they understood it.

That does not mean that they were "above the law" because they were religiously motivated, but that their violation of the law—if any—was not the result of a premeditated plot to do wrong. It was incidental to their main preoccupation—to create an ideal colony of the heavenly Kingdom apart from the evil of the present world. Their armaments were designed to protect their isolation, not to assault others. They were not planning bank robberies, like the Symbionese Liberation Army, but conversion forays to spread their gospel, in which their weapon was the Word, not the Sword. But the federal agencies seemed to see in Howell/Koresh a Charles Manson rather than a charismatic "prophet" or "messiah." (That does not mean that his actions were all laudable or even excusable, but that they were not necessarily "criminal.")

It would be important to discover if the ATF was assisted in its scripting of the situation by the Cult Awareness Network or other anti-cultists, who see demonic victimization in such new religious movements. Some of them have claimed to have been "advising" the ATF for months on the (supposed) nature of such "cults." Their definition of the situation is predicated upon the concept of "mind control," "coercive persuasion," "thought reform," or "brainwashing"—that the cult leader has enslaved gullible victims by this means to carry out his own ambitions for power and wealth.

Under this view of the matter, Howell/Koresh was victimizing his hapless followers, who had but to be "freed" by outside intervention in order to resume their "normal" lives. Of course, that belies the reality that his followers were there of their own volition ("willingly," as the FBI recently acknowledged), because they believed in his vision and were trying to follow it. One may not like that vision, but there is no law against preaching a vision of a different way of life or trying to follow it. (The theory of "mind control" has been rejected by a federal district court in your state as generally not accepted by the relevant disciplines of psychology and sociology (cf. *U.S. v. Fishman*, 745 F. Supp. 713, 719 (1990)) and should not be entertained in a legislative hearing either.)

The contemplated hearings should not allow themselves to be diverted into placing the religious group on trial for acts that are not illegal. "Child abuse"—if it occurred—is illegal and should be prevented or punished, though the allegations to this effect remain to be substantiated. But sexual relations with various (adult) partners, as has been alleged against Howell/Koresh, has become a commonplace—unfortunately—in our society, and is apparently not frowned upon when recreational, though somehow is thought to be heinous if religious. Unconventional domestic arrangements are not unusual in the precincts of utopian movements, and should not be allowed to discredit the devotees or discount their civil rights. (Cf. the "celestial marriage" of the Mormons, or the "complex marriage" of the Oneida Community, where all the men were married to all the women, though if any pair got too attached to each other, one of them was exiled to Wallingford, Conn., until their ardor cooled.)

It is also important to remember that "atrocity tales" tend to be generated around unconventional or nonconforming religious groups. The early Christians were accused of all kinds of nefarious acts because they kept secret the holiest part of the Mass, and during the Middle Ages Jews were accused of drinking the blood of Christian babes (Cf. Bromley, David G., Anson D. Shupe, Jr., and Joseph C. Ventimiglia, "Atrocity Tales, the Unification Church and the Social Construction of Evil," *Journal of Communication*, 29 (1979):42-53). So one needs to take with more than a grain of salt the allegations made against religious groups by outsiders or disgruntled apostates.

Lastly, the question whether the Branch Davidians immolated themselves by setting fire to the compound or the federal forces ignited the conflagration when the tanks knocked over Coleman lanterns into bales of hay and smashed a propane tank seems a bit beside the point. It would not have happened if the FBI had not been determined to "increase the pressure" by means that cannot but have seemed to the besieged devotees to be the beginning of the end.

If it was a mass suicide—as it may have been—the only surprising aspect would be that the FBI was surprised by it. Had they learned nothing from the tragedy of Jonestown? There the rocket went up after the mere intrusion by a member of Congress, a bunch of apostate accusers and a television film crew; here the invasion was by a military onslaught of (relatively) huge proportions. That no bullets were fired from the government side in the last round may seem like marvelous forbearance, but may not have been noticed by those whose walls were being broken down.

This critique may seem like 20-20 hindsight, but on March 11, 1993, I wrote the President urging the demilitarization of the standoff in Waco and suggesting that tragedy was otherwise unavoidable:

> [The officers do not] seem to have any real understanding of what is involved in a high-energy religious movement, where the members are drawn into a tight circle of devotion and commitment to a charismatic leader whose spiritual insight and guidance they value more than life itself . . . . Threats of vengeance and the mustering of troops and tanks are but proof to the "faithful" that the powers of the world are arrayed against them, evidence of their importance in the cosmic struggle—confirmation of their worst fears and validation of their fondest prophecies. Their level of commitment to their faith is higher than most people give to anything and is therefore very threatening to others. To invade a center of energy of that kind is like sticking a finger in a dynamo. *Whether it explodes or implodes, the result will be tragic for all* . . . . It would be even more tragic if the government has invested so much money and credibility in this no-win situation that it cannot be satisfied with less than a total eradication of the offending sect.

(I quote this, not to reproach the President for not taking my advice—if he even saw it—but to suggest that the outcome should never have been such a surprise to anyone familiar with similar encounters between high-energy religious groups and outside powers, which—alas—law enforcement agencies and the psychologists they consult do not seem to be.)

The hearings will have their optimum outcome if they make plain to all that new religious movements are unlike other groups and need to be handled carefully. They can be a precious resource of vision and commitment, living out new ways of ordering human society, and should not be treated like pariahs or outlaws simply because their vision is different from the commonly accepted—and none too perfect—ones with which we are familiar. (The Mormons are an example of what religious movements can contribute to the world.)

If Rodney King had a civil rights claim against the cops in Los Angeles, what do the Branch Davidians have? No one is likely to start a riot if the ATF and the FBI are exonerated, but that should not mean that the fate of an obscure little cluster of religiously committed American citizens in Texas is unimportant.

Yours sincerely,
Dean M. Kelley
Counselor on Religious Liberty, National Council of the Churches

P.S.: This letter is my personal view and does not necessarily represent the position of the National Council of Churches, though it is not inconsistent with its policies.

Chapter 44

Letter from Laura Murphy Lee to Jack Brooks

April 27, 1993

The Hon. Jack Brooks
Chairman, House Judiciary Committee
U.S. House of Representatives

Dear Congressman Brooks:

The ACLU welcomes the decision of the Judiciary Committee to investigate the events that led to the tragedy near Waco, Texas, and urges the Committee to focus especially on a number of civil liberties questions which are outlined below. The American people deserve a full and fair accounting of the actions of the federal government, specifically the Federal Bureau of Investigation (FBI) and the Bureau of Alcohol, Tobacco, and Firearms (ATF), with respect to these questions. To that end, we respectfully suggest that the Committee include with its investigation the following:

* whether the government had probable cause to justify the original arrest and search warrants of the residence and compound;

* whether excessive force was used in either the initial encounter or in the final assault on the compound, which may have led to the loss of life, including the lives of a number of children;

* whether the events near Waco justify new government authority to investigate unpopular or unusual religious groups, without reasonable suspicion that criminal laws have been violated, in violation of the

Constitutional guarantee of the free exercise of religion (as may have been suggested by some Department of Justice officials); and

*   whether there were undue restrictions on press coverage of the events near Waco.

Although we know that law enforcement officials acted on the basis of a warrant, there are many unanswered questions about the adequacy of the government's probable cause showing. The information available to the public does not indicate whether firearms violations were sufficiently supported. In that regard, we note that the ATF affidavit which supported the application for a search warrant has not yet been made public.

There are legitimate questions as well about the amount of force used and whether this was excessive on February 28, 1993, or on April 19. There are questions as to whether the type of tear gas chosen for the final assault was safe for this situation, and whether the method for introducing the tear gas was excessive. In answering these vital questions, the Committee should draw upon a variety of informed sources including non-government sources. It is highly appropriate that the Committee conduct oversight hearings. However, if the investigation yields evidence of criminal wrongdoing, this evidence should, of course, be referred promptly to the Department of Justice.

According to news reports, some Department of Justice officials have suggested that the Department will be considering guidelines to allow investigation of unusual religions to prevent another Waco-style confrontation from taking place. If true, this raises the specter of unconstitutional surveillance of religious or political groups that was widespread during the COINTELPRO-type investigations which occurred through the mid-1970s. The Constitution requires that law enforcement investigations be based on reasonable suspicions that a targeted individual or group is planning to engage in or has engaged in criminal conduct. This should continue to be the standard.

Finally, did law enforcement officials improperly prevent the media from doing their job? While safety is a legitimate concern, that rationale has been used improperly in the past to prevent the media from covering confrontational or controversial events, which severely circumscribes their watchdog function on behalf of the people. What was the justification for the two-mile cordon?

The ACLU thanks the Committee for its consideration of these important civil liberties issues.

Sincerely,
Laura Murphy Lee, Director
American Civil Liberties Union

Chapter 45

Letter from Edward C. Lehman, Jr., to Janet Reno

April 29, 1993

The Honorable Janet Reno
U.S. Attorney General
Washington, D.C.

Dear Attorney General Reno:

I am writing to you in behalf of the members of the Society for the Scientific Study of Religion (SSSR). We are a scholarly organization composed mostly of social and behavioral scientists affiliated with colleges and universities in the United States and abroad. SSSR enjoys the participation of our members primarily on the basis of their mutual interest in studying religious institutions and religious experience within the rigorous constraints of a scientific perspective.

We share your revulsion over the tragic events involving the Branch Davidian community near Waco, Texas. And we were glad to hear that you intend for your offices to learn more about cults and other new religious movements in the United States. That is the main purpose in my writing you today.

It is clear that since the fire the media have been exploiting the situation for their own purposes. In pursuing their stories, they have interviewed and otherwise presented the opinions of a variety of persons identified as

247

authorities on the subject of cults and sects mostly in the United States. Many of these persons consulted as "experts" represent a very narrow perspective on such groups and movements, i.e. the frame of reference of the anti-cult movement. We want you to know that there are important other perspectives from which to examine such groups and their activities.

Some of our members can be of great help to you in the process of developing greater understanding of sects and cults. Several social scientists who participate in SSSR have devoted major portions of their scholarly activity to analyses of particular groups as well as religious movements in general. I believe those individuals can make a significant contribution to your search for information and especially for perspective on those groups. Should you wish to take advantage of their knowledge and insight, you might contact one or more of the persons listed below. The list of names is not exhaustive, but it does include most of the leading scholars working in this area. They can provide names of other persons should you wish to have that information.

Professor David G. Bromley
Department of Sociology
Virginia Commonwealth University
Richmond, VA 23284

Professor J. Gordon Melton
Institute for Study of American Religion
Box 9079
Santa Barbara, CA 93190-0709

Professor James T. Richardson
Department of Sociology
University of Nevada
Reno, NV 89557

Professor Anson Shupe
Department of Sociology
Indiana Univ.-Purdue University
Fort Wayne, IN 46805

Professor Jeffrey K. Hadden
Department of Sociology
University of Virginia
Charlottesville, VA 22901

Professor Stuart A. Wright
Department of Sociology
Lamar University
P.O. Box 10026, Lamar Station
Beaumont, Texas 77710

Professor Arthur L. Greil
Alfred University
Box 545
Alfred, NY 14802

Professor Rodney Stark
Department of Sociology, DK-40
University of Washington
Seattle, WA 98195

Dr. Thomas Robbins
College Apts. 8-A
427 4th St. SW
Rochester, MN 55902

Dr. William Simms Bainbridge
Director, Sociology Program
National Science Foundation
1800 G Street, NW, Room 336
Washington, DC 20550

The study of new religious movements is also quite active in the United Kingdom and elsewhere. Two persons in England who are especially knowledgeable about such groups are:

Professor Eileen Barker
Department of Sociology
London School of Economics
Houghton School
Aldwych
London   WC2A 2AE
United Kingdom

Professor James Beckford
Department of Sociology
University of Warwick
Coventry   CV4 7AL
United Kingdom

It may also interest you to know that the British Government has established an office devoted to dealing with possible problems in dealing with sects and cults. They are explicitly organized to consult with these scholars studying sect and cult phenomena in order to take advantage of their insights when a need arises. I suspect that either Professor Barker or Professor Beckford could give you more detailed information about that structure.

Finally, I would invite your attention to three prominent scholarly journals that regularly publish articles reporting research on sects, cults, and new religious movements. They are:

The Journal for the Scientific Study of Religion
(published by our Society—SSSR)

Sociology of Religion
(published by the Association for the Sociology of Religion)

The Review of Religious Research
(published by the Religious Research Association)

These journals can be found in virtually any university library.

Again, we are pleased that you plan to direct the Justice Department to obtain more information and perspective on sects, cults, and other religious movements. I think you will find the resources named above to be very helpful in that quest. Please contact me if you think I can be of assistance.

Sincerely,
Edward C. Lehman, Jr.
Executive Secretary
Society for the Scientific Study of Religion

From the Ashes

Edward C. Lehman, Jr., Executive Secretary of the Society for the Scientific Study of Religion, is Professor of Sociology at the State University of New York at Brockport. He is a former President of the Association for the Study of Religion and former Editor of the *Review of Religious Research*.

Chapter 46

Letter from Larry Shinn to Hon. Donald Edwards

April 23, 1993

Congressman Donald Edwards
Judiciary Committee
U.S. House of Representatives
Washington, D.C.

Dear Congressman Edwards:

Perhaps I may be of some use in your committee's cult investigations. I am a scholar of world religions trained at Princeton University and a teacher/scholar who has taught at Oberlin College and Bucknell University. I have studied the religions of India, especially Hinduism, for twenty-five years; I am also a Methodist minister. Hence, my twelve years of research on the Hare Krishnas and the cults which resulted in the publication of *The Dark Lord: Cult Images and the Hare Krishnas in America* provides me with a perspective that may be useful in your deliberations. I have testified as an expert witness in four cult trials and in numerous media contexts.

David Koresh and the Branch Davidians are simply the most recent example of a cult that has ended in tragedy. What concerns me is that we Americans not over-react to this single event with broad-sweeping generalizations about the cults and seek to pass repressive laws that abridge the freedom of religion in America. That freedom can lead to tragedies like

251

Koresh, but also to new religions like the Mormons. What I can offer your committee's deliberations is a perspective that acknowledges the dangers of "cults" like David Koresh's while differentiating those cults from more benign groups like the Hare Krishnas, Moonies, and Scientologists who are often inaccurately lumped with them.

My deep concern, as expressed in an article, "The First Amendment and the Psychology of Fear," is that media, legal institutions, and law-makers too often rely on the word of self-styled experts like CAN (Cult Awareness Network) whose overly negative agenda often slides into a purely anti-religious attack. I realize the complexity of this issue and worry that at such moments as Jonestown or Waco we will go too far in our judicial or legal constraints on religious freedom. How to describe and find that balance is something I can offer your deliberations.

Sincerely,
Larry D. Shinn
Vice President for Academic Affairs
Bucknell University

Epilogue

A Fiery Ending

J. Gordon Melton

Even though it was my wedding anniversary, I did not feel like celebrating. Even though it was Sunday morning, I knew I would not make it to church. I awoke that morning to find myself plugged into IVs in both arms, and several tubes ran out of my midsection. I had vague memories of the doctor removing other tubes from my throat some hours before. I had gone into the hospital on the previous Friday for a long overdue test, but when the doctors found the blockage in my artery, they sent me to the operating room rather than back home.

A little fruit juice helped me clear my head. The nurse took my temperature and blood pressure and shoved some pills in my face. Once the routine slowed down, I asked my wife what was the latest from Waco. She had heard no news; and in spite of the way I felt, I suggested we turn on CNN for a few minutes and find out what was the latest word from the standoff.

As the image focused on the scene, the first tank was punching a hole in the wall of the Davidian compound. It caught my attention, and for the next three hours I watched with a mixture of unbelief, anger, and sorrow as I saw the assault on the flimsy compound and the all consuming fire. Some initial hope that at least the compound's residents would get out alive turned to despair as no one appeared, and it became apparent that most had perished—men, women, and children. It had been so unnecessary.

253

When the situation in Waco erupted in February, 1993, I found myself one of the few scholars who had written about the Davidians, and so had spent a week on the phone talking to reporters. If they were calling from Texas, I swapped interviews with them in an attempt to learn everything I could about what had happened. What possible reason did the BATF have for such a disastrous and foolhardy stunt? What was David Koresh actually saying? What had happened to start the shooting? There was not much information coming out; and to keep the story alive, the press quickly shifted the issue to "cults" and why "cults" turn violent.

The process of putting together the story and monitoring the situation continued until I entered the hospital April 17. As the standoff turned from a few days into a few weeks, Robert L. Moore, my co-author in a textbook, *The Cult Experience*, phoned the Chicago office of the FBI and offered our assistance. Like other new religions scholars, we never heard back. However, as I watched the fire run its course, I also knew that continuing to relate to Waco and attending to my immediate recovery needs were incompatible activities. I could not talk to reporters whose calls started that afternoon. I gave my wife a list of colleagues to whom she could refer any who telephoned. Suzie was already experienced in clipping newspaper articles, and she faithfully assembled the news magazines.

Looking back with some perspective, I realize it was probably just as well that I had a legitimate excuse not to deal with the Waco fire. During the next week, the few people who knew about the fire were not talking; and when they did speak, it was in self-defense. We separated truth from lies with the greatest of difficulty. Very early in the standoff we realized that we could not trust the daily briefings, at least for any account of what had passed between the Davidians and the FBI. The FBI had decided to control all access to Koresh and to let the press and public know only what it wanted them to know. We later verified what we suspected: that during the briefings the FBI handed out conscious lies (in the name of disinformation), as it chose to use the televised sessions to communicate messages to Koresh who was also watching.

Only in the weeks since the fire have we been able to put together the story of what happened; and even as this volume goes to press, some of the essential documents we need to reach a final assessment sit in files as yet unavailable to the public. The opening of these files, especially those accumulated by the grand jury in Texas, will undoubtedly shed further light on what happened both before and after the shootout, standoff, and fire.

Violence and the "Cults"

While I had some interest in rounding out my knowledge of the Branch Davidians, the time devoted to monitoring the events through March and April—and my quick return to the growing stack of clippings as soon as my health allowed—was dominated by a singular concern: the issue of violence. In the wake of Jonestown, spokespersons of the anti-cult movement had made broad charges that new religions were inherently violence prone. In response to these charges, during 1983 and 1984 the Institute for the Study of American Religion which I headed had conducted an extensive study of violence in the new religious movements.[1]

Our survey of all the reports of violence connected with new religious movement over a two-year period produced some idea of the patterns of violence. First, while we investigated numerous reports of violence, very few violent incidents were reported in connection with the more well-known and controversial new religions—the Unification Church, the Church of Scientology, the Way International, and the International Society for Krishna Consciousness. Those which had occurred were random and isolated. The major incidents of ongoing violence were connected to two groups about which the anti-cult movement had been largely silent: the Church of the Lamb of God, and the Nation of Islam. Both groups had been at war with rival organizations—Mormon polygamy groups, and African American Muslim groups—and the body count grew as the conflicts continued. Incidents related to the Church of the Lamb of God continued through the 1980s. There was also a high body count from several loner serial killers who had described themselves as satanists (but were not connected to any group). Otherwise, there was no pattern of violence from the new religions.

Two other patterns, however, did emerge. First, there was a pattern of child abuse emerging in mainline churches, though we did not yet know of the extent of the child abuse that was occurring and being covered up among Roman Catholic priests. Second, we found some patterns of violence directed toward the cults. It included the assassination of leaders and attacks upon property by night riders and bombers. The most vicious incident concerned the bombing of the Philadelphia Krishna temple. Early one morning during the group's devotional service, a bomb exploded. Only their devotion to their rituals kept them from rushing to the sight. Had they done so, they would have been met with death as a second and larger bomb exploded a few minutes later. The bomber made an obvious attempt at multiple homicide, using the first bomb to attract its prospective victims to the bomb site.

The most systematic pattern of violence, of course, was being carried out by the Cult Awareness Network which was promoting and assisting in the kidnapping and forceful deconversion of members of targeted religious groups, a process called deprogramming. The vigilante activities of the anti-cult groups continue to this very day in spite of the lies of their leaders that they do not involve themselves in such physical attacks. As we shall note, the Cult Awareness Network's involvement in the Waco situation was integral to the conflagration.

What Makes New Religions Turn to Violence?

The questions which arose out of the Waco situation were, "What made the Branch Davidians turn violent?" and "What other new religions are likely to follow the same course?" "Does it have anything to do with millennial, end-of-the-world beliefs?"

As I pondered the Waco incident in the light of what we had learned about violence and nonconventional religious groups, and integrated all we were learning about the BATF investigation and the events of February 28 and April 19, I was forced to the conclusion that we were being misdirected by the question, "Why had the Branch Davidians turned violent?" In our desire to locate a simple solution to this most complex situation, we were looking for answers in the wrong places.

The main trail of events leading to the conflagration began with Koresh's taking control of the Davidians and introducing some fresh new teachings out of his own appropriation of the Bible. The most controversial of these teachings concerned sex. While considerable sexual liberty had been allowed the group's previous leaders, and Koresh's predecessor had introduced polygamy to the group, Koresh took the teachings one step further. As an end-time ethic, he claimed all of the women for himself while the other men were to remain celibate. Coupled with his new sexual guidelines, Koresh possessed an emotionally expressive personality. He could be loving and charming, was an accomplished musician and a more than capable orator, and possessed of a fiery temper when crossed. While many admired him as a spiritual leader, others, initially attracted to him, became disillusioned after seeing him in operation on a day to day basis. They came to doubt his teachings, did not accept the changing sexual arrangement, did not like the way he disciplined children, and/or had a personal negative encounter with him. Reassessing their relation to the group, they simply chose to leave the Branch Davidians. Many of those who departed lived in Australia.

During 1990, some of the Australian ex-members were organized by Marc Breault, a former leader in the group. They pooled their resources and began a systematic attack on Koresh and the Branch Davidians. It should be noted that at least some of these former members had some righteous grievances derived from their own interaction with Koresh. However, according to Breault's rather detailed account, they were motivated to act by Breault's hysterical announcement that Koresh had plans to sacrifice a child following the model of Abraham and Isaac in the Old Testament.

In response to Breault's alarm, nine people drafted affidavits accusing Koresh of a laundry list of crimes. Breault had come to believe that the best way to attack Koresh was through the law and he submitted the affidavits to various government agencies, including the Internal Revenue Service, the Department of Immigration and Naturalization, the Waco sheriff's office, and the police in LaVerne, California. These affidavits, while vehement in their denunciation of Koresh, failed to offer any information upon which the legal authorities could operate. They dealt primarily with the alternative sexual mores which Koresh taught and to which the members of the group acceded. However morally reprehensible some might consider Koresh's sexual life and the Davidians' sexual arrangements, neither were illegal. In spite of their putting together their accounts of life in the Branch Davidians, they were unable to establish probable cause that any crime had been committed. Frustrated, Breault began a campaign of contacting other agencies, including the FBI and several members of Congress. As his frustration grew, the content of his letters became more frantic, and he charged Koresh with more and more serious crimes.[2]

In 1992 Cult Awareness Network deprogrammer Rick Ross was hired by the family of David Block, a Branch Davidian who had consented to go through a voluntary deprogramming (to be distinguished from those deprogrammings which begin with a violent kidnapping). Ross talked Block into giving up his membership in the group and, after absorbing Ross's anti-cult rhetoric, Block emerged as another vocal critic. Meanwhile, Koresh had taken steps to develop the financial base of his community. With the assistance of David Fatta and Henry McMahon, both federally licensed firearms dealers and Branch Davidians, Koresh began to purchase a variety of firearms and make himself knowledgeable of the firearms business. As Koresh began to accumulate stock, the movement of firearms into the Davidians' headquarters did not go unnoticed.

The Authorities Enter the Situation

The complaints of the former Davidian members began to bear fruit after David Block and Rick Ross joined the attack on Koresh and his followers. The *Waco Tribune-Herald* began a lengthy investigation of life in the compound. Child welfare agencies responded to reports of child abuse on at least two occasions but were unable to find any evidence of abuse. The sheriff of McLennan County visited on several occasions and checked reports of illegal weapons. He found no evidence of such weapons, though he did note that Koresh had a device which simulated machine-gun fire. It was not until after the fall presidential elections and the selection of a president-elect who had promised to make significant changes in the nation's budget that a federal agency suddenly discovered the Branch Davidians. The agency was the Bureau of Alcohol, Tobacco, and Firearms (BATF). In December it opened an investigation and by the middle of the month had contacted the *Waco Tribune-Herald* and then phoned Marc Breault who put them in touch with his circle of ex-members. On January 25, a BATF agent interviewed David Block.

The BATF was in a severe time bind. Rumors were flying that they were headed for a budget cut, and there were a number of proposals that the

BATF be dissolved and its duties reassigned to the FBI and other law enforcement structures. They had a budget review hearing coming up in March. They needed something impressive to take to that hearing. They selected the Branch Davidians.

Hastily they assembled all the evidence they could. There were lengthy allegations of child abuse (though no evidence), and they learned of Koresh's relation to the women. But, however much individual agents believed the charges, blamed Koresh, and despised everything he stood for, child abuse and illicit sex fell outside the agency's job description. Agents were fed on the anti-cult rhetoric of the Cult Awareness Network. But, however motivated by a belief in Koresh's megalomania, it was not part of their assigned area of concern. Thus, they searched for any evidence of illegal weapons, including a review of a previous dead end investigation of Koresh's purchases. That proved a nearly impossible job, for while they were able to track numerous sales of weapons to Koresh and other branch leaders, none of the transactions were illegal.

In spite of their findings, during February, the BATF had to move. A hastily drawn-up assault plan was laid out and agents assembled from around the country. Helicopters were needed but only available for drug enforcement. The BATF quickly manufactured a story that the Davidians had a drug lab. Agents then approached a judge to obtain a search warrant. In spite of numerous demands to see the document after the raid, its contents were not revealed until some weeks after the final fire. Its content, largely taken from David Block's statement, suppressed all that the agency had learned of Koresh's business, including his distribution of inert grenades as advertising novelties, and accused the Davidians of making several illegal conversions of weapons in ways which were impossible to accomplish. Had the warrant been made public earlier, it would have been determined that the BATF had failed to establish probable cause. But time had run out. The budget hearing date was rapidly approaching.

Thus on the morning of February 28, the BATF moved. There is no need to rehearse the fiasco again. Scheduled for the wrong reason, poorly planned, based upon inaccurate data, the raid was a disaster. Staged for the press and its audience in Washington, D.C., the raid literally blew up in the agency's face. It matters little who fired the first shot. Both sides thought the other did. The BATF agents followed orders. The men in the compound moved to protect their wives and children (several of whom were killed by some of the first shots) from the armed invasion of their home. It took Koresh some two hours on the phone to negotiate a cease fire, which occurred only after the BATF ran out of ammunition.

If the primary goal of the raid had been to detain Koresh and search the compound for illegal weapons, that objective could have been accomplished quietly by alternative means by arresting Koresh while he was out in the city.

However, quietly searching his compound would not have served the agency's purpose.

From Fiasco to Fire

The BATF retreated from the scene and a few days later were replaced by the FBI. Finally, someone who knew what they were doing. Finally, some experienced negotiators. Finally, some people who would patiently let the situation work itself out. Or so we hoped.

In fact the opposite occurred. The FBI negotiators quickly showed themselves ignorant of the religious rhetoric of Koresh and the religious life-style of the Davidians. While they had negotiated with criminals, the FBI soon showed they had little experience in talking to a committed religious leader who was unmoved by the kind of carrots which could be held out before, for example, terrorists holding hostages. Belatedly, the FBI proved that they lacked the necessary patience.

The FBI's crucial mistake was its complete misapprehension of the situation in which it now found itself. It sought information from "experts," but chose a set who, whatever their credentials otherwise, had never studied nonconventional religions. It ignored all that religious scholars and social scientists have learned since Jonestown. It brought in Bible scholars who could argue the Bible with Koresh, but neglected to consult students of millennialism who could understand and interpret Koresh's message.

In the end, like the BATF, the FBI listened to the anti-cult critics and accepted the adequacy of anti-cult rhetoric. And at this point the Cult Awareness Network and its spokespersons become morally, if not criminally, responsible for what eventually occurred. For twenty years the Cult Awareness Network has been attacking nonconventional religions. It has done so under the rubric of protecting people from "destructive cults." Destructive cults practice something called "coercive mind-control" or "brainwashing." In the same twenty years the anti-cult movement and its scholarly spokespersons have failed to provide any empirical evidence of the existence of such "mind-control," hoping that if they say it often enough, it will be believed. At the same time a massive amount of evidence has been assembled which demonstrates the continuity of the techniques and practices of new religious movements with those of more familiar and approved religious groups, the ones to which you and I belong.

In most cases the antics of the Cult Awareness Network have been limited to the deprogramming of one person here, or a court case there. However, in this incident the lives of a number of people, dehumanized as fanatics and brainwashed zombies, became expendable and were ultimately lost.

And the FBI should have known better. It is not headed by ignorant people. Its agents are not stupid. The course it pursued was not from lack of alternatives. Numerous qualified people offered to assist them. In the end the FBI grew tired. They did not have to move. They had other choices. They had control of the situation; the Davidians had nowhere to go but into their arms. There was no reason to believe other than that eventually Koresh would give up. The men could be arrested, and the women and children "rescued." The FBI's own impatience with the "cultists" led to their deaths. The impatience engendered the negligence. And with a plan as ill-conceived as that of the BATF, this episode reached its fiery ending.

An Afterword

There is one lesson which might be learned out of the Waco incident. It would be some consolation if the government, the media, and the religious community could drop the prejudicial and pejorative language surrounding the concept "cult." While it may have had some use at one time, it has now joined terms like "nigger," and "wop," as a label of hate, a name for any religious group we fear, cannot control, do not understand, or otherwise dislike. The deduction is obvious: *Cults don't exist; and therefore, anyone who would pass himself or herself off as a "cult expert" is an expert about nothing!*

Notes

[1] The final report was published in the first edition of the *Encyclopedic Handbook of Cults in America* (Garland, 1986) and has been repeated along with a lengthy addenda in the second edition (Garland, 1992).

[2] Breault left a detailed account of his life in and fight with the Davidians, including his increasingly outlandish claims of Koresh's supposed plans for using his guns, in his quickly post-Waco volume, co-authored with Martin King, *Inside the Cult* (New American Library, 1993).

J. Gordon Melton is Director of the Institute for the Study of American Religion and Specialist in Religion at the University of California, Santa Barbara. The author of such standard reference works as the *Encyclopedia of American Religions* (1987-1992) and the *Encyclopedic Handbook of Cults in America* (1992). Dr. Melton is widely recognized as a leading authority on non-mainstream religions.

Index

-P-

Palmer, Susan J. 99
Palo Mayombe 64
Paolini, Talita and Kenneth 161
Pate, James L. 73, 80
Paulie, Jane 161
Pember, D-on R. 157
Pentecostal revival 126
People's Temple 52, 100, 149, 193
Philadelphia 46
Phillips, Stone 161
Pitts, Bill 33, xiv,
Polygamy xiv, 12, 102, 103, 165-168, 207, 256
Posttribulationists 47
Prabhurpada 123
Presbyterian Church (USA) 222
Prophet, Elizabeth Claire 159, 160-163, 226, 227
Protestants 38
Pruden, Wesley 115
Pyle, Howard 165, 166

-R-

Randall, Terry 8
Rather, Dan 161
Reagan's administration 87, 236
Religious Research Association 249
Reno, Janet ix, xiii, 3, 79, 80, 84, 85, 96, 97, 106, 142, 153, 166, 170, 172, 177, 179, 194, 206, 213, 215, 230, 231, 236, 247
Reunion Institute 15
Reverre, Paul 86
Richardson, James T. 143, 181, 248

Ricks, Bob 78, 80, 96, 106, 111, 116, 229
Riddle, Ruth 21
Robbins, Thomas 125, 193, 248
Roberts, Paul C. 80
Robertson, George xiv, 142
Roden, Ben 36
Roden, George 36
Roden, Lois 36
Rodriguez, Robert 17, 73, 74
Roman Catholics 37, 192, 205, 255
Rosedale, Robert 141
Ross, Rick xii, 138, 186, 257
Royster, Ted 93
Rowe, David 2
Rulo, Nebraska 52
Ryan, Michael 52
Ryan, Patricia 139, 141

-S-

Saipaia, Doreen 92
San Antonio, Texas 23
Santeria 64
Satanists 255
Schmook, Kathy Grizzard 160
Schroeder, Mike 77, 102
Scientology 108, 122, 125, 130, 193, 252, 255
Sects 126
Sessions, William 84, 117, 139, 231
Seventh-Day Adventist Church 34, 229
Seventh-Day Adventists 2, 34, 35, 36, 37, 38, 43
Sexual abuse 11, 72, 170, 179
Shakers 46, 192, 205
Shepherd's Rod 35
Shinn, Larry D. 185, 251, 252
Shupe, Anson, D., Jr. 243, 248

From the Ashes